Forty-Six Years of Pretty Straight Going

Forty-Six Years of Pretty Straight Going
The Life of a Family Dairy Farm

**The Wyman Farm
Weybridge, Vermont**

George Bellerose

Vermont Folklife Center
Middlebury, Vermont

Forty-Six Years of Pretty Straight Going: The Life of a Family Dairy Farm

Copyright © 2010, George Bellerose and The Vermont Folklife Center

All rights reserved. No part of this book may be reproduced in any form or by any electronic or mechanical means, including information storage and retrieval systems, without written permission from the publisher, except by a reviewer who may quote brief passages in a review

Design and production: Mason Singer, The Laughing Bear Associates, Montpelier, Vermont

Printing: Capital Offset Company, Concord, New Hampshire

Scans of negatives: John and Stephen Stinehour, Stinehour Wemyss Editions

Photography reproduction consultant: David Goodman

ISBN 978-0-692-00433-3.

Publication of this book was made possible by grants and community support.
See acknowledgments for a listing of supporters.

Vermont Folklife Center
88 Main Street, Middlebury, Vt. 05753
Telephone: 802 388-4964
Fax: 802 388-1844
Website: www.vermontfolklifecenter.org
Email: info@vermontfolklifecenter.org

George Bellerose
80 Meetinghouse Lane, Weybridge, Vt. 05753
Telephone: 802 545-2035
Email: georgebellerose@gmavt.net

Cover: Dan Kehoe, fall cutting

Title page: Grayson, left, and Larry Wyman

For the men and women who till the soil and care for the land. Every farm family has a story to tell. This is the experience of one family, the Wymans.

Contents

Collecting and Preserving
The Voices and Traditions of Vermont

For over 25 years the Vermont Folklife Center has been deeply engaged in documenting the cultural heritage and traditions of our region. Since our founding we have used the oral interview to collect and preserve the compelling stories of Vermonters and those who call the state home. In addition, through workshops and outreach programs, we have instructed teachers, students, and individuals from all walks of life in the documentation of their own communities.

One of our longstanding interests has been the preservation of the voices and experiences of those tied to the land. Our teacher's guide, *Measured Furrows: Vermont's Farming History*, and traveling exhibits like "Making and Remaking Vermont Farmsteads" are part of that commitment. More recent exhibits, such as "Almost Utopia: In Search of the Good Life in Mid-Century America" and "The Golden Cage: Mexican Migrant Workers and Vermont Dairy Farmers," have explored historical and contemporary agricultural themes and issues.

As we lose more and more dairy farms every year, Vermonters have become increasingly concerned about the future of agriculture.

In *Forty-Six Years of Pretty Straight Going: The Life of a Family Dairy Farm* George Bellerose has followed brothers Larry and Grayson Wyman of Weybridge, Vermont, through their yearly farming cycle. Using photographs, historical accounts, and first-person narratives, this portrait provides readers and researchers with an engaging visual and detailed written documentation of a working farm.

Their story illustrates the difficult choices—economic, social, and environmental—that farmers everywhere face in being good stewards of the land. We are pleased to publish this documentary and to share it with Vermonters and everyone concerned about the future of the family farm. ◅

Brent Björkman is the executive director of the Vermont Folklife Center.

Imagining a Vermont Without Farms:
The Landscape Could Be Changed Forever

My grandfather, Homer Kennedy, farmed 200 acres in North Duxbury that stretched alongside the Winooski River, right at the base of Camel's Hump. He worked that strip of land between the river and the mountain for almost all of his adult life, and he made a living at it, but not much beyond that. He was, as another farmer, Keith Wallace of Waterbury, once said, "a real old Vermonter —lived not so much on income as on lack of expense!"

I spent most of the summers of my young life on that farm. Much of my understanding of what Vermont is about was shaped there. And now that Grandpa Kennedy is gone, now that the old barn where I jumped in the haymow has collapsed, now that the old yellow farm house with its black-iron cook stove and creaking floors has been pulled down and the land itself is growing back to trees, I think of that wonderful old, doomed farm as a cautionary tale, an omen for Vermont agriculture as a whole.

I hope it is not. But I worry that it may be.

• • •

Summers, during the late 1940s and early 1950s, the Kennedy farm seemed like about the best place in the world to a young boy. At that time, the little yellow farmhouse was uninsulated and had neither electricity nor indoor plumbing, so it was undoubtedly less appealing to the adults who had to get through the winters there.

But to the young boy I was then, the farm was a summer-long adventure. It had a brook to splash in, open fields to run in, a red barn filled with hay to jump in, and two dogs to play with. It also had big, slightly scary farm animals— two or three milk cows in the back of the barn and Old Joe, the aging Belgian draft horse. We could watch them and gingerly pet them, wonder at them, and feed them swatches of hay.

Homer Kennedy must have been in his late 60s by the time I first remember him. He was of average height and had a rugged build, the result of a lifetime of farm work. His wife, Mary Kennedy, was a firm and constant presence around the little yellow farmhouse. She wore rimless glasses and though she was unfailingly kind to us junior members, she seldom smiled.

I think the one relief from her life of nearly constant work was her gardening. She was said to have a "green thumb," which I asked once to see, and built and kept for years a quietly gorgeous rock garden in the farmhouse's front yard.

The farm was no hobby farm. It was the Kennedy family's livelihood and the scene of several family tragedies. But mostly what that farm was, was hard work. Homer Kennedy tried various ways to make a living there. He milked a few cows. He raised and sheared sheep. He cut timber on the hillsides above the rolling meadows. For a time, he even tried running a small grocery store in a shed attached to the side of the old yellow farmhouse. None of those ventures ever amounted to much, and part of the reason may have been Grandpa Kennedy himself and his approach to life.

Grandpa was a conservative, in every imaginable way. On one summer evening, I remember my father saying, heatedly: "Dammit, Homer, Vermont can't live in the past—Vermont has to keep up with progress!"

Homer responded laconically: "But y'know, Ron—it's awful hard to keep up with progress."

My Uncle Charles wanted to modernize the farm, invest in a bulk tank, expand the operation and try to make it profitable, but Grandpa flat out refused to let it happen. He was probably determined not to go into the kind of major debt that modernizing the old home place would require. Whatever the reason, that was the old man's most serious error of judgment.

He kept right on doing what he knew best, which was tend a few cows, feed them mostly with hay he cut and cured himself, and make a few dollars here and there with his small flock of sheep and what garden crops he could grow. His most significant cash crop was yellow wax beans—string beans that he sold to the Demeritt Canning Company in Waterbury. I remember picking those beans for a penny a pound and quickly spending the 30 or 40 cents I earned on comic books.

But eventually the canning company closed, and the farm's income shriveled even more. The old ways—subsistence farming, self-reliance, frugality, and good old-fashioned doing without—kept the farm together. (We would call it "renunciation" today.) A big vegetable garden and hard work sustained the family, and their few cows and sheep kept the land cleared. Somehow they managed.

In the end, there was no one to reimagine the farm so that it could prosper or even survive. The meadows that I used to walk are now scrub alder forests pierced by jeep tracks. The pasture brook I used to catch frogs in now runs through a dark, tangled woods, and there are no frogs there. In the alders that have smothered the pasture, I cannot find Acorn Rock, a big open ledge under a giant oak tree where the family used to go for picnics.

Only the ghosts of the Kennedy family remain. Soon the forest will close in on the last few open acres, and the land will have forgotten that they ever existed.

• • •

The Wyman Farm depicted in George Bellerose's photographs and essays is, quite obviously, a much more modern and sophisticated operation than my grandfather's subsistence farmstead. Just about any dairy farm in operation these days has to be.

But as of this summer of 2009, Vermont dairy farms are facing the most serious crisis they have had to cope with in many, many years. Put most bluntly, dairy farmers in Vermont are not being paid enough for their milk. Federal milk support prices are disastrously low. Vermont dairy farmers are now receiving about the same price for their milk that they got 30 years ago—even though their expenses and the cost of living have risen dramatically. As a result more and more dairy farms are failing—going out of business.

Every failed farm is, of course, a personal tragedy for the family that owns it. But the crisis is broader even than that. Conventional dairying still dominates the farm scene here. Roughly 80% of Vermont agriculture is dairy farming. Consequently, what happens to dairying affects all of Vermont. The loss of dairy farms in Vermont would put both our countryside and our culture at risk.

What would a Vermont without working farms look like? The short answer is: New Hampshire or inland Maine with lower mountains.

Vermont's beauty is unique in New England because much of it is still farmed. Although Vermont's Green Mountains are lovely, they are not as high or as spectacular as either the White Mountains of New Hampshire, the mountains of northern Maine, or the Adirondacks of New York. But to many people, Vermont is more beautiful than upstate New York, Maine or New Hampshire, and the reason is that Vermont has retained much of its "working rural landscape"—its farmland. Although Vermont has lost, by one estimate, about 400,000 acres of farmland since 1982, it is still the most-farmed state in New England.

Despite the fact that many farms have already been lost and Vermont is now close to 80% forested, enough farmland remains, in Addison County and elsewhere, to keep the general statement true: the Vermont landscape that everyone loves is a farmed landscape. And the loss of that landscape—either to scrub forest or housing development—would be a disastrous blow to Vermont's economy. Not only agriculture, but tourism would also suffer, since much of Vermont tourism is based on the pastoral landscape and image that farmers have provided us (at no charge), along with the milk, cheese, apples, and maple syrup they produce.

But further: the loss of dairy farms in Vermont would affect more than just our economic well-being. It would also weaken our culture and identity—our soul, if you want to be a bit melodramatic about it. The values we associate most deeply with Vermont — a belief in hard work, a deep connection to the land, individual independence, and a community-based egalitarianism — were forged on the farm. Vermont's identity, like its landscape, is farm-based.

Imagine, if you can, a Vermont without farmers. You'd drive toward Lake Champlain through a forest instead of open farmland. Lake Champlain would still be busy in the summer with sailboats and motor launches, but the only farm fields in sight would be the few farms growing berries and hay.

The openings in the ever-growing forest near the lake would contain more vacation homes and condominiums than farm houses.

Country stores along the way would have a wide selection of wines and DVDs, but very little farm-related hardware, and no hunting rifles or shotgun shells. Farm-related businesses—the "infrastructure" so vital to agriculture like creameries and feed dealers and tractor dealerships and farm equipment stores—would have withered away. There would be bike tours on the highway, but darn few manure spreaders. There would be very few large-animal veterinarians around. Some real work would still be done. But not much real farm work. And so a major part of what is genuine about Vermont would be lost.

Admittedly, that's an exaggerated picture. There are, in fact, signs of hope in Vermont farming. The busy retail chaos of farmers markets throughout the state, the emerging "localvore" movement, the re-emergence of grain farming in the Champlain Valley, the birth of a top-quality cheese industry, and the new organic dairies now struggling to secure a stable market are all hopeful signs. But that 80% of Vermont farming represented by conventional dairying is at this moment in serious trouble. And without a strong working agriculture, we could be left with a "Disneyfied" Vermont—nice perhaps, but not based in the reality of hard work on the land.

We must find a way to keep real farms, especially dairy farms like the Wyman Farm, alive and working. Otherwise, an important part of our heritage will be lost and the Vermont we love could be changed forever. ⟆

Tom Slayton is the editor emeritus of *Vermont Life* magazine.

Who Are These People Who Work So Hard To Produce Our Cheap and Abundant Food?

In the summer and fall of 1990, my wife and I, interested in living closer to where I worked, began traveling the back roads of Addison County looking for land to build on. That often meant investigating multi-acre chunks of land, marginally profitable for farming. The three acres in Weybridge that we eventually bought was just such land, part of a dairy farmer's 20-acre pasture.

To scout our home site, we had to slither under a barbed-wire fence and shoo away a dozen curious heifers. Then, watching for cow flops, we'd walk the rolling hills, ideal for grazing but too uneven for crops, that led to Otter Creek.

Townspeople knew the land as the part of the Gervais farm, 275 acres that Ed Gervais had taken over from his father in 1969 and had farmed until he sold the farm and 200-head herd in 1982 to the Otter Creek Farms Partnership. When we moved in during the fall of 1991, the dairy barn, several hundred yards to the west, had been empty for most of the past five years.

The partnership, a lawyer/developer and a farmer, had sold the herd in 1986 during the federal Whole Herd Buyout. This one-time offer, designed to reduce the perennial over-supply of milk, prohibited participants from milking or housing female cows in their barns for five years.

In 1990, Chris Roeloff bought the farm, minus our 20-acre pasture and an adjacent 30-acre piece set aside for house lots, with the intention of milking as soon as the moratorium ended in June of 1991. Until 1996, we were the lone house in what would become a four-house development. Our one lot left acres of prime grassland, which Armond Brisson, another Weybridge farmer, cut for hay. Armond, who had been grazing heifers on the land when we first visited, round baled the northern half, leaving the rockier southern half for us to brush hog.

Occasionally, city people would see the land-for-sale sign, stop, and ask, "Can you smell the cows from here?"

"Yes," we would reply.

They would raise their eyebrows. They wanted country living without the cows.

We were (and are) quite happy to have cows and farmers for neighbors. To the west, the Roeloffs' 400-foot-long barn lights the morning and evening sky with a UFO-like glow. Occasionally in our first years, venturesome Roeloff cows, seeking fresh grass, waded into the Otter, looped around the boundary fence, and spent the day in our greener backyard.

The Wymans are a half mile to the southeast. From early November to mid-May, when the oak, birches, and maples along the Otter Creek are leafless, we can see the roof of the Wyman barn from our living room window. The rest of the year, we hear milk-time moos and beeping machinery.

From the top of our driveway, we can see the Hagar Farm, part of the Monument Farms Dairy complex, sitting on the horizon, just to the south of the Wyman farm. Family dairies that raise crops, milk cows, and bottle their own milk were once common. Today a handful of cooperatives and large private corporations dominate milk processing in New England. Monument Farms, run by the James and Rooney families, is the lone, non-organic family dairy left in the state. To the northwest, a mile and a half distant is the Chalker Farm, just across the Weybridge town line in New Haven. On a ridge half a mile farther north is the Briggs Farm, a 400-cow operation with a commanding view of the Champlain Valley.

We did not need to be told that we were in the middle of dairy country. For generations, Addison and Franklin County to the north have been the state's principal dairying centers, each with about a quarter of the state's dairy production and 40-plus percent of their land base in farms.

These two counties have a significant economic heft as well. A 1997 study estimated that they contributed $450 million and 10% of jobs to the state's economy and were responsible for 10% of all farm sales in New England. Nationally, Addison ranked 43rd and Franklin 42nd in the value of their dairy production in 2007 in a universe of 2,493 counties. Their seas of corn are similarly statistically impressive. Addison ranked 35th and Franklin 30th in their corn silage acreage in a universe of 2,263 counties.

Growing up in Vermont, I had a schoolboy's rudimentary knowledge of the importance of dairying and agriculture. In grade school, we learned that a statute of Ceres, the Roman goddess of agriculture, topped the Statehouse's golden dome and that the State Seal included sheaves of wheat, a lone pine tree, and a cow. And we reveled in Vermont's bragging rights as the only state that once had more cows than people. Not true, it turns out.

Later, as a newspaper reporter in Rhode Island, Wyoming, and Vermont, I enjoyed writing an occasional agriculture feature story: septuagenarian Rhode Island farmers whose land was coveted by developers; a day with Idaho's potato farmer of the year; roundups and traditional branding with hot irons on a Wyoming cattle ranch; the dual life of an IBM engineer-weekend farmer in Vermont.

But like many non-farming Vermonters, my knowledge of dairying was often little deeper than newspaper headlines. Some stories, such as county fair 4-H reports, presented dairying as an appealing way of life with pint-sized, freckled kids leading equally scrubbed quart-sized heifers around the judging ring.

But rarely will these cows ever again receive the attention they did in their show days. And rarely will these future farmers become attached to an animal as they have here. Their job in the future will be to produce milk and lots of it. Ribbons will not earn their keep.

But many more headlines described the family farm as an endangered species:

"USDA Announces Sign-up for Crop and Disaster Programs"
"Dairies on Roller Coaster Again"
"Farmers Face Feed Shortages This Winter"
"Efforts Undertaken to Address Low Dairy Prices"

Books offered similarly bleak assessments:
Fields Without Dreams
The End of the Family Farm
American Dreams, Rural Realities: Family Farms in Crisis
Changing Works: Visions of a Lost Agriculture

What was the non-specialist to make of these gloomy forebodings?
Was the family farm in the first decade of the 21st century any more threatened than it has been during the past 200 years?

Historians point out that the family farm has been in a state of constant change since settlers in the late 1700s cleared the forested landscape, several acres at a time each summer. During the subsequent two centuries, the ups and downs of Vermont agriculture have included wheat, sheep, butter, and dairy booms, and near collapse during the Depression.

Numbers told part of the story. Since 1880, when family farms peaked at 35,000, the number of family farms and people working on them have steadily declined. In 1790, about 90% of Vermonters lived on and earned part of their livelihood from farming. By 1850, that number had dropped to 64% and by 1950 to 12%. In 2006, about 1% of the state's population lived on Vermont's 1,100-plus dairy farms. As historians have noted, America was born in the country and has moved to the city.

Vermont's experience is not unique and parallels that of other dairy states. From 1965 to 2005, Vermont lost 79% of its dairy farms, nearly identical to the losses in major dairy states, such as New York, 82%, Wisconsin, 82%, and Pennsylvania, 78%. Vermont continues to lose about 5% of its dairy farms every year, although "lost" land and cows are often absorbed by neighboring farms or the land is kept open with land trust agreements that prohibit commercial and residential development.

In 1965, Vermont's dairy farms had 233,000 cows; in 2006, there were 141,000 cows, a 39% decline, nearly identical to the 40% decline nationwide. But as some traditional dairy states, like New York and Pennsylvania, have experienced major declines, Western dairy states, with cheaper production costs, have been booming. California, the nation's largest milk producer

with about 21% of the country's milk production, adds the equivalent of Vermont's herd every several years.

But all is not gloom. Despite these changes, Vermont continues to be the dairy heartland of New England, producing over 60% of the milk in the region, with over 80% of the state's production exported and sold either as fluid milk or manufactured products, such as cheese and ice cream. Dairy sales range from $450 million to $550 million annually with the multiplying effect of related businesses— cheese and ice cream makers, vets, insurance agents, equipment and feed dealers—increasing that economic impact two and a half times.

Family farmers' fundamental challenges have changed little over the years: uncertain weather, fluctuating harvests, long hours, scarce help, marginal returns. Today, national and global competition and biotechnology developments further complicate the survival of the family farm.

By several measures, 1880 was the statistical high-water mark in Vermont agricultural history: the most farms, 35,522, over five times today's 6,000-plus farms; the most acreage in crops, 3.3 million acres, nearly six times that of today; and the most open landscape, with an 80-20 farmland-to-forest ratio, roughly the reverse of today.

Dairy's role as one of the mainstays of the state's economy can be measured by its contribution to the state's gross domestic product (GDP). In only 13 states does dairying make up more than 1% of the state's GDP. Dairying in Vermont is responsible for 7% of the state's economy, second only to the fast-growing dairy industry in Idaho with 11.5%.

Will these trends and the roller-coaster economics of dairying continue? Yes, say industry experts and the task forces that periodically examine the future of the family farm across the country. (Like Vermont, over 90% of the country's 62,000 dairy farms are family owned, even farms with multi-thousand-head herds.)

But their crystal balls remain cloudy on permanent solutions to dairying's perennial problems: the uncertainties of weather and harvests; a shortage of people willing to work the long hours; federal and state programs that have rarely been able to control the oversupply of milk or fully stabilize wildly fluctuating milk prices; and, specific to Vermont, the challenges of competing with the Midwest and West, with their lower costs of production.

The questions and challenges have long been apparent. Answers and solutions have not. Can, for example, the average-sized family farm—in Vermont about 125 milking cows—survive the bigger-is-the-only-path-to-economic-survival that has been the pattern of agriculture almost since its start?

In 2007, 4% of Vermont's dairies, roughly 50 farms, had more than 500 cows, an unthinkable size a generation ago. These dairies produced 34% of the state's milk. Nationwide, farms with over 500 cows, 3.7% of all dairies, produced over 47% of the country's milk.

Is the consolidation of small farms into larger farms, with their economies of scale, such as bulk purchasing, an inescapable reality? A 2003 Cornell University study on the future of small farms answered yes, projecting that 6,000 New York dairy farms with fewer than 200 cows would be replaced by about 100 consolidated operations, averaging 1,400 cows, by 2020. Two-thirds of the state's milk

output, the country's third largest, would then be produced by a little over 200 farms.

Another 2003 Cornell study, projecting this "industrialization of agriculture" nationwide, forecasts that there will be 85% fewer dairy farms in 2020 and that the average herd size will be 500 cows. Milk production will increase 17% to 20%, but with ever increasing productivity, 15% fewer cows will be needed.

These operations, whether in New York, Vermont, or the West, are sustainable, critics contend, only with cheap fuel, immigrant labor, and federal farm policies and subsidies that favor large operations. Wouldn't it make more economic sense, supporters of smaller farms argue, to slow the ruthless pursuit of economies of scale and ever-greater production?

Their solution to the family farm crisis is to get off the treadmill of oversupply and resulting rock-bottom prices. But would independent-minded farmers accept production quotas and restrictions on the use of biotechnology in the barn and field to eliminate the oversupply of milk in return for guaranteed higher prices?

Will individual farmers, who have almost no control over the price they receive, always be captive to a market and processors who view milk as a low-priced commodity? Or can Vermont farmers and entrepreneurs continue to create value-added products and businesses, such as premium ice creams and artisanal cheeses—Vermont's 30-plus artisan cheese makers are the most per capita in the country?

Can organic dairying, which has been growing at a double-digit rate annually for the past decade, be the family farm's salvation? Family-sized organic dairy farms—the average herd size is 60 cows —have grown from three certified farms in 1994 to 195 farms in 2007.

Or will organic milk, which is roughly twice as expensive on the store shelf as conventional milk, continue to be a niche market? About 7% of fluid milk sales in Vermont is organic, the highest percentage in the country. In 2005 about 1% of the country's dairy cows were certified organic. Will organic farmers and processors work together to control production so supply does not exceed demand? Or will oversupply drive down milk payments to organic farmers, which can be 50% to 100% higher than those to traditional dairy farmers?

Technology has always been a double-edged sword in agriculture. The expansion of rail lines in the mid-1800s made transporting cheaper Midwestern wool to New England mills economically feasible and hastened the end of Vermont's sheep boom. At the same time, the railroad, especially with the coming of refrigerated cars at the end of the century, allowed Vermont farmers to ship fluid milk to what would become their principal market, Boston.

Today, Vermont agriculture, like agriculture nationwide, faces a host of new biotechnology and global economic challenges. How should genetically modified seeds be regulated? These seeds, already widely used, provide higher crop yields with reduced use of fertilizers and pesticides, supporters argue. These crops don't have a proven health-safety record, and their seeds can spread to neighboring organic farmland, critics caution.

Should there be any restrictions on the supplemental use of rBST, a synthetic, genetically engineered copy of a cow's naturally occurring growth hormone, to boost a cow's milk production at a time when there already is an oversupply of milk? Does rBST "burn out" cows and create breeding problems or does it provide the economic margin needed to stay in business? Is rBST milk safe for human consumption, as supporters believe, or could there be long-term health consequences from its use?

Food production and its transportation currently consume about one-fifth of our annual oil use. How will global economic trends, such as the increasing cost of fuel, affect farm management and policies? Will the use of corn for ethanol biofuel be counterproductive and continue to create feed shortages, higher grain prices for farmers, and higher food costs for consumers?

Vermonters spend five times the national average on locally produced food, even so less than 5% of the food in Vermonters' diet is grown locally. Will the cost of shipping low-priced commodities encourage and require that even more food be produced locally?

Economics aside, does society have an obligation to "save" the family farm? How do we value, with our head, heart, and pocketbook, the preservation of open land and a rural way of life? Americans spend the smallest percentage of their disposable income, about 10%, on food of any industrialized country. Would we, accustomed as we are to cheap, industrial-scale food that on average travels 1,500 miles from field to store be willing to spend more to support locally produced food?

How would rural communities and their accompanying small-scale agricultural infrastructure change if dairying is dominated by Wal-Mart-sized farms? Similarly, what would the Vermont landscape look like if our dairy industry shrank 85% to the size of neighboring New Hampshire?

Many contemporary writers have tackled these questions with rigor and historical sweep. Several books come to mind: Ronald Jager's *The Fate of Family Farming: Variations on An American Idea*; Jan Albers's *Hands on the Land: A History of the Vermont Landscape*; Michael Pollan's *The Omnivore's Dilemma: A Natural History of Four Meals* and *In Defense of Food: An Eater's Manifesto*; and Gregory Sharrow and Nancy Price Graff's *Measured Furrows: Vermont's Farming History*.

Bill McKibben in his recent book, *Deep Economy: The Wealth of Communities and the Durable Future*, sums up the longstanding importance of family-sized farming—locally produced food creates a network of community-affirming social and economic relationships that are lost when food is imported from factory farms thousands of miles away.

Another book that looks at the big picture is Paul Roberts's *The End of Food*. The continuing industrialization of U.S. agriculture is not environmentally or economically sustainable when one considers the true cost of cheap food, such as the cleanup of land, air, and water pollution, he argues. Furthermore, competition from low-cost countries, like Brazil, which is now the world's largest exporter of

Being a family farmer means caring for one's land. Such love cannot be taught in agricultural colleges; it is a practice that one learns at the feet of a master. It is knowledge of the heart, not the head, and it's best passed from generation to generation. That longstanding sentiment sums up the family farm's historic role.

economist, historian, legislator, task force member or policymaker. My overriding question has changed little over the years: Given the long hours, the toll on the body, and the scant economic returns, why would anyone want to be a family farmer?

Few of us get our hands dirty today at anything that approaches the intensity of the farmer. A large garden is a summer-long hobby with perhaps some best-in-the-neighborhood tomatoes and an abundance of zucchini in September. A farmer's fields are an April-to-October obsession that determines economic survival.

Few of us work the hours of the dairy farmer. By our breakfast, they have put in half a day's work. By noon, many have logged an eight-hour day. By nightfall, they have often added another eight-hour day.

Who are these people who work so hard so we can have cheap and abundant food?

There are the obvious answers. Farming appeals to those of independent spirit; those who want to be their own boss; those who never lose their sense of wonder that a seed a little larger than a BB-gun pellet can become a 12-foot stalk of corn. Farming attracts those who enjoy being jacks-of-all-trades—helping deliver a calf in the morning, fixing a harrow in the afternoon, planting corn in the evening—in an age of ever-increasing specialization. Farming is for those who value the rhythm and routine of the seasons and the diversity of each day's challenges; farming is for those who accept that farming is a tough way to make a living but steadfastly believe that it can be a fulfilling way of life.

But this is an outsider's assessment. What would it be like to be a farmer for a year? My stiff knees, a balky back, and the prospect of

beef, will lead to the United States becoming a net food importer in the coming decades. At the end of the book, I list other books and reports that discuss the transformation of and challenges facing American and Vermont agriculture.

My neighbors, strong-minded as they are, had little ability to affect national and international developments, but they did answer these questions every day in their ground-level decisions: whether to use rBST, to sell marginal land for house lots, to increase the size of their herd. My interests, too, have always been found on a smaller canvas—the farmer's world seen from the tractor seat and milking stool, not from the more distant vantage point of the agricultural

4 a.m. milkings have always vetoed that prospect. Documenting the life of a family farm has always been more appealing.

But what kind of family farm? Farmers just starting out? Farmers in the twilight of their careers? Farmers who embrace the latest technologies? Wait-and-see, make-do farmers?

What size? The average-sized family farm? The megafarm, 500 to 1,000 cows in the East and multiple thousands in the West, the building block of industrial agriculture's future?

One rainy morning, I described my interests to Peter James, a third-generation farmer who oversees farm operations at Monument Farms Dairy. "Who would be candidates for such a project," I asked.

"Not us," Peter replied. "We're a 30-employee corporation."

Go no further than your neighbors, Larry and Grayson Wyman, he recommended. They were, he and others later said, the traditional family farm: two brothers who had farmed together for 40-plus years and knew their cows and crops. They didn't have the latest tractors or equipment but did well with what they had.

Many farms had gone to labor-saving, but initially costly, milking parlors; the Wymans, nearing retirement, put in long hours in the traditional tie-stall barn. In an era of computers and spreadsheets, the Wymans managed with encyclopedic memories and pencil-entry notebooks, but perhaps best of all, Larry and Grayson are compelling storytellers, as anyone who has ever visited them in the barn will attest.

In March of 2004, I began photographing and taking notes on a year in the life of the farm. Larry was 69 and Grayson 64, making them two of the oldest full-time farmers in the state. Since the mid-1990s, when they had trouble finding help, the Wymans had been considering retirement. In the winter of 1997, Dan and Jeanne Kehoe had been hired to help part time with milking and over the subsequent years had become an integral and essential part of the farm's operation.

When I began the project, retirement was on the Wymans' horizon. On March 31, 2005, Larry and Grayson planned to stop milking, ideally turning the operation over to the Kehoes. Farming, however, is about dealing with the unexpected, as monthly summaries, from March 2004 to December 2005, will show.

In the spring of 2006, I sat down with Larry and Grayson, now retired and rested, with a tape recorder to talk about the longer arc of their lives in farming—how they started farming and how the operation grew, how their thinking about crops and cows and machinery has evolved, how dairying's tight-margin economics has and will shape the family farm.

Larry and Grayson began farming during the post-World War II golden age of dairy farming when productivity soared from better seed, more nutritious and scientifically balanced feeding, artificially inseminated cows, and labor-saving equipment in the field and barn. But they can remember stories of their grandfather who farmed with horses and mules at the beginning of the century.

Today's farmers have more knowledge and resources than their predecessors could have dreamed of. But any review of historical accounts of farming over the past 200 years reveals that the satisfactions, frustrations, and challenges have changed very little. Narratives and historical accounts from those times are interspersed with the Wymans' commentaries.

What could I call these strands of storytelling, reflection, and historical narrative?

Grayson gave me the answer one morning when I asked him to sum up their farming lives. "It was forty-six years of pretty straight going," he replied.

What follows is that story. ❧

Family farmers like Larry Wyman (right) are among our last generalists. Survival requires that they be part veterinarian, mechanic, nutritionist, soil and crop expert, and small businessman.

The Life of a Family Dairy Farm

Chapter 1

Starting Out

The Family Farm Is Not A Factory

There is no one-size-fits-all definition for a family dairy farm. They include 10,000-cow herds in California, Wyman-size herds of 100-plus cows, and one-person operations with several dozen cows. The expansive definition of the Economic Research Service of the U.S. Department of Agriculture simply stipulates that a family farm can't be a non-family corporation or cooperative or be run by a hired manager. It does not require, as other more restrictive definitions do, that the family supply at least half the labor and that the majority of the family's income come from the farm; nor does it set gross income limits. Such definitions are more than hair-splitting as they may determine the farm's eligibility for private-sector and federal programs and loans.

The Vermont Agency of Agriculture does not attempt to define the family farm, nor do state statutes. Finding a consensus definition is thorny and invites lawsuits. The Agency does follow the farm size classifications of the federal Environmental Protection Agency in regulating farm operations: large, over 700 cows; medium, 200 to 699 cows; and small, 199 cows and smaller.

The National Family Farm Coalition has a down-to-earth definition: The family takes the risks, makes the decisions, and should receive the economic gains; a farm should be owned by the operating family with the intent of passing the land in better condition to the next generation. And it has a vision: the family farm should be "an ideal by which we measure our progress as a society in offering economic opportunity and freedom, conservation of resources and biodiversity, and a healthful, safe food supply."

Agricultural economist John Ikerd offers another working definition and warning:

> A family farm is not a factory. Plant and animal production are not mechanical processes like those of a factory assembly line. Farming isn't just about minimizing costs or maximizing profits; it's about caring for living things—plants, animals, people, and even the wild things of the fields and forests and living things in the soil.

This culture must be nurtured and passed on from one generation to the next. In an effort to make American agriculture more efficient and productive, agribusiness has removed this family farm culture from agriculture, John Ikerd argues.

And finally, the federal census has a dollars-and-cents definition: Any place from which $1,000 or more of agricultural products were produced and sold, or normally would have been sold, during the census year. Using that definition, the Wyman farm was one of 6,984 farms in Vermont in 2007, and one of approximately 1,100 dairy farms.

Opposite page, the Wymans' Weybridge farm. The Wymans began farming in the late 1950s, when there were 10,000-plus dairy farms and many 15- to 30-cow herds. In 2009, there were about 1,050 dairy farms, but they were far bigger, with a herd size averaging 125 cows.

Most of these farms, unlike the Wyman farm, cannot support a family. Thirty-seven percent of the state's farms, "hobby farms" or "quality-of-life farms" for many, sold less than $2,500 in agricultural products, according to the 2007 U.S. Department of Agriculture census. Their sales were slightly less than 3% of the state's agricultural income.

While these farms keep land open, they cannot support the extended infrastructure—major machinery, equipment, and feed dealers—needed for a healthy agricultural economy. This infrastructure requires the buying power of larger farms. In Vermont, 1,468 farms with sales over $50,000—the majority are dairy farms—provide that critical mass. These farms, about 21% of the state's total number of farms, generated about 90% of the state's agricultural income. In a sign of the agricultural times where bigger and bigger is the perceived path to economic survival, 291 farms with sales of $500,000 and greater, about 4% of the total number of farms, generated about 54% of the state's farm gate income.

Though small compared to 500-cow megafarms, the Wyman farm, with 100 to 120 milking cows, was slightly bigger than the median dairy farm, 90 milking cows; it was slightly smaller than 2007's average herd size, 125 cows. Depending on milk prices and ancillary revenues, such as the sale of bull calves, heifers, mature cows, and crops, Wyman farm sales were a step below these largest farms, with sales at the low end of the $250,000 to $499,999 bracket. Three hundred and fourteen farms, about 4.5% of the total number of farms, fell in this sales category, generating about 17% of the state's agricultural income.

The family farm is subject to the measurements of the statistician and marketplace, but to define its worth so narrowly is to miss its significance. Can we put a dollar-and-cents valuation on the preservation of rural communities? How much is open space worth in our often selective bookkeeping that favors development over preservation? How do we value the work ethic and land stewardship at the heart of family farming?

Family farming has always been a way of life as much as a way to make a living. The farm is as much a home as it is a workplace. Farming has never been a speculative venture that can turn a quick profit. It is a generational commitment. Larry and Grayson Wyman have always had that long view. They began at the "hobby farm" end of the scale. Not by choice but by necessity. There was no family farm to inherit. No herd, no barn, no land, no farm machinery to be passed down.

There were, however, farming genes in the family—starting with Grandpa Wyman who managed a 100-cow dairy farm in Maryland just before and during World War I. Guy Wyman, their father, would later milk cows as a teenager on his father's West Granby, Conn., hill farm. But the farm, like many hill farms, was too small to support both.

For the next 30 years, Guy Wyman was part of the flight from thousands of hardscrabble, uneconomic family farms to jobs in the city. When he took early retirement from a major tool manufacturing company in New Jersey in 1957, his get-your-hands-dirty, low-technology farming days were a distant memory. Farming was not his goal for a second career; living in rural Vermont, where he had once worked and the family had enjoyed summer vacations, was.

Dairying today with a 100- to 150-cow herd requires six- and seven-figure investments, well beyond the resources of most who don't have a family head start. Fifty years ago, the financial challenges facing Larry and Grayson and their father in returning to family roots and dairy farming were more modest but daunting nonetheless.

"If only we had known what we were doing, we might not have had to make so many moves," Larry would laugh and reflect years later on a lifetime of painstaking, incremental gains that began with the purchase of the first family cow in 1957.

In the following narratives, Larry and Grayson discuss their decisions to take up farming and their years of on-the-job training on White River Junction and Brownsville farms. By 1968, the Wymans, pushing the limits of their Brownsville farms, were ready for one last move, to the seeming greener pastures in the Champlain Valley. ❧

Grandpa Wyman hand milked and plowed with horses and mules at the start of the 20th century. At the end of the century, Larry and Grayson Wyman were part of an agricultural revolution that had transformed the family farm into a high-tech, capital-intensive but low-margin business.

Family farms, given their high start-up costs, are with few exceptions passed from generation to generation. Larry (above) and Grayson Wyman are the exception. They started from scratch with a single cow in 1957. Over two decades they built a herd of 200 cows.

The Grass Has Never Been Greener Somewhere Else

LARRY WYMAN: I grew up in the 'burbs of New Jersey— Chatham, about an hour west of New York City. In those days Chatham was relatively rural—a typical middle- to upper-income town. Ninety-eight percent of the kids went to college. People had good jobs, and in the 1940s and 1950s the husband worked and the wife stayed at home.

My father worked for a major tool making company in New Jersey for 25-plus years, but he had grown up on farms in the country. Both my parents had Vermont connections, and every July we would vacation in Grand Isle at my grandfather's camp.

I just loved the outdoors and people and pace here; I lived 11 months for that one month. Going home, I'd look out the back window all the way. Route 7 was dotted with farms from Burlington to Pownal then, and I wanted to drink in that last view. It was always hard to accept that we wouldn't be back for a year.

In New Jersey people were so competitive and petty. Everything was keeping up with the Joneses. That didn't interest me one bit. Vermonters weren't trying to impress me or anybody else. I wanted to be in the same place and walking in their shoes. I've said many times that I came here to live the way people here live. I didn't come here to try to make Vermonters into what I came from.

When I was in high school I worked summers in the paint and glass factory where my father worked. I did all kinds of hand assembly, just about everything except run machines because I was too young. I could earn $500 in a summer, which went a long way toward the cost of the local private high school. I enjoyed the people, but it wasn't a life that I would want.

In the fall of 1953, I went to Drew University, which was several miles away, and didn't like it at all. It wouldn't have made any difference if it had been Harvard; I just never liked school. That winter, I dropped out of Drew and started working in the greenhouses where I had worked two nights a week in high school. I enjoyed the work and people, but it was New Jersey.

I had heard about Marlboro College and wanted to get back to Vermont and figured that was a good way. In the fall of 1956, I stopped working in the greenhouses and came to Marlboro. It was a small college, about 40 students in a class. They say the best learning situation is a professor on one end of the log and student on the other. That was the way it was there.

I didn't quite finish the third year and was close to fulfilling academic requirements for a diploma when I met Fern. She was a freshman and had grown up on a farm in West Guilford, which is just a couple miles away. I left because we got married in 1958 and had a child arriving in March of 1959.

And I had an opportunity to work in greenhouses again, which I liked very much. So I started working in Brattleboro part time in 1958 and full time in 1959. This was a very large operation—the greenhouse was about the size of a football field. I worked in the greenhouse and had a truck route delivering flowers around the state.

I wouldn't say that it was cast in die that I'd become a farmer. I could have done something else, but it would have had to be outdoors. I had a chance to work in Boston in the wholesale flower market, which would have been very lucrative. But Fern would probably have divorced me. She liked rural living and so did I.

Grandpa Wyman, who we never knew, may have had more to do with our approach to life than we really know. He used to say he liked to travel as long as he could sleep in his own bed at night. So when Grayson and I decided to farm together that was like B'rer Rabbit in the briar patch. I could work just where I wanted to live, Vermont, and be outdoors.

For me, the grass has never been greener somewhere else. This is where I wanted to be, and I was married to someone who wanted to live here. We raised three kids in a place that I wanted not just for

In moving to Weybridge after farming in White River Junction and Brownsville, the Wymans were seeking not just better land but Addison County's healthy agricultural infrastructure, an infrastructure that has been lost in much of the state.

me but for them. How much more perfect could it be? Our younger brother (Dale) has lived in the suburbs all his life, and he's happy. I've been back to New Jersey just once since I left 40-plus years ago and that was to show the kids where I grew up. For me, New Jersey was wall-to-wall people. There was none of the natural beauty that you have here.

Farming was not so much milking cows or driving tractors or doing fieldwork but living the rural life. Grayson shares my feelings. That's one of the reasons why we have been able to work together all these years.

Grayson started farming during college summers, first working on a wealthy businessman's state-of-the-art farm and then on a young couple's barebones operation. The lesson? Both paid attention to detail.

I Knew After That First Summer That I Wanted to Farm

GRAYSON WYMAN: Larry and I always had an interest in growing things. It didn't make any difference if it were plant or animal. I didn't have any experience growing up on a farm and didn't work on one until after my first year at college. But I knew growing up in New Jersey that I didn't like being cooped up in a factory or office all day. I liked anything that I could do outdoors.

Larry and I both worked in my father's factory. It was all right as a summer job, but I wasn't interested in it as my life's work because I didn't like the idea of sitting at a bench doing the same thing day in and day out. One of things about farming is that you never lack for variety. When you get up in the morning, you can never be sure what you're going to do that day. There is no quicker way to throw a monkey wrench into your schedule than to think the day is all set.

Larry, Fern, and I all went to Marlboro. It was the old liberal arts education. If you don't know exactly what you want to do take a liberal arts course and maybe it will help you find a direction. It helped me. I started out as a chemistry major. When I was in a lab for four or five hours and saw the sun shining and everything turning green, I knew that I wanted to be out there and didn't wanted to be penned up inside.

You don't meddle with that feeling. It's right in your genes. Both Larry and I and our younger brother, to a lesser extent, have it. I think we got it from the grandfather that we never knew.

After that first summer at the College's farm, I knew that I wanted to farm. We lived five minutes from the farm, and I looked forward every morning to going to work. Marlboro had been founded as a college for World War II veterans and had a lot of growing pains. This millionaire businessman whose son went there gave his side hill farm to the College with the idea that they would sell it to raise money. He had given all the cows to land grant colleges in New England and New Jersey, and the land was being cropped until the farm was sold.

The donor still decided how things were to be done, and he wanted them to be done just so. If you were irrigating the fields and he showed up, you wanted to be sure that the water was down 12 inches before you moved pipe. If it wasn't you went back and did it.

Side hill farms with loamy soil were where you grew alfalfa. You didn't grow alfalfa on flat land, which has a tendency to pond and hold water because alfalfa doesn't like wet feet for a prolonged period. This was good land, but you had to be careful on a tractor because everything was very tippy. Alfalfa had been around for a long time, but not much had been done to improve it and many farmers were wary of growing it. But we had beautiful alfalfa.

My first summer we cut our first crop in May. Second crop, the end of June. The afternoon we put up the second cutting, we put heavy potash on the field. The next morning we laid irrigation pipe. By noon it was "raining" and three weeks later we cut our third crop. That alfalfa just jumped out of the ground.

You could almost stand there and see it grow. We cut five full crops and one partial crop. One field we cut six times. If Mother Nature didn't provide the moisture, we put the water right to it and made it rain.

I was working on what I'd call a rich man's farm and had the advantage of working with the latest of everything. That first summer machinery companies were introducing the hay crusher/conditioner; we had the first one in the state. Hay was picked up as it was mowed and run between two rollers so the stems were crushed and it dried faster. The faster hay dries, especially alfalfa, the better the bond with leaves. Leaves are where the protein is so you're making better feed.

There was another machine, a downdraft hay dryer, that was also new to the market. We baled hay when it was still moist and after two, three, four hours we had hay that was fully dry with fully intact leaves in the bale. And we were using preservatives in our silage to stop the development of mold. We were among the first to do that.

Win Way, UVM's extension agronomist, was a farm advisor and all our fertilizing was done according to soil tests, which we followed to the nth degree. It was like going to ag school, but it was all practical experience. So I learned a lot about crops working there.

Halfway through my second summer, the farm was sold to a doctor. He was interested in the main house, which was a typical home for a millionaire, and started selling off this, that, and the other thing to help pay for it. The farm manager left and in midsummer I was told there was nothing there for me.

After that I went to work on another farm, a farm along the Connecticut River. This was just the opposite—a young couple who were milking cows and had only been in business a short time. They were on a very tight budget, and I only worked part-time at the end of that summer when they needed help.

In the spring of 1959, after I had just gotten out of my last exam, I had a phone call from the wife who said that her husband was in the Brattleboro hospital with an infection in his finger and couldn't milk. Could I help? I helped until he got out of the hospital and stayed there all summer.

I left in the fall when my father and I started milking our small herd. I had already decided not to return to Marlboro for my junior year because of reoccurrence of the undulant fever that I had had since I was a kid. The doctor recommended taking some time off and getting my strength back from physical work.

I didn't have experience farming growing up, but I got to see both sides of farming those summers. I went from a farm that had everything to a farm that was struggling but that had a good herd of cows. From them, I learned the value of quality animals, buying good cows, and breeding them right. Their cows weren't fancy or registered, but they got the most out of what they had.

I was very lucky starting out in the 1950s and 1960s, working where I did, and at a time when the science of agronomy was taking over. Seed companies were becoming very competitive and were introducing new varieties. If one seed company had a corn that would do such and such, the other guy had to come up with something the next year or be left in the dust.

There were changes and improvements everywhere, and the difference was showing up at the milk pail. ❧

The Peer of Any Man

The first discouragement we have to meet is that of Climate. We have such long seasons of winter to provide for that to many of us the outlook often appears desolate. Have we not all, as the winter waxed strong and biting upon us, had more or less of anxiety and apprehension lest our supplies for the winter should prove short of the demand?

Another thing, and it may prove a discouragement to some of us—we must learn to moderate our expectations; we must learn to be content with an average of one cent per pound or twenty dollars per ton net return for our milk when manufactured into butter or cheese.

But another matter of vexation at least is the unskilled inefficient labor we have to employ. You can scarcely find one American young man who is content to work on the farm even for himself, much less for hire.

But a greater discouragement than all comes to us by way of taxation. The mode and manner or organizing the "grand list" of our State is made to operate unequally and oppressively upon the farmer.

I have been discoursing thus far of discouragements— always an unwelcome theme. But, brother farmers, there is a brighter and better side to this matter of farming. Your bank is the earth, and your investments are the broad acres you possess, while all the deposits you shall make there by way of manures, high cultivation, planting fruit trees will be safe and secure. Your milk and meats, your bread and butter, your fruits and vegetables, all come to you direct and fresh upon your tables; and better still, they have been prepared and served up by interested and loving hands.

The farmer, too, knows something of the value of personal independence. He orders all his hours of labor and rest without let or hindrance. He is not subject to the call of the factory bell, nor obliged to report himself "on time" at the store, the shop, or the office. Neither is he constrained to stifle his own convictions or compromise his actions for the sake of patronage, while he has very small inducement to play toady to any man class or clique, but himself in full liberty to be an honest, industrious, intelligent worker, a kind and hospitable neighbor, a good citizen of his town and State, as well as a Christian man in heart and life.

So the honest, industrious intelligent farmer is the peer of any man that walks the earth, and he has no cause or occasion, aside from courtesy and politeness, to lift his hat to any one.

G.H. Rice, *Fourth Report of the Vermont Board of Agriculture*, 1877

Larry, here fixing a waterbowl, was the "pragmatist"; Grayson was the unrepentant "optimist" always willing to give a cow a second chance. What they shared was pride in the herd they developed, says their long-time vet Walt Goodale.

We Had No Labor-Saving Devices: Everything Went Into Building a Quality Herd

GRAYSON WYMAN: My father was born in 1907 and grew up on farms, but when we started farming together it had been over 30 years since he had worked on a farm. He had a basic knowledge of farming, but it was from a different era. His father managed a big dairy farm in Maryland just before and during World War I where everything was done by manpower. A dozen to fifteen men hand milked over 100 cows, which was a big herd then. Horses and mules worked the land. There were no tractors.

When the War came along, the military took all the mules, and he packed up and came back to New England where he had grown up. My father and his brothers and sisters and my grandfather and grandmother had all their belongings in a freight wagon pulled by horses. They camped out at night and were on the road for over a month. That was the way they went down there and that was the way they came home.

My grandfather found a small hill farm in West Granby (Connecticut) and milked a one-man herd, probably 20 to 25 cows, until he died in 1933. My father helped out on the farm when he was in high school, but the farm wasn't big enough to support two people.

My father was always very mechanical and interested in engineering and after high school he moved to Windsor (Vermont) where he worked in a machine tool factory started by "Grandpa" Fancher. We always called him "Grandpa" because he took my mother in as a young girl after both her parents died. My father and mother had known each other from Granby and that's how he knew Mr. Fancher, who had lived in West Granby, too, before moving to Windsor.

"Grandpa" Fancher invented the bread wrapping and letter canceling machines. After he sold his inventions, he set up his own business that his son and grandsons ran. Over the years, the Fanchers expanded the business through mergers and buyouts. They moved it to Hill, New Hampshire, where my mother and father were married, and then to Irvington, New Jersey. I used to say that if you were a

"We were very labor intensive with the cows, both feeding and milking. That was why we basically lived in the barn. Everybody said, 'You're crazy.' Maybe we were but that's the way we did it," says Larry.

painter or glazier you were probably using tools made by "Grandpa" Fancher's company, Red Devil Tools, where my father worked.

After my father had a heart attack in 1956, the doctor told him that continuing to work in the industrial pressure cooker was going to finish him off. Larry was going to Marlboro College then and was interested in moving to Vermont. We had spent summer vacations at a family place on Grand Isle, and my parents liked Vermont from their days in Windsor.

Larry had seen a place in Dummerston, just north of Brattleboro. We looked at it on a weekend, bought it, and moved in the week before I graduated from high school in 1957. There was a brook and a pond, a lot of woodland and pastureland and some cropland. I was going to start at Marlboro in the fall, and we figured that if I didn't want to pay the room and board fee I could live at home. My first year I lived at Marlboro. The next year I commuted.

There was a barn with about 60 acres. We started with several hundred chickens. We crated eggs and sold them. We had two big fields and plowed a good portion of them for vegetables, which we sold. We hired the woodlot out for logging. My father and I raised turkeys for Thanksgiving and Christmas, which we sold and dressed. We started buying calves, and Dale, my younger brother, bought a cow, a registered Gurnesey for $300, which became the family cow that we hand milked.

All this was during our free time. I worked when I got home from Marlboro; my father, who couldn't afford to retire yet, worked as an insurance agent for National Life of Vermont and pitched in when he could. Larry was doing woodlot maintenance, working at a greenhouse in Brattleboro, and helping here in Dummerston and at a farm that Fern's father and brother had in West Guilford. It was a case where we were doing a little bit of everything. But almost everything had ties to being outdoors.

At this point, it was obvious that we couldn't stay here with all the calves and heifers that we were buying, raising, and selling. The heifers were getting ready to freshen and we had no place to milk

them. When Larry and I said we wanted to start farming full time, our father didn't say, "You're crazy" or anything like that. He was totally supportive and said, "If this is what you want to do, let's go for it." He helped in every way he could, but physically he couldn't do an awful lot because of his heart attack.

We kept our eyes open for farms and looked at operating dairies in Wilmington and the surrounding towns but didn't find anything that was big enough to support three people—my father, me, Larry and Fern. We looked at The New England Homestead, which always had ads. Dad was traveling all over the state for meetings, and he'd look for farms. This was before the interstate so it was pretty much back roads driving.

A real estate man told my father of a White River farm that had been out of operation for 10 years. The land had been kept up, but the barn needed a lot of work. We went and looked at it and that was how we ended up in White River. The farm had over 400 acres, but most of it was woodland. I think my father paid $17,000 to $18,000 for the whole thing.

We moved the cows on Labor Day of 1959 and shipped our first milk on October 12. We started with 8 or 10 cows. Our goal right away was to fill the barn with milkers. All that winter we bought one here and one there. My father and mother bought some. I had saved some money and bought nine cows. Larry joined us the following June and bought some machinery that summer.

We had just about anything and everything for cows—registered Holsteins, Guernseys, some Jerseys. We had most anything that would give us a good amount of milk. One of the hardest things the first year was trying to build numbers. Every time a bull calf came along you were disappointed because that meant that you didn't have another milker. To cull a young cow that didn't pan out was also tough when we were trying to keep every stall full.

In the spring of 1960, we got our first farm credit loan and bought a small herd from a man in North Hartland. The loan was for about $5,000. Once we had accumulated some animals and machinery, it wasn't hard to get the loan. A woman in Windsor, who had known my mother in high school, was also a big help. She had a herd of registered Holsteins that she had taken over when her father died.

Larry and I did a lot of business with her on a trust basis. She would sell us animals and say pay me when you can or give me $300 each month or $400 when you sell the animal. We bought some blemished cows, cows that only milked in three quarters or cows that she would have to carry while she tried to breed them. They were going to be dry for longer than she wanted to deal with. She also seemed to have an abundance of heifers, and we'd buy bred heifers from her.

We bought another small herd from a man who became one of our closest friends in White River. He and his cousin eventually started a farm machinery business, and we traded work back and forth to help them get started and to help us get started. He worked part time as a dairy farmer and worked at a machine shop in Windsor.

We had many neighbors like that in White River and Brownsville. They would milk 12 to 15 cows in the morning, work eight hours in one of the machine tool factories in Springfield or Windsor, and then milk at night. They had a week's pay that was supplemented by seven days of milk checks. Many had been brought up on farms but couldn't make a living just farming.

But even if they only had a few cows, they still had to comply with all the regulations of the full-time farmers. They put up with it for many years. Then bulk tanks came along and milk companies started picking up in bigger trucks and would tell these small farmers on remote back roads that it wasn't worth driving a big truck to pick up their milk. For that reason many small farmers dropped out.

We had the barn, which had room for 36, pretty full by the fall of 1960. Most were milkers, but a few were heifers and calves. In those days, we could buy quality cows for $250 to $300. The milk price then was $4, $5, up to $6 [for 100 pounds of milk, about 11.6 gallons], which was big money. Forty years later the milk price was only $11 to $12, which has been part of our problem.

The following winter we started planning for an addition to the barn and finished it in August of 1961. The addition, which was an open barn with a feed bunk, roughly doubled the space we had. We milked the cows in the barn and if we had 4 or 5 or 10 that needed to be milked, we'd let 10 out of the barn and bring 10 in. It was like musical chairs.

We built a silo at the end of the barn for corn silage. We filled a wheelbarrow, walked down the bunk, dumped it, and got another load until the bunk was full. Everything was done by hand. We had no labor saving devices. Our primary interest was getting more of the one thing that was making money for us and that was cows.

We did a lot of things the hard way because everything extra went into keeping the herd up to snuff, improving it, and increasing the numbers. Whatever we did, whether it was buying feed or building an addition, the goal was always to improve the quality of the herd and the milk check.

The first year, we shipped in cans until the dairies said no more cans. We didn't have any other options but to buy a tank. Things were tight, but I'd have to give credit to my mother who was a good money manager. She knew how to get everything she could out of a dollar. Most years we came out with our head above water. We supplemented lean years by letting out logging jobs on our woodlands.

We stayed in White River from 1959 to March of 1963. All that time, we knew it was just a stepping stone. The addition and silo helped, but we were limited by three or four very well-established, old family farms that surrounded us and had taken up most of the available land.

Larry and Fern had bought a small farm in Brownsville just before we bought the White River farm, but it was 15 miles away. Every time we did something there we had to get in a truck or tractor with a piece of equipment and drive from White River to Brownsville over the back roads. He had quite a bit of tillage land but a very small barn. It was good for heifers but not for milking cows, so all the milking was done in White River.

In a business that constantly tests one's patience, Larry and Grayson Wyman farmed together for 46 years. Their secret? A shared love of the outdoors and an appreciation of each's unremitting dedication to the farm's success.

In the early years, my father and I were doing most of the milking. Larry was taking care of the heifers in the early morning and then driving to White River to help us during the day. At night when we milked, he'd go back to Brownsville to take care of the heifers again. Then my father fell one morning when we were unloading milk cans at the milk plant in West Lebanon where we shipped our milk and fractured his wrist and hand. He ended up with a slight disability so Larry started helping me more on the night milking.

In 1963, a farm that bordered Larry's in Brownsville came up for sale so we decided that the best thing was to sell the farm in White River and move over there. The farm had a brand new barn that tied 56 cows with additional room for heifers, a good milk room, and an up-to-date ventilation system.

And it had a gutter cleaner in it. That was our first encounter with a gutter cleaner. At White River we shoveled manure into wheelbarrows every day. You went out the door and up a plank and into the manure spreader. When the snow got too deep to use the manure spreader you piled it up until the

"Every time you went there it was like a step back in time. You knew you weren't going to get out of there quickly when it came to their cows," says vet Walt Goodale of a farm visit. "If they weren't in the barn I was to call them from the barn phone or Larry's house. Even in busy fieldwork time one of them wanted to be there."

snow went. Who knew when that would be? White River is a place where the snow really comes early and stays late.

We had no trouble selling it. It was quite a spot. We were on a hill and on a clear day we could see Mt. Washington. A man who worked in the White River post office and his brothers had hunted there for years. When we moved in, he said if we'd ever like to sell it that he'd like to buy it. He didn't want to farm it but just live and hunt there.

We sold the house, the barn, and land to him and his nine brothers and sisters for $19,000. The house, barn, and 150 acres in Brownsville cost us a little over $30,000. We had gained some tillable land and Larry's land, which was next door.

Once we consolidated operations in Brownsville things began to come together. The barn in White River had all wooden stalls and wood stanchions, which was the way they constructed barns in the 1930s and 1940s. Wood stalls had been declared illegal, because you can't clean them well. In White River, we had to replace the wood floor in the barn with concrete. When we left the floors were concrete but the stanchions were still wood.

When we went to Brownsville, we had all concrete floors and steel stanchions. Everything was right up to code for milk production. We had a better milk room and a gutter cleaner. We had washable walls and ceilings, which had become part of the code. It was an easy move to make because there were so many things we would gain.

The one thing we didn't gain was enough land to support our cows. Even there our cropland was rather limited. We got into an arrangement with a hay dealer in town who baled on land he owned or rented. We traded some of our labor for hay and paid for the balance. That got us the extra feed that we needed to muddle along.

We raised a couple good-sized fields of corn and stored it in a bunker silo. Our tractor didn't have a bucket loader on it, so we dug the corn out by hand. We had to dig everything out and feed the cows, which were on two levels, all by hand.

By that time we had gotten into a flow where Larry and I did most of the work. My father couldn't do heavy work and by then he was technically retired and had stopped selling insurance. He continued to work every day, however, this time at a hardware store in Springfield.

So the Brownsville years were stepping-stone years. We knew the land and that the availability of hay in Brownsville would continue to be an issue and we would have to find something that was more appropriate. Dale had majored in ag ed at UVM and had gone to work for Eastern States Farm Exchange in Middlebury after graduating in 1965. He said if you are interested in staying in the business and want to be where agriculture is going to be viable, you want to be in Addison County because Middlebury is going to be the hub of agriculture in the Northeast in the not-too-distant future.

So we started looking up this way.

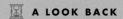

A Spirit of Industry, Enterprize, and Intelligence

We believe in small farms and thorough cultivation.

We believe that the soil loves to eat, as its owner, and ought to be manured.

We believe in large crops which leave the land better than they found it, making both the farmer and the farm rich at once.

We believe in going to the bottom of things—and therefore, in deep ploughing and enough of it. All the better if with a subsoil plow.

We believe the best fertilizer of any soil is a spirit of industry, enterprize, and intelligence—without this, lime and gypsum, bones and green manure, marl and guano, will be of little use.

We believe in good fences, good barns, good farm houses, good stock, good orchards, and children enough to gather the fruit.

We believe in a clean kitchen, a neat wife in it, a spinning piano, a clean cupboard and a clear conscience.

We disbelieve in farmers who will not improve—in farms that grow poorer every year—farmers' boys turning into clerks and merchants—in farmers ashamed of their vocation, or who drink whiskey till honest men are ashamed of themselves.

Vermont Family Visitor: A Monthly Newspaper Devoted Exclusively to Agriculture and Miscellaneous Matters, 1845

April 2004: A Little Dirt Under Your Fingernails

For 30 years, Larry Wyman captured in his DayMinder note-books the details, routine, and seasonal rhythms of the dairy farmer—daily milk production, vet visits, barn inspections, births and sales in the herd, spring plowing and planting, summer field work, fall harvests. From December through March, winter's slower pace is reflected in each day's dozen-line summary. This is a barebones accounting—milk production at the top, above the 7 a.m. appointment line, followed by weather observations, chores, cow notes, and non-routine business like a barn inspection. Milking partners and feed, beneath the 5 p.m. line, complete the entries.

April 1, 2004 thus becomes:

Milk Production: *8,581 pounds*

Weather: *40 degrees at 4 a.m., showers-heavy rain p.m.*

Chores: *clean feed alleys, wash 2 tanks, clean heifer barn & part of free stall*

Cow Notes: *herd check—Nate*

Miscellaneous Work: *errands in town (brush)*

  * *Briggs brought a load of sawdust—push into bin*

  * *heard 1st peepers this a.m.*

Milking Partners: *Jeanne & Larry, Grayson & David*

Feed: *1 hay, 1 silage*

There is relatively little variation in the notes during the locked-in months of winter: a truck load of sawdust is delivered for bedding, four days of hay are dropped from the haymow, a several-day-old bull calf gets sold to Addison County Commission Sales, a broken stall is fixed, cob webs are cleaned in the feed alley, spoilage is removed from the feed bunk.

Few winter events rise to the importance of being cited with an asterisk or multiple asterisk: *February 23 ******Matt did a DA (stomach operation) on #701; January 15 ********lost all water at 9 a.m. —pulled pump & replaced wires.*

Calendar spring arrives March 21. A farmer's spring begins when the fields say so. Winter's snow and ice may have melted by the 21st, but the fields can also still be under a foot of snow and rock hard. More than a calendar date, spring peepers, geese flying north, or the first robin, the awakening of the manure spreaders and the unlocking of the land are the true start of a farmer's spring.

By law, the farmer's metronome can speed up on April 1. On the 1st, Vermont's Accepted Agriculture Practice Rules permit spreading of manure and commercial fertilizer, with the window closing on December 15. Most springs the soil is sufficiently pliable by then to permit manure and fertilizer to be quickly plowed under, avoiding possible runoff into streams, lakes, and groundwater supplies. With 4,000 feet of frontage on the Otter Creek, the Wymans must be more conscious than most of the land's readiness.

Spring was accommodating. Following a week of mild weather at the end of March, when temperatures climbed into the 50s and 60s, Grayson began the spring's manure spreading on April 2. Over the next three weeks, Grayson and a contract manure spreader would be busy bees, traveling from manure pit to field and back.

Larry's DayMinder chronicled the activity: *April 2, manure on long field; April 7, liquid manure on long field with 6,300 gal tank*

A tractor's dusty tail is a welcome sight in a wet spring, signaling that Addison County clay is now dry enough for plowing.

and tractor; April 12, urea on grassland; April 16, manure on cellar hole piece; April 19, manure from pile in barnyard; April 20, fertilizer on alfalfa; April 21, spread more pile manure; April 22, fertilizer on Smith lot; April 23, more manure out of pile in barnyard on cellar hole piece; April 27, finish spreading manure from free stall—start pile in back of barn.

By month's end, the Wymans had solved one of farming's messiest problems—what to do with the roughly 12 to 18 tons of manure a mature dairy cow produces annually. Fields now had a nitrogen, potassium, and phosphorus mix that had been plowed under, the first step in reinvigorating fields in an eight-month planting, harvesting, and replowing cycle.

April will not end the barn's morning and evening milking routine, but overlay it with an often eight-hour day in the fields.

The pace of these days and the relief when fields are planted, the first cutting is completed, and corn is stored for the winter warrant not just asterisks in Larry's notes but underlinings and exclamation points.

Grayson does not keep a daily log—he does have an equivalent black book for breeding information—but he, too, recognizes and welcomes the coming of spring. "Once you get a little dirt under your fingernails and know that farming is what you want to do, you can't help being a little bit excited that the planting season is going to start," says Grayson. "It's like the baseball player going to spring training, the excitement of the upcoming season is ahead of you."

Call April spring training for farmers.

Chapter 2

Coming to Weybridge

The Land of Ham, Mooney, Frost, and Fletcher

On November 3, 1761, New Hampshire Governor Benning Wentworth, in issuing a charter for the town of Weybridge, granted land along the Otter Creek, now the Wyman Farm, to Samuel Ham, Benjamin Mooney, Zachariah Frost, and Ebenezer Fletcher. Wentworth, following King George's instructions, was to charter communities only when at least 50 grantees agreed to settle the land immediately.

That rarely happened in the 129 charters he issued from 1749 to 1764 and did not happen in Weybridge. Of the community's 64 grantees only one claimed the roughly 150-acre grants. While Weybridge histories have no information on the Wyman farm's grantees, they most likely had political connections and were investors interested in selling this valuable river-bottom land to farming- and frontier-minded residents from increasingly crowded Connecticut and Massachusetts.

In 1760, the territory that was to become Vermont was still very much the frontier, with forests covering most of the land; transportation via Lake Champlain, the Connecticut, and other rivers was difficult. The population of the disputed territory—both New Hampshire and New York governors claimed the land and issued conflicting land grants—was only several thousand but would grow to 150,000 by the end of the century.

As Jan Albers notes in her history of the Vermont landscape, *Hands on the Land*, real estate speculators faced a challenge and responded by depicting the land as little short of Eden:

> [The land] is of a very fertile nature, fitted for all the purposes and productions of agriculture. The soil is deep, and of a dark color; rich, moist, warm, and loamy. It bears corn and other kinds of grain, in large quantities, as soon as it is cleared of the wood, without any ploughing or preparation.

Few found such conditions. Thin soil and rocks underlay much of the forest, which covered about 95% of the land. Those settling in Addison County often found a taffy-thick clay, a challenge today for 200-horsepower tractors and an even greater challenge then to a pioneer with a hoe and, if prosperous, an ox.

If the land's fertility was oversold—by some estimates only about a sixth of Vermont has first-rate agricultural soil with most of that in the Champlain Valley and Orleans County—Vermont's forest floor, enriched by centuries of organic decay, was nonetheless productive in its first years. And because there were few other economic opportunities, over 90% of Vermont's first settlers were either full- or part-time farmers.

Unlike today's technology- and capital-intensive agriculture, farming once required little beyond perseverance and a strong back. As the *Fourth Report of the Vermont Board of*

In coming to Weybridge, the Wymans exchanged a rocky, side hill farm on the eastern side of the state for the relatively flat expanses of the Champlain Valley, Vermont's dairy heartland.

Agriculture (1877) notes, in the early 1800s "with the exception of the cart and harrow all of the farming tools of an average farm might be carried upon the shoulders of a strong man."

In this first phase of subsistence farming, which ran roughly from 1760 to 1830, the first rule was "never buy what can be produced at home." A pig, chickens, sheep, and large garden fed the family. A sturdy cow that doubled as a plow animal supplied the family's milk and butter. Cleared trees were burned with the ashes processed into potash, a salty chemical residue used in the production of lye, gunpowder, soap and glass and finishing of cloth. The standard barn, roughly 30 feet by 40 feet, with three bays—one for animals, one for hay, and one an open threshing floor that could also store wagons—could be built cheaply from available timber.

Seth Hubbell, in one of the classic accounts of the pioneer's life, *Narratives of the Sufferings of Seth Hubbell & Family*, describes his family's typical rocky start in the late 1700s:

> When I came into Wolcott, my farming tools consisted of one axe and an old hoe. The first year I cleared about two acres, wholly without any team, and being short of provision was obliged to work the chief of the time till harvest with scarce sufficiency to support nature….I could not get a single potato to plant the first season, so scarce was this article. I planted that which I cleared in season with corn; and an early frost ruined my crop, so that I raised nothing the first year….

Hubbell faced sterner conditions as a hill farmer in northeastern Vermont than settlers in the more hospitable, warmer, flatter and relatively rock-free Champlain Valley. But his resilience would be the hallmark of Vermont farmers for decades. They would be tested constantly by weather, demanding soil, lack of transportation, and competition from the Midwest. Despite these disadvantages, Vermont agriculture has always had periods of prosperity.

In the "wheat boom" following the Revolutionary War, Vermont farmers, taking advantage of the still fertile soil, became major wheat exporters, much of it sold in Canada and shipped via Lake Champlain. But by the 1830s, the wheat boom was over, killed by devastations from wheat weavil and wheat rust, the soil's exhaustion from a nutrient-demanding crop, and cheaper midwestern wheat, transported east by the new Erie Canal.

This pattern would be repeated with the "sheep boom." Vermont's hilly, rocky land, often marginal for crops, was ideal for sheep and by the 1830s, Addison County was producing more wool per acre than any county in the country. In 1837, at the boom's peak, the state's nearly 1.7 million sheep outnumbered people by six to one. But this boom was largely over by the 1850s, a victim of cheaper wool from the West and lower tariffs on foreign wool.

For the past century-plus, Vermont's farming niche, albeit with many ups and downs, has been dairying. With better rail transportation, most importantly refrigerated rail cars in the late 1800s and early 1900s, Vermont dairy farmers could now sell fluid milk, not just cheese and butter, to the ever-expanding Boston market. Today, Vermont produces more milk than the other six New England states combined.

Larry and Grayson Wyman are relative newcomers in this sweep of agricultural history. There are no records of when their 320-plus acres were first farmed. The farm's homestead dates to 1850, but settlers most likely farmed the prime river-bottom land before then.

The farm's first residents are known: Sylvia Drake and her companion, Charity Bryant, aunt of poet William Cullen Bryant. Asaph Drake, Sylvia's blacksmith brother, came to Weybridge from Massachusetts in the late 1700s to run a sawmill, later expanding his commercial empire with a grist mill and forge. Sylvia, a seamstress, followed in 1806. Today, the foundation ruins of Drake and Bryant's home lie in a copse of trees in a field just to the north of Drake Road.

In coming to Weybridge, the Wymans did not need a land speculator's hard sell. As Grayson and Larry recall, the prospect of exchanging patched-together hill farms for the expansive fields of Addison County was appealing. For Fern Wyman, moving with three young children from a new house to a drafty, run-down 100-year-old farmstead was much less attractive.

In coming to Weybridge, the Wymans sought a self-contained farm, where home, barn, pasture, feed bunks, and cropland were contiguous. Larry had a 100-foot walk across Quaker Village Road to the barn. Grayson did as well until building a home two-tenths of a mile away.

This Place Could Get Us Somewhere

LARRY WYMAN: My father retired from Red Devil Tools in 1957 after he had a heart attack and was looking for a less stressful job. I was going to Marlboro College then, and my mother and father bought a home with a small barn in Dummerston. He was only 49 or 50 when he went to work in the insurance business with National Life of Vermont.

Grayson, Dale, and I started buying calves for the barn, but the place wasn't set up for dairying and farming. It was a country home with some acreage. My father couldn't do much physical work, but he knew that Grayson and I were interested in getting into farming and when he traveled around the state he always had his eye on farms that were for sale.

In 1959, he sold the Dummerston place and bought a hilltop farm in White River Junction with the idea that we could milk cows there. The farm had a small barn set up for milking and a house that looked off toward Hanover and Lebanon and over the town of White River. There were 450 acres but nearly all was woodland and very little was tillable.

Grayson had been going to Marlboro and started milking with our father. They shipped their first milk October 12, 1959. I had been working in a greenhouse in Windsor that grew roses and joined them the following spring. Fern and I had bought a farm in Brownsville and were living there. It was only 15 miles away, but some nights it seemed like 150 after I was through milking.

My father's White River farm gave us a place to start. But it was difficult farming in two different places. I didn't have any dairy cows at my place but had 25 or so heifers that we pastured behind the barn. At White River we started buying cows and soon filled the barn to capacity, 36. We shipped milk in 10-gallon cans and took four or five every morning to Buttrick's Dairy in Lebanon. Most of it was made into ice cream or sold as milk to the hospital in Hanover.

During the winter of 1963, a Brownsville neighbor who had been having financial problems decided to sell. Our White River barn was old and too small so we looked at this farm, which was about a quarter of a mile from mine. With this farm's land, what I had, and with what we could rent in town, we figured there was plenty of land around. Being closer together would make life a lot easier. My father put the White River farm on the market that winter and sold it in a heartbeat.

The two farms gave us the opportunity to expand the herd. The big problem was that Brownsville and West Windsor were becoming ski towns (surrounding the Mt. Ascutney ski area). People who had never seen a dollar in their life were seeing their land values go way up.

Fern and I bought the Brownsville farm for $8,000 in 1959. That was for a house, barn, and 115 acres. Nine years later when we moved to Weybridge that same property would have been worth $40,000 to $50,000 if we hadn't had to sell much of the farm. We had three kids then and the old house was very small so in 1965 we sold the house, barn, and some land, but none of the tillable land.

We used that $35,000 to help pay for a new house on my father and mother's land.

The Wyman barn includes a 200-foot-long by 40-foot-wide central unit, built in the 1960s with 102 stalls and a hay-mow above; a 100-year-old smaller wing on the southern side that holds 40 to 50 young calves; and an open free stall for 50-plus older heifers and dried cows on the southwest side of the main barn.

Our new house was within walking distance of the barn, which was convenient. I could go home for breakfast and lunch and dinner. The kids could walk back and forth to the fields.

We now had a good barn, but we still didn't have the acreage to support our herd. The problem was that people had become very reluctant to let you rent their land even though they were no longer farming because if a hot deal came along they wanted to get in on it. By the mid-60s we figured that we had to get someplace where dairy-ing had a future, because people in Brownsville were speculating all

the time, whether they wanted to admit it or not. When we came in 1959 there were 26 dairy farms in the area. When we left there were only about a dozen. There isn't a dairy farm left there today.

The bottom line was that we needed more land and better facili-ties. So we started looking around up here (Addison County) because the county had the best land and agricultural infrastructure in the state, and we figured that if dairying were going to survive anywhere it would be here. You had tractor dealers, feed companies, vets, breeding technicians here. All that was being lost in Windsor County.

Plus, land prices were still manageable here and you could buy a farm for far less than you could closer to the interstate and urban areas.

We wanted a farm big enough for 100 cows, which was a big herd then. We wanted a size that Grayson and I could run because we didn't want to hire people. We wanted a farm on a hardtop road and not on a hill top.

In Brownsville, we could see the side of the Mt. Ascutney ski area. Our house was higher yet, and we could see way down the Connecticut River Valley. It was picturesque but hillsides are hardly the easiest farmland to work when you're trying to carve out a living.

We didn't want to be on busy Route 7 or on a backcountry dirt road either because more and more tractor trailers were transporting milk. At the tail end of our time in Brownsville, some farmers on the backroads were having trouble finding truckers to pick up their milk.

My father and mother were both agreeable to the move. They had already made a million moves and had bounced around all their lives. As it turned out, when my mother died at 95, she had lived longer in Weybridge (1968-2004) than any other place in her life.

We probably looked at a dozen farms in Addison County, in Charlotte and the Rutland area. A lot of farmers were getting out then. They were selling off their cows or being gobbled up by bigger farms or selling their land for house lots. There was a lot of demand, too, for farms from people from Massachusetts and the Connecticut River Valley like us.

We always came back to Euclide Quesnel's farm even though the house was old and in horrendous shape. The barn was what sold us. The barn was brand new—a little over a year old. It had a drilled well, and we had just gone through drought years, dealing with water problems.

Quesnel was a cattle dealer and hadn't installed a milking system so we would have to do that. But the barn tied 102, which was double the stalls we had in Brownsville, and gave us a lot of room for growth. And it had adequate pasture and at that time we were still pasturing. We had about 75 tillable acres in Brownsville. Here we would have roughly triple that. It just seemed so much better than what we had.

The realtor tried to interest us in the Smith farm, too, which is just to the west of us. The idea was that my mother and father and Grayson would stay in the Quesnel homestead. Fern and I and the three kids would live in the Smith homestead. But we didn't feel that we had to farm all of Addison County and said we'd take just this one.

Quesnel and Francis O'Brien, a machinery dealer, bought the farm from Martin Young in 1959. Young had owned it since 1924. They sold it to Henry Highter, who couldn't make a go of it and sold it back to Quesnel, who sold it to us.

As it was, this was a very big step for us and we had to go well into debt to buy the place. After my father and I had sold our Brownsville farms we were able to come up with about half the $92,000 price for the house, barn, and 320 acres. On top of that we probably spent another $30,000 on cows and machinery because what we had wasn't adequate to run the place.

We were shipping $5 milk then and thought we had gone head over heels in debt. We didn't pay off the farm until the summer of 2006. We rolled over a line of credit and carried debt right until the end because we needed the tax deductions.

We probably could have gotten more for our Brownsville places if we had been willing to wait. But we were impatient and decided it was better to just bite the bullet and get started. The potential was there, and we thought this place could get us somewhere. ⚭

The Otter Creek, a highway through the woods for the Abenakis, is a different kind of highway for today's farmers, bringing, as it does, rich loads of loamy silt to their fields during spring floods. Fields contiguous to the Wymans' 4,000 feet of river frontage have some of the best yields on the farm.

There Was a Lot of River Bottom Land

GRAYSON WYMAN: We had ideas about what we wanted. We needed housing for two families. We needed a barn that was far bigger than what we had. And we wanted a farm with land that could support what we milked. At that time we were looking to double our size to 100 milkers and 50 replacement heifer calves.

The rule of thumb was that you needed 3 to 4 acres per animal and their offspring. I don't think they have a figure like that today because land is so much more productive and your farms are milking 500, 600, 700, 1,000 cows. The approach today is grab all the land that you can whether you buy it, lease it, or rent it. Finding land today isn't the issue it used to be because there are so far fewer farms.

Back when we were thinking about moving to the Champlain Valley, most everything was an integral unit. Your house, barn, and land were all in a block. You didn't go down the road 10 miles to get extra acreage the way they do today.

We started looking in earnest in the winter of 1968. Larry and Fern came up first and saw this farm. Larry thought right away that it had potential. At the time Euclide Quesnel, a cattle dealer, owned the farm. He had bred heifers in the barn, but there were only stalls, water bowls, and a gutter cleaner. Euclide had torn the old barn down and built a new one in 1967. He had cows all over the county with people milking for him. He planned to milk here but a change in family plans made this farm available.

Dale and I came up, and a real estate man from Brandon took us around to some farms. Dale graduated from UVM with a degree in ag ed in 1965, but he wasn't interested in farming. He started out working for Eastern States Farm Exchange as a trainee in Middlebury so he already knew the area.

Back in 1966-67, we were already talking about finding something bigger and more appropriate. He said then if we were interested in staying in the business and wanted to be where agriculture would be viable in the future then Addison County was the place to be. Middlebury was going to be the hub of dairying in the Northeast in the not-too-distant future. So we started looking up this way.

When we were looking at farms, we didn't see anything that compared with this. Most farms were available because their owners were older and physically worn out. They were selling the farm and would live off what they could get.

Finally my father, mother, and I came up and looked at the next farm over and then the Quesnel farm. What impressed us with this farm was that there was a lot of river-bottom land with a sandy loam from years of spring floods. It wasn't the typical heavy clay in the Champlain Valley. We wanted to grow a lot of corn and corn likes sandier soil. And sandy loam is a lot easier to plow.

So here we had good fields, a good barn, and a farmhouse for two families. When we moved in, Larry and Fern lived in the front of the house with the three girls; my father, mother, and I lived in the back. That was the way it was until my father died in 1976.

I Had to Support My Family Without a Cow

I moved from Connecticut with the expectation of having fifty acres of land given me, but this I was disappointed of, and was under the necessity soon after I came on of selling a yoke of oxen and a horse to buy the land I now live on, which reduced my stock to but one cow; and this I had the misfortune to loose (lose) the next winter. That left me wholly destitute of a single hough (hoof) of a creature: of course the second summer I had to support my family without a cow.

I spent the summer before I moved, in Wolcott, in making preparation for a settlement, which, however, was of no avail to me, and I lost the summer; and to forward my intended preparation, I brought on a yoke of oxen, and left them, when I returned in the fall, with a man in Johnson, to keep through the winter, on certain conditions; but when I came on in the spring, one of them was dead, this yoke of oxen that I put off for my land was made of the two surviving ones. But to proceed, in the fall I had the good fortune to purchase another cow; but my misfortunes still continued, for in the June following she was killed by a singular accident. Again I was left without a cow, and here I was again frustrated in my calculations: this last cow left a fine heifer calf that in the next fall I lost by being choaked.

Here I was left destitute—no money to buy, or article to traffic for one: but there was a door opened. I was informed that a merchant in Haverhill was buying snakeroot and sicily. With the help of my two oldest girls, I dug and dried a horse-load, and carried this commodity to the merchant; but this was like most hearsay reports of fine markets…[he] would not even venture to make an offer; but after a long conference I importuned with the good merchant to give me a three year old heifer for my roots. I drove her home, and with joy she was welcomed to my habitation, and it has been my good fortune to have a cow ever since.

Narratives of the Sufferings of Seth Hubbell & Family,
1789

Rarely Pancake Flat: The Farms of Addison County

The fields of the Wyman farm, like those of many river-bottom farms, are rarely pancake flat. They are full of gentle rises and side hills with just enough pitch, contour, and wet spots to keep planting and harvesting a challenge. And like many farms that hug valley bottoms, the Wyman land has a pleasing sweep but rarely panoramic, far-as-the-eye-can-see views.

Snake Mountain, a 1,200-foot-high ridge across the valley, blocks views of the Adirondacks to the west. A much lower ridge that butts up against the farm's eastern-most fields blocks views of the Green Mountains to the east.

This lower ridge with its several lookouts provides the best view, the hawk's view, of the farm's patchwork of field, creek, road, and forest. From above, Quaker Village and Drake roads and Route 23 trisect the land like a tic-tac-toe board. Fields from several to 40 acres fill the squares of this grid.

Larry and Fern's home, the barn, the Kehoe home, and repair shop are just north of the intersection of Quaker Village and Drake roads. The homes of Grayson and Beverly Wyman, Larry and Fern's daughter, are just to the south of the intersection.

The farm is bordered on the south by fields of Monument Farms Dairy, one of the last family-owned dairies in the state. To the west, Wes Smith raises beef cattle. The farm's northern border is the Otter Creek; sluggish in the summer, the Otter floods in the spring, leaving prime sandy loam soil at river's edge.

About three-quarters of the Wyman's 300 acres are open, but the broken-down stone walls and thick growth at the top of ridge reveal how quickly the landscape can change. Most likely, the stone wall fenced in sheep during Vermont's short-lived mid-1800s sheep boom, a time when eight Weybridge farmers had flocks of over 400 sheep while the largest dairy herd was 14 cows.

Had the sheep boom continued, Vermont would look very different today. Forested hillsides would be clean shaven like the dales of Wales, Scotland, and Ireland, nibbled clean by generations of Merinos. Instead, the dairy cow, more comfortable grazing on flatter land, has been the predominant landscaper for the past 150 years. Hillsides have grown up while lowlands and valleys have been kept open for pasture and crops.

This ridge top, once suitable for nimble-footed sheep but not for crops or cows, is testament to this change. It is now a wood lot, overgrown with hardwoods. That the ridge remains relatively open is testament to Larry's annual thinning for winter firewood.

The fields below are of much higher quality, containing some of the most productive, relatively rock-free soils in the state. That glaciers have shaped Vermont is readily visible in the craggy, sculpted summits of the highest peaks of the Green Mountains. Their impact is much less visible but equally significant in lowland Vermont, where the receding ice sheet 12,000 years ago deposited glacial till dozens of feet deep. Vermont and New England's thousands of miles of stone walls and the annual crop of rocks unearthed during spring plowing are reminders of this deposition.

The Champlain Valley has this same glacial debris, but deposits of fine sediment, as much as 100 feet deep, can overlay this till. Credit Lake Vermont, a freshwater lake five times the size of today's Lake Champlain, for Addison County's clays. During the 1,000-year period when the glacier retreated and the lake flooded the western half of Vermont, the Wyman farm would have been under several hundred feet of water and the summit of Snake Mountain would have been the only dry ground until the foothills of the Green Mountains 10 miles to the east.

Lake Vermont would be replaced by the Champlain Sea, when the mile-thick glacier had fully retreated. Where Holsteins now graze, whales and seals would swim for more than 2,000 years in a saltwater sea. Not until the northern end of the Champlain Basin rebounded several hundred feet after the glacier's retreat would Atlantic Ocean waters stop flowing downhill into the state from the St. Lawrence River Basin.

Over the past 9,000 years, the Champlain Valley, responding to a warming climate, has evolved from a tundra ecosystem, where nomadic paleoindians hunted wooly mammoths and caribou, to a forested landscape occupied by an estimated 4,000 Abenakis when Samuel de Champlain explored the area in the early 1600s. More recently, the hand of man in clearing forests for fields has dramatically changed the Vermont landscape. The view from the ridge, with its quilt of field and woodland below, reminds us how quickly 200 years of farming has reshaped the land.

Glaciers have shaped Vermont's landscape. But so too have the million sheep that grazed from valley to ridgeline in the mid-1800s. Tumbled-down pasture rock walls, here on the ridge to the east of the Wyman Farm, remind us of their several decades of preeminence.

In coming to Weybridge, Fern exchanged a new home for a drafty century-old homestead. Nearly 40 years later, the house still needed work. The farm came first.

It Doesn't Matter Where You Live

FERN WYMAN: It was very difficult to move to Weybridge, and I probably didn't have the proper attitude at the outset. We had just built a new house in Brownsville that had a beautiful view of Mt. Ascutney. This was hard to leave. And it didn't help that our friends and relatives would say how could you leave that house.

I had to be careful what I said because it could make things worse for Larry. So I tried to be cheerful about the whole thing. "It's home. It's for the family. It doesn't matter where you live if you are with your family."

I finally grew into it, but cleaning up this house was a chore and a half. The house goes back at least to 1850 and had never been modernized. It was cold and had no central heating so we had to install a furnace right away. There was a bathroom but no kitchen.

I scraped wood and painted. I pulled paper off the walls. I worked and worked and worked and really never got the house in good shape. There is still so much to do, but at least we got it cleaned up.

One reason they chose the farm was because the barn was right on the road across from the house. In White River and Brownsville, we were at the end of long hills and it was hard for milk trucks to reach us. I hated the road, but they thought it was wonderful because the milk and feed trucks could back right up to the barn. But there wasn't much traffic, which I liked. Today there is and you want to be careful when you cross the road. People weren't in a hurry, the way they are now.

When we came here, I had three small kids and that was my main interest, that and the garden. We raised a lot of our food and meat and were quite self-sufficient. Larry and Grayson were really into farming by then. But when I first knew Larry, he wasn't talking about being a farmer. We met at Marlboro where we both took forestry courses and worked in the woods. I thought he was a real nice guy and liked the outdoors the way I did.

We married in 1958 after my freshman year. I didn't finish college. Larry completed another semester and then stopped. We lived in an apartment in Brattleboro when we were first married, and he worked for a florist there. He also helped hay and occasionally milked on my parents' farm when we were going together and were first married.

The next year (June 1959), we bought an old hill farm in Brownsville, which is a couple miles west of Windsor. There were 115 acres, but we didn't plan to use it as a farm. The barn was small and ancient, and the land had not been farmed for a while. And there weren't any cows.

The main reason we bought it was the price, $8,000. After we moved, Larry worked in a greenhouse in Windsor and delivered flowers around the state. Grayson and his parents were still in Dummerston, but several months after we moved they bought an old hill farm in White River because Grayson was interested in farming.

Larry worked at the florist's for about a year but would go over and help his father and Grayson in White River. After a while, they brought the heifers over here. Even then I didn't think that farming was going to be his life's work. In the beginning, I thought Grayson was more interested and Larry was just helping out. But when Larry's parents bought the farm next to us they began to get pretty serious about farming because now they had the capacity for a lot more cows.

But I don't think they ever had a master plan; it just evolved.

Larry and Grayson are like many farmers. They prefer to be their own boss and work for themselves. Neither wants to be cooped up in a factory. And neither likes a lot of regulations.

But they were also a little different from most farmers. Dan can talk tractors and pickup trucks for hours. Larry and Grayson could care less about machinery. When they first started, their father repaired machinery. Grayson and Larry came to that eventually, but they never enjoyed it. That's way different from most farmers.

What they shared was a love of the country and a respect for each other. I think that's how they were able to work together all those years. ᴁ

Fern worked off the farm for nearly 20 years after the children were grown, enabling Larry, in lean years, to devote all milk income to farm expenses.

May 2004: At the Mercy of Factors We Can't Control

Each spring after the fields bordering the Otter Creek have been turned over, travelers on Drake Road can observe hunched figures in the distance, heads bowed, their feet scuffing the sandy loam. With any success, these distant walkers will go home with a handful of Abenaki artifacts. Centuries before Weybridge's white settlers began farming in the late 1700s and early 1800s, the Abenakis set up small settlements along the Otter, Winooski, and Lamoille. There they grew corn and beans.

Today, the Wymans plant corn on this prime bottomland. Some springs the Otter overflows and again, more ominously, in mid-summer. These floodings, which can destroy a corn crop, have also left layers of nutrient-rich soil that produces Jack-in-the-Beanstalk-high corn.

Unlike the clay mixtures found in other fields, these fields dry quickly and plow easily, and are usually the first to be planted. On May 7, 8, and 10, Dan seeded these 20 acres to corn during a spell of sunny 60-degree days. By May 21, all corn fields, 80-plus acres, had been planted and Larry can reflect on a spring where nearly everything has gone according to schedule:

> Planning is good in theory. In practice it's something else. We're at the mercy of factors 24-7 that we can't control. Your machinery breaks down. You can't get a part for a week. Or you wake up and you have three or four new calves to deal with.
>
> And weather. That's the biggest unknown. Last year we finished on June 28. There's nothing that you can do when it rains and rains, and you can't get in your fields.
>
> This year we finished on May 20. We got in the fields and just kept working. Last year, we would have a day of sun and days of rain. Dan didn't so much as plant the corn as mud it in.

Now we need some sunny 70- to 75-degree days. The corn is already germinating, and it will take off with a little sun. But we have a long summer ahead of us.

Larry sums up the spring's strong start and flurry of activity with a series of celebratory DayMinder entries on May 20:

    * *harrow barn field again!*
    * *Bourdeau sprayed all corn land that had not been done!!*
  ** *cultipack & plant barn field!!*
    * *corn all in ground for 2004!!*

May 11, 2004 was planting perfect. Warm, 62 degrees at 4 a.m., with dry fields. The only hitch was the broken bearings on the disk harrow. Fix the bearings, harrow the Drake Road piece, roll it, and then after a quick supper, Dan began the evening's planting.

June 2004: A Near Perfect Spring

There is no such thing as running a farm on automatic pilot. But there is a pattern for each day, season, and year. Farmers set their clocks by morning and evening milkings. Fields have to be planted and harvested in an unforgiving spring/fall window. Machinery and barns have to be maintained, repaired, and replaced. The herd has to be culled and upgraded.

But farming is also full of variables and, at times, the totally unexpected. A mid-June hail storm can severely damage the corn crop. Should those fields be plowed under and reseeded with short-maturity corn, an expensive and time-consuming proposition? Or will enough of the crop survive and can reserves carry the farm through one bad harvest?

The transmission on an aging but mainstay tractor goes. Should it be repaired at a cost of thousands of dollars or be replaced by a new or used tractor? Will the backup tractor last until milk prices improve?

There are no sure-fire answers to such questions, and farmers become experts at making do.

For the most part, this has continued to be a near perfect spring. The Wymans' corn had good germination before a cold and wet spell at the end of May and early June that killed later-starting corn on neighboring farms. By the second week of June, the mower had new a set of blades and fields were ready for their first cutting.

But June threw the Wymans and the Kehoes some major-league curves. On June 30, Esther Wyman, 95, died at home after several years of declining health and a last year where she see-sawed between hospital and home.

On June 7, Jeanne Kehoe's day began as it had for the past seven years, milk with Larry and then clean the heifer barn. A diagnosis of leukemia that afternoon would end her work with heifers. Dan would take over as "Mom."

"At the service people were saying this was the end of an era," Larry would recall. "She had paid the bills for years until she became so blind that Grayson took over.

"It's the end of an era but not the farm. We just don't know what form it will take when Grayson and I stop. There are just too many questions now."

The biggest question was Jeanne Kehoe. On the afternoon of June 7, Jeanne, who had been feeling tired, not unusual for a farmer, received the results of lab tests. She had a fast-developing acute form of leukemia.

For the next 14 months, Jeanne's health would shape the farm's operation far beyond the vagaries of weather, harvests, and milk prices.

Chapter 3

The Land

Sticky and Soft When Wet; Hard and Cracked When Dry

Farmers have a rough rule of thumb; it takes five years to learn the quirks of a new farm—fields that can withstand the heavy nutrient demands of corn year after year, land that needs to be rotated frequently between grass and corn, pieces that dry early or late in the spring or are prone to late and early frosts. In moving to Weybridge, the Wymans added another variable in this learning curve; stonier soils from their hill farms on the eastern side of the state would be replaced by the sticky but relatively fertile clays of Addison County.

Maps 35 and 43 in the U.S. Soil Conservation Service's soil survey of the county, with their amoeba-shaped tracings outlining the boundaries of soil types, provide a soil scientist's perspective of this challenging terrain. Each aerial map, which covers an area of about 2.5 miles by 3.75 miles, is overlain with roads, Monopoly-like squares for structures, and an alphabet soup of soil types, Cw, FaE, Hh, NeB, VgB.

In the conservation service's classification system soils are ranked by capability, Class I to Class VIII. Class I is a farmer's and developer's heaven—a soil that has "few" limitations restricting its use; it's usually relatively flat and fertile, well drained, and not subject to flooding or standing water. Class VIII is unsuitable for cultivation but has value for recreation, wildlife habitat, and water supply. Think steep hillsides, rocky ridges, forest, and "esthetic purposes," not crops.

Then add a subclass: "e" indicates that erosion is a risk without close-growing plant cover; "w" warns that water in or on the ground can interfere with plant growth and field cultivation; and "s" cautions that the soil is shallow, stony, or droughty. A scale of 1 to 10 ranks the quality of the land within the class.

Like much of the lower elevations of the Champlain Valley, the Wyman farm is a combination of looser-grained loams and fine-grained clays with classifications ranging from Class II along the Otter Creek to Class VII, the rocky ridge rising to the east over the Wyman homestead. Like most farmers, the Wymans can walk potential cropland and from experience gauge the land's potential. Should they need a second opinion, there are these conservation maps and soil analyses.

Their frontage along the Otter, for example, is Hh and NeB. Hh is part of the Hadley series, a very fine sandy loam that is deep, well drained, and retains moisture very well. The only drawback? The land floods.

Not surprisingly, the greatest yields on the Wyman farm, 25-plus tons of corn per acre most years, is grown on Hh. This 12-foot-high corn lives up to the land's classification, IIw-1: Class II, "moderate" limitations that may reduce the choice of plants or may require "moderate" conservation practices; "w," the land's wetness must be watched; and 1, this

At the end of March the land unlocks. By the end of October over 200 acres of grass and 10-foot high corn have been cut and stored in the Wymans' feed bunks and haymow.

land is the best of its class. NeB, the Nellis stony loam, on more sloping, erosion-prone land is ranked a notch lower, Class IIe-3.

Inland from the silt-laden, easily-plowed soils along the river, the Addison County clays—the Covington and Panton silty clays and the better-draining Vergennes clay, take over. Should farmers need any forewarning, the conservation service's observations suggest the problems that Covington and Panton clays present: they are difficult to plow and harrow, cold until late in the spring, very sticky and soft when they are wet, and harden and crack when they dry. They also should be plowed in the fall so winter's freezing and thawing will break the soil and make harrowing easier in spring.

These mainly Class III and IV soils are easy to spot. Each spring, look for Grayson and Larry plowing under manure and pulverizing cannon ball-sized clods of clay, loop after loop, with moldboards, disc harrows, and cultipackers. The old saying, "The best fertilizer is the footsteps of the landowner," perhaps needs some modification with Addison County. The best fertilizer starts with a tractor and a very comfortable seat for hours of plowing.

Should a farmer consider short cuts, the conservation service's table *Predicted Average Acre Yields of Principal Crops under Two Levels of Management*, "Ordinary" and "Improved" should stop that temptation. "Improved" management—erosion control, proper fertilization, crop rotation, weed control, and seedbed preparation—improves yields from 30% to 100%.

Addison County's preeminence in dairying stems not so much from the quality of its soils, which the soil survey cautions "range from moderate to very low in natural fertility" but from its relatively flat terrain, longer growing season, and still robust agricultural infrastructure. Addison County clay, farmers joke, is not much good for growing houses because the soil won't percolate to meet septic systems regulations. What's left is farming.

That Vermont farmers have surmounted these soil conditions is testament to their resourcefulness and perseverance. As University of Vermont geographer Harold Meeks points out:

> Vermont's agricultural soils then are acid, infertile, low in organic content, and often either poorly or excessively drained. In a word, they are generally poor soils, especially in a national context, and their quality, or lack of it, certainly was one factor in the great westward migration. In a New England context, the soils of the Champlain Valley are some of the best in the region; but they too suffer by comparison with those of most of the Middle West.

In the following commentaries, the Wymans discuss the challenges in working Addison County clay and the necessity, with a bigger herd, tight margins, and a larger mortgage, to squeeze the most out of every tillable and pasture acre. ᐛ

Take care of your fields and they will take care of you. That means timely crop rotation, appropriate fertilization, and no skimping on seed bed preparation.

Ever increasing herd size means more feed, which requires additional acreage and/or greater productivity per acre. Commercial fertilization per acre has roughly tripled since 1960. Dan, above, adds nitrogen to the soil during corn planting.

A Fertilizer Salesman Would Have Starved to Death

LARRY WYMAN: When we came to Weybridge, a farm with 60 cows was a big farm. Some farms had 300, 400, 500 acres of land. Heavens, with all that land farmers didn't have to worry about feed. They made hay, hay, and more hay. Everybody had all they needed. Farmers didn't see that the quality of their feed was going to have to be better.

As it was, most farmers figured that part of their income would come from selling surplus hay. Tractor trailers loaded with hay were very common in the winter. Most went to horse farms in Massachusetts and Connecticut and some over to New Hampshire and Maine because farming in those areas was dying out. Fields were growing up or being covered with concrete.

People here didn't give a hoot if they rode their tractors over all their acres. Fuel was cheap. The grass was thin, and it dried very quickly. Consequently, they could put up hay in no time.

Our ideas, coming from the eastern side of the state, were different. We didn't have the acreage and used lots of fertilizer on our grass and corn to get as much feed per acre as we could and to improve its quality. When we ordered fertilizer for every square inch, the salesman was aghast. He didn't know what kind of gold mine he had struck.

Farmers here hadn't been on the eastern farms. There was no reason to go there. We were the poor cousins. Our farms were full of stones and on side hills. You needed one leg shorter than the other to work most of them. You had to be out of your mind to even try to farm there, let alone think that you could make a living. But the Connecticut River valley farms were a whole different ball game. Those river-bottom farms were going places and in many ways outstripped anything that was over here, not only in their size but also in their production and feed.

When we started in the late 1950s, heavy use of fertilizer and pesticides was a new issue and concept. Up until that time, farmers basically used manure out of the barn. If that didn't do it, nothing did. And most farmers didn't need more feed because their herds

Early May is optimal field preparation time. Ideally, April showers are over, fields are dry and the soil has warmed. Farmers plant, weather permitting, in a several-week window that follows.

were still small. Farmers here had some catch up to do when it came to improving the yield of their fields.

At that point, even upcoming farmers weren't convinced that you had to get bigger and bigger and milk more cows. Higher taxes changed that. The only way farmers could compensate was to milk more cows and spread out their fixed costs. That's what started it. As time went on the cost of machinery, fuel, and electricity increased and you began to see a significant increase in cow numbers and the greater use of fertilizer, insecticides, and pesticides to improve your crop yields.

People still sell hay today, but it's a fraction of the 1960s and 1970s because most farms need all they can produce. Another change is very few farms deal with small square bales. There's too much labor in them. It's either big square bales or big round bales, which weigh hundreds of pounds. People who are looking for small bales are horse people. Women take care of them, and they can't horse around a mammoth bale.

The Wymans discovered that moving cows from pasture to daily milking was too time consuming and that they could provide a better-balanced diet by feeding the herd in the barn. But they still maintained 10 acres to pasture dried-off cows for several weeks before they freshened.

We made round bales but kept making small square bales right up until the end because a lot of our hay was fed in the calf barn or to the heifers. Jeanne did that and 30- to 40-pound bales were easier for her to handle. But on a lot of farms you can't find a small bale of hay today. They may break hay out of big bales or not be feeding any hay. It's hay, haylage, and corn silage as your base with corn or soybean meal to get your TMR (total mixed ration).

In the late 1950s what did the experts know, let alone Grayson and me. You just started and when you got done haying, fine. Whether it was two weeks or ten weeks, you covered the ground the best way possible and then started all over. Then experts began to stress cutting before the head matured and went to seed. Everyone started picking it up a notch and cutting before the grass went by.

Farmers cut much earlier and faster now. We go out when grasses are just about in the boot stage and when the head is beginning to show. Trucks and mowers and choppers are bigger and faster, and we mow and chop just as fast as we can and get it into silos or bunks to preserve maximum nutrient value.

Then you deal with the second cutting. If it's alfalfa, you'll normally have another cut ready to go in four weeks. And then four weeks later and four weeks later. It's about every four weeks for alfalfa. You can just about mark your calendar.

Grasses will be a little different. If you start after Memorial Day, by the second or third week of June you're all done and it's in the silo or bunk. Grasses grow pretty well in the month of June but come to a screeching halt in the hot weather of July. Whatever you have by the first of July you better cut because the grass will be maturing and showing heads and in July's heat it won't grow that much. Plus July is a good time for second-cut hay because of sunshine and long days. When you put it in the barn you will probably have a pretty good product.

As the month of July moves on, with luck you'll get some showers and the grass will start to come back. By the time you hit Addison County Field Days in early August and have cooler nights, the grass begins to take off again. So by the end of September you may have another crop to mow. In a good year you can get three cuttings of grass and four of alfalfa. But every year is different. Cooler and wetter and you'll get a little more grass. Hot and dry you'll get more alfalfa.

Over time, variations in feed quality became less and less of an issue. The better the quality, the less feed we had to buy. So it behooved us to cut it at its peak value and get the most out of our fields. That has all changed over the years. When we came here, a fertilizer salesman would have starved to death. ⚘

Such Be the Pains in Improving the Soil

During the first stage of agriculture in this county, but little thought or attention was given to manuring or recruiting exhausted land. The accumulation of vegetable matter was deemed rather a nuisance than a storehouse from which to keep up the fertility of their fields. If it was used at all, if a farmer occasionally took pains to restore it to the soil, it was not until after it had been suffered to lie for months, and in many instances years, exposed to bleaching rains and the scorching sun. And when it is considered that the farmers knew next to nothing of the elements of the soil, or the properties or action of manures, is it a matter of surprise that the early cleared fields were rapidly becoming impoverished?

There are many farmers yet among us, who cling to the old manner of farming. Such farmers have now no thought of looking beyond the yards of their own farms, for the means of enriching the soil.

They have yet to learn that nature has furnished many fertilizing substances for their use. To them it would be news, that the thousands of bushels of leached ashes, lying about the county, are so valuable, as to pay for transportation from the western borders of this county to Long Island to dress their sandy soils.

This year and last year, a speculator purchased in Shoreham in our county, many tons of bones, which are taken away by boat loads, to be ground and shipped to England; to that England, which annually uses many thousands of tons of guano, a deposit recently and first discovered on Islands in the Pacific Ocean.

If such be the pains and expense bestowed in improving the soil, in perhaps the best cultivated country in the world, and by occupants who are mainly tenants for lives or for years; what strong inducements are presented to the farmers of the United States, to improve and enrich their farms, not for the ultimate benefit of a titled aristocracy, but for themselves and their posterity.

Silas H. Jenison, President,
Addison County Agricultural Society, 1844

Haying: A Time of Storm and Stress

Haying is the period of 'storm and stress' in the farmer's year. To get the hay in, in good condition, and before the grass gets too ripe, is a great matter," naturalist John Burroughs wrote in 1886 of haying operations on his New York farm. "All the energies and resources of the farm are bent to this purpose. It is a thirty or forty days' war, in which the farmer and his hands are pitted against the heat and rain and the legions of timothy and clover."

In his history, *While the Sun Shines: Making Hay in Vermont 1789-1990*, Allen Yale notes that Burroughs' anxiety has been a constant in haying over the past two centuries. Feed remains a dairy farmer's largest expense, with a good crop critical to survival, but

Cutting alfalfa requires Goldilocks balance. Let alfalfa windrows wilt in the field, but not too much. Some wilting, to about 65% moisture content, reduces water content and weight of the haylage. But alfalfa that has dried too much in August's sun gets sticky and clogs the chopper—ask Grayson.

On June 24, the Wymans began the first cutting, delayed at least two weeks by Jeanne's health and poor weather. Cutting when some of the grasses had gone to seed would reduce their protein content but not as much, the Wymans would later learn from testing, as they feared.

nearly everything else has changed. Farmers in the early 1800s went to war with scythes, wood hay rakes, pitchforks, and oxen-pulled hay carts. Half a dozen men scything in the optimal pre-dawn and early morning hours when dew was still on the field could harvest about 30 tons of hay in a month, enough to feed a dozen cows over the winter.

Today's technology-intensive farmers, by comparison, hardly get their hands dirty. A chopper cuts a 12-foot swath and leaves a 3-foot wide windrow. A tedder spreads the windrow for faster drying. The windrower recollects the grass, and a square baler then vacuums the field, spitting 40-pound bales into a hay wagon. Conveyor belts lift the bales to the barn's haymow. In another labor-saving innovation, farmers since the 1980s have plastic wrapped 500 to 1,000 pounds of grass and stored the round bales in the field like giant snails.

Unlike their counterparts of a century earlier, who cut once a summer starting in July, the Wymans had to make a series of short- and long-term calculations throughout the summer, beginning in early

June with the first cutting and ending in October with the third cutting. How many hay bales are left in the barn? How much haylage, tightly packed fermented grass, is left in the outside bunks? What's needed to get through the winter and the coming year? Is there a good market for leftover hay?

And the biggest question, what will the weather be like when the fields are ready? Baling requires a several-day window of good drying weather, which can be hard to find in typically rainy early June. In these wet conditions, fields can be cut and chopped for haylage and packed immediately.

On June 24, the Wymans began the first cutting, a four-acre piece adjacent to the Drake Road bunk. The entire first cutting, as usually is the case, would go into haylage, which when cut and stored properly retains more of the grasses' nutritional value. The second cutting, in the dry dog days of mid-summer, might be baled or chopped for hayage. Wait and see. Third cutting at the end of the summer was too distant to worry about now. In 30 minutes, Grayson cut the four acres. In the next 90 minutes, in a care-

fully choreographed tag team, Grayson chopped the windrows into a trailing dump wagon. When the wagon was full, he offloaded 500 cubic feet of grass into a dump truck. Dan drove the load several hundred yards to the bunk, where Larry spread and packed it with a six-ton John Deere tractor, running over it back and forth like a metronome. By 12:30 the first field was cut and in the bunk. Seventy-plus acres to go.

"It's good to get something in. It packed pretty well, except for the first windrow that had dried out and was pretty stiff," said Larry.

Farmers can fill a bookshelf with books and bulletins on when to cut their fields for optimal nutritional content and how to mix a cow's ration with long fibers from hay and shorter fibers from chopped silage for most efficient digestion and

Above. Where have the long rows of grass drying in the sun and hay bales gone? For many farmers, it's become haylage. Grasses can be cut, chopped, and quickly packed for haylage even in damp weather, retaining more of their feed quality in the process. Grayson has chopped a windrow into a dump wagon and is transferring the chop to a dump truck that Dan will unload at the silage bunk for Larry to pack.

Left: Preservatives, which Dan is adding to the chopper, speed fermentation and inhibit toxic molds.

optimal milk production. But in a small operation like the Wymans, theory meets reality: harvesting plays second fiddle and is squeezed between morning and afternoon milkings.

On August 5, Dan began the second cutting of a 40-acre piece at the farm's western edge with the drying of the morning's dew and continued until the sun slipped behind Snake Mountain. "If you ask me, grass cut at the end of the day has more energy than grass cut in early morning. You catch the plant's energy before it descends, like sap in a maple tree, into the plant's roots at night. Some people would say I'm nuts, but that's what I try and do," says Dan of his long days and post-dusk cutting.

By the end of October, the success of the year's harvest is immediately visible in the bulge of the

Opposite, above: Cutting grasses at maximum nutritional level and baling them at proper moisture content can, like planting the corn, be a make-or-break operation. This often means 16-hour days during August's good haying weather, sunny and dry days.

Opposite, below: Every 4 to 10 seconds, depending on the density of the windrow, the baler spits a 40-pound cannonball toward the hay wagon, a target roughly 10 feet wide, 18 to 20 feet long and 8 feet high. Sounds easy. It's not. Square bales don't stack neatly, and the driver must constantly adjust the bailer's ejection angle in an attempt to evenly fill the wagon. Turns are the real test as the wrong angle sends bales swan diving to earth.

Right, above: Tidying a hay wagon to squeeze in a few more bales at the end of the day is like playing pick-up sticks. There is no guarantee that the mess can be fixed, but it's worth a try.

Right, below: "When the mow was full you knew you had enough to get you through the winter," says Larry of the dirty work of stacking bales.

Wymans' two storage bunks — the 150-foot long bunk off Drake Road and the 100-foot-long bunk just to the north of the barn. The quantity of the hay harvest is not visible. In a good year, hay stacked 10 bales high will fill the 200-foot-long haymow.

"Stacking bales is a lot more work than just dropping them off the conveyor belt, but you know just how many you have. A full loft is like looking at money in the bank," says Larry of the most labor-intensive part of haying. A full mow is roughly 10,000 bales, if you're counting. Plenty to last the winter, with some left to sell.

They Were Never Meant to Be Farms

In 1915, the Vermont Bureau of Publicity, concerned that "the people of Vermont have been overmodest in their failure to do a little wholesome boasting concerning their natural advantages with which a generous Creator has endowed the state," published a 140-page booklet. The document, *Vermont Farms: Some Facts and Figures Concerning the Agricultural Resources and Opportunities of the Green Mountain State*, shed Yankee reserve in arguing that Vermont could hold its own and more with the Midwest.

Vermont, in fact, had not been holding its own for decades, in part because thousands of Vermonters had moved West seeking, literally, greener pastures. The state, which had one of the fastest growth rates in the country from 1790 to 1830, had had one of the slowest rates since the 1850s. More precisely, 129 Vermont towns, over half the communities in the state, had fewer people in 1910 than in 1850. Historians would later term the state's stagnation from 1850 to 1920 "Vermont's Winter of Decline."

The booklet would tackle these developments head on:

An impression has been created, and has been accepted in many quarters as a fact, to the effect that upon the broad prairies of the West is the place of all others that where money may be made in farming, but impressions often are misleading, and sometimes are incorrect. This little book will undertake to show, not by empty boasts and rhetorical statements, but by well authenticated facts and figures, that the state of Vermont offers opportunities for profitable farming equal to all and superior to most of the states of the Union.

Under the heading "A Few Fertility Facts," the writer noted that Vermont ranked first in average yield of bushels of corn per acre from 1870 to 1909; that only Maine raised more bushels of potatoes per acre than Vermont in 1914; and that "Vermont is by far the most notable dairy state in the Union, being really in a class by itself."

Vermont, he pointed out, produced more pounds of butter per capita than any other state and that the state's per capita value of dairy products exceeded that of all other states and was six times the national average.

These facts should be sufficient to prove that Vermont is one of the most fertile regions in the country. If further ammunition were needed, J.L. Hills, dean of the College of Agriculture at the University of Vermont, contributed a statement, "Concerning Vermont Soils," contending that the state should not be judged by its many abandoned farms:

These abandoned farms were never meant by the Almighty to be farms, and the men who wrestled them originally from the forests were working against his Plans. In the valleys and on the lower hill slopes, agriculture may be, and is being, conducted successfully and profitably. On such areas, Vermont soil is not exhausted, though it may be temporarily weary.

Vermont soil is inherently fertile. The detritus of the granitic rocks of the Green Mountain Range, ground in the mighty mills of the old time glacier, sorted by the rushing waters which followed its melting, commingled with the debris of thousands of years of unharvested vegetation, worked over by heat and by cold, by wind and by wave, by water and by ice, by frost and by snow, by flood and by rain, and by the multitudinous effects of the weather throughout the ages past, it has made of this state a more fertile land than some of her less favored sisters. Not for naught are our mountains verdure clad. Not idly, not without a reason, is Vermont called the Green Mountain state in contradistinction to her eastern neighbor, the Granite state.

The dean did concede that Vermont's topography was "irregular" and that "barely one-third of her entire land area is made up of pasture (of the better sort), of mowings and of plowed fields; nearly two-thirds of her area is occupied by woodlots, forest areas, and rough lands. Such as is good is good; such as is not adapted to agricultural purposes is largely covered by forests, is being set out to forests or is reverting to forests."

The Almighty, he noted, was unable to make "two ranges of mountains without a valley in between." But ever the optimist, he counseled that farmers would generally find these valley soils to be fertile. Furthermore, "Considerable upland soil in Vermont is of a strong character, and, if not acid, produces well. If it is to be found to be acid, liming tends to remedy the situation."

Nature has richly endowed the state and generations of Vermont farmers have further improved the soil's fertility with conscientious application of a renewable resource, manure.

"In no other state in the Union are there so many cows crowded upon so small an arable area," the dean wrote. "She far out-classes all her sisters in this respect."

Seventy years later, geographer Harold Meeks would probably have given the dean's assessment an A for optimism and a C for sound science. Vermont, he observed in *Vermont's Land and Resources* not only had a lower percentage of prime agricultural soils, Class I and II, than the national average but was far outdistanced by Iowa, where slightly more than 50% of its soil was prime compared to 10% in Vermont.

Scything near Rockingham, Vermont, circa 1910

Science of Mowing: Take a Quick, Easy Gait

Gentlemen: Having long since promised you an article on the science of mowing, I now sit down to redeem my pledge.

1st. The scythe should hang natural and easy, and as I have said before, must be kept in first rate order.

2nd. As you approach the standing grass, let the heel of the scythe move to the point of commencement, and let it stop the instant it has done its work. If the grass stands up, measure with the eye the utmost capacity forward of your scythe, take a quick, easy gait, moving your right foot well up towards the standing grass, and your body with it, though leaning back, by bending the knees a little forward, so as to bring your whole weight to bear upon the scythe without twisting the body from right to left.

Note: If you swing 6 inches too far back, and 6 inches too far in pointing out, it makes 24 inches loss! This applied to a scientific forward motion will give you a greater gain on ordinary mowers.

Vermont Family Visitor, 1845

Cows are curious and inveterate explorers, but the first day of pasturing requires careful investigation. Approach new environment, sniff it, lick it, and if the object is small and pliable, chew it. That process cannot be forced and even herd leaders may deliberate for hours before venturing far into untouched fields.

The Farm Where They Never Let the Cows Out

GRAYSON WYMAN: When we came here, farmers weren't buying much fertilizer; our neighbors saw us putting fertilizer and looked at us like we were crazy. But we had come from hill farms and had to make up for our smaller acreages there with higher yields.

We brought 56 milkers with us but wanted to milk 102 cows, which was what the barn would tie. Those cows were producing offspring so we got to the point where we had 200 to 250 head and a little more than 275 tillable acres to support them. So we were out of balance with our animals and acreage. That forced us to get the most out of our land.

We had also gone through several drought years where we not only had to harvest everything on our land but also had to buy many trailer loads of hay out of Canada. And with poor-quality feed in the pasture, our cows were coming back with slack udders, and we weren't getting the milk that we should.

When we recognized that using productive land for pasture would be an absolute blowout we decided to stop grazing, tie the cows up in the barn, and bring the feed to them. We put in rubber mats and did everything we could to make them as comfortable as possible.

Once we got into a cycle where we were producing quality silage to feed cows in the barn 365 days a year our milk production began to take off. We could realize the potential that had been bred into them. With bigger milk checks we could start making improvements like a pipeline where the milk went straight from the cow to the bulk tank instead of to a pumping station on wheels that we moved up and down the center aisle. We didn't have to move anything and that saved us a lot of time.

In those first years, people would ask where we farmed and we'd tell them and they'd say, "You live on the farm where they never let the cows out."

We became known for that. But if you drive by farms today you don't see many farms with cows outside, except for heifers and cows that have been dried off. We stopped pasturing our milkers early on. I'm not saying that what we did was better but that it suited our needs and paid off for us. ❧

July 2004: Medical Limbo

Throughout July, Dan and Jeanne were in medical limbo. There was some relatively good news—after three weeks of chemotherapy at Fletcher Allen Medical Center in Burlington, the loss of her hair and 40 pounds, the leukemia appeared to be in remission. "She still has the same Jeanne spirit, but with a very tired body!" Larry would write in his DayMinder.

The tired body could not be missed: overnights at Porter Hospital, the community hospital in Middlebury, to monitor heart irregularities and infections; weekly trips to Fletcher Allen for blood tests; and at the end of the month a consultation at the Dana Farber Cancer Institute in Boston on a bone marrow transplant, the only possible long-term solution.

On July 1, the Wymans completed their first cutting—some by Grayson, Larry, and Dan—but given Dan's uncertain schedule most was contracted out to a crew from Monument Farms Dairy.

And July saw much smaller milk checks. By the end of June, the Wymans, short on help with Jeanne sick and Dan often unavailable for morning chores and afternoon milkings, had sold 32 cows, roughly a third of their milkers. Dan's brother, David, who had been helping with afternoon milkings, would take Jeanne's place in the morning and fill in as needed.

The lone bright spot? The pending bumper corn crop.

One traditional benchmark, that corn should be knee high by the 4th of July, didn't apply in the summer of 2004. Two weeks earlier, on the first day of summer, corn leaves were already tickling shins, knees, and thighs. Such early growth is even better as it shields the soil from July's baking sun and slows the growth of weeds.

By the end of July, the corn, 10 feet high along the Otter Creek, was approaching rain-forest thick in all the fields and was nearly impenetrable except by ground-hugging rodents, turkeys, and the odd beaver pilfering corn stalks for its lodge.

With Jeanne unable to milk, the Wymans struggled to find help and sold roughly a third of their milking herd. Unused water bowls quickly became cobweb ridden.

Chapter 4

Machinery's Lure

A Faustian Bargain With Technology

The Wymans, from Grandpa Wyman in the early 1900s with his horses and mules to Larry and Grayson with their half dozen specialized tractors, have been part of the technological transformation of American agriculture. In a century, the family farm has become a capital- and technology-intensive business, where a single farm can produce what 30 farms once did. This industrialization of agriculture, historians could argue, began with a local boy, John Deere, who made good.

In 1968, the Vermont Board of Historic Sites erected a historic marker in Main Street's Cannon Park in downtown Middlebury recognizing his role:

> **John Deere**
> **Inventor**
>
> "THE PLOW THAT BROKE THE PLAINS"
> *John Deere learned the blacksmith trade*
> *here as an apprentice in the shop of*
> *Capt. Benjamin Lawrence from 1821 to 1825.*
> *The shop was located below this spot*
> *on Mill Street in what is known as*
> *"Frog Hollow." In 1836 Deere removed to*
> *Grand Detour, Illinois where, in 1837, he*
> *built the world's first steel moldboard plow.*

The John Deere Company, now the world's largest manufacturer of farm equipment, started modestly—from 1838 to 1840 Deere sold 53 plows. But this self-scouring, curved plow saved prairie farmers endless hours of scraping clumped clay from their wood and iron plows, and by the end of the 1840s, Deere, a savvy businessman, was mass producing thousands of plows a year.

Fast forward to the early 1900s and the transition to the next major technological change in farming, the tractor. Like the handymen who tinkered for decades to get the self-scouring plow right—gentleman farmer Thomas Jefferson designed a plow; it didn't work—getting the farm tractor right would also take decades.

Farm tractors first appeared in the 1870s, but these costly, explosion-prone, coal-burning, steam-powered "behemoths" weighed 15 tons and more and were of little use to the average farmer, who had less than 50 acres of tillable land.

In the 1890s, their sales, mainly to vast Midwestern farms with hundreds of acres of tough prairie sod to break, never exceeded 2,000 tractors a year. Enter the automobile and the rapid development of the gasoline-powered internal combustion engine. Piggybacking on automobile advances, scores of backyard inventors, along with a handful of companies that dominated the market for harvesting machines, began to

The first rule of tractors is size them for your fields and checkbook, not for bragging rights. The second rule, don't skimp on maintenance and they'll last for years. The Wymans' two 20-year-old Allis Chalmers tractors were still in their working prime.

At the end of World War I, only one farm in 125 had a tractor. By 1930, tractor power had surpassed animal power on the farm. This World War I-era tractor had steel wheels needed, farmers thought, for good traction. Rubber tires were introduced in the 1930s, providing a much smoother and faster ride, equally good traction, and reduced field compaction.

They were right. In 1915, the number of workhorses on farms peaked at 21 million. By 1930, the Department estimated that tractors had surpassed animal power on the farm. Within a generation, the impact of the "agricultural automobile" would ripple through rural and urban life in ways that even its most fervent backers could not have envisioned.

World War I, with the military's requisitioning of draft horses and mules to pull wagons, caissons, ambulances, and hearses, and the draft, which created a shortage of farm labor, would speed the tractor's use. Tractors could help address both problems and the need for greater food production; to meet this demand 200 tractor makers produced 62,000 tractors in 1917.

Even with this surge, very few of the country's six-million-plus farms would have tractors by the end of the war. One need only look at Depression-era photographs of Vermont farms with their horse-drawn hay wagons and plows, the hand-planting of corn, and hand-scything of side hills to understand that labor-saving machines spread slowly among nearly all small farms.

Only since World War II has production and use of tractors with their multitude of specialized attachments exploded and transformed the family farm. By the end of the war, the use of tractors had freed millions of acres—about a quarter of a farm's cropland had once been devoted to hay and oats for work horses and mules—for other commercial crops. Tractors had helped further increase crop yields by more timely preparation of fields in the spring and rapid harvesting when crops were at optimal value.

respond to the farmer's wish list for an affordable, lighter, reliable, agile, multi-purpose tractor.

It would take time. In 1915, a United States Department of Agriculture bulletin noted that "the tractor appears to have made for itself no important place in the agricultural economy of the country." While tractors were not presently a good investment for the average farmer, their future appeared bright:

> With the decrease in the price of farm tractors and an increase in their mechanical efficiency, simplicity, and durability, all of which seem to be assured…it is safe to predict that the tractor will soon become an important factor in reducing the cost of crop production on the average farm.

One prediction did not hold true. Tractors, some advocates forecast, would improve the quality and desirability of rural life by reducing the physical drudgery of farm work. This, in turn, would slow the rural to urban movement of the labor force. Not so, the tractor and its accompanying equipment have turned the farm into a low-employment business. In 1900, farmers made up 38% of the labor force; in 1950, 12%; today less than 2%.

Few farmers would trade a tractor with an air-conditioned cab pulling an eight-row planter, chopper, or cultivator for a return to hand labor and horse-drawn plows. But the ever-increasing mechanization of the farm comes with a new set of economic challenges. In 1927, E.G. Nourse, an agricultural economist, presciently forecast one outcome of this Faustian bargain with technology: "The outlook for agricultural production is so good that the outlook for agricultural prosperity is distinctly bad."

Today's farmers with their barnyards full of tractors and disk plows, chisel plows, row-crop cultivators, finishers, tillers, rippers, tedders, windrowers, forage harvesters, bucket loaders, round and square bailers, planters, and fertilizer spreaders are both beneficiaries and victims of this technology treadmill. To pay for today's labor-saving but costly farm machinery—bigger tractors cost six-figures plus—farmers must spread this fixed cost over more cows. Greater milk production has led to surpluses and lower prices, which can force the farmer to increase production even more. Only the most efficient, which generally means larger farms with their economies of scale, such as bulk purchasing, can survive this economic slippery slope.

In the following commentaries, Larry and Grayson reflect less on this big picture and more on their day-to-day concerns of matching equipment to their growing farm's needs and to their pocketbook. Dan discusses the challenges of making do and keeping high-cost machinery running and running and running. ⚘

Today's farm equipment comes in two sizes, big and bigger. Moving and changing a 500-pound tire can be a dangerous two-person operation or a job for the tire dealer.

For their first dozen years of farming, the Wymans couldn't afford a tractor with a cab. Before retiring, they had three, making winter work more tolerable. The bucket loader, used for snow plowing and feed mixing, was a cold exception.

We Dreamed of Having a Tractor With a Cab

LARRY WYMAN: You put a bunch of farmers together and what are they going to talk about? They're going to talk about their machines. They won't talk about their cows. Oh, no. It would be about their tractors and how many horsepower they have.

For some, farming isn't cows. It's not crops. It's machinery. You take their tractors away, and they would just as soon work in a bank. Then there are those of us who could care less about machinery. We'd rather milk cows and deal with animals.

Grayson and I were never involved in the one-upsmanship of having the latest and biggest tractors. We didn't have the pocketbook for it. We were always looking to get what we could at the lowest possible cost.

Dan was like a detective at auctions. He could eyeball equipment and tell if it was a good investment. He's been around a lot of farmers' equipment, repaired a lot of it, and is used to buying someone else's problem and figuring out how to make it work.

With tractors it's awfully easy to get carried away. I know one farmer who bought a big tractor and was having trouble with it. The field man asked him why he bought it, and he gave half a dozen reasons. The field man shook his head and said there wasn't a place in all Vermont that needed a tractor that big. It was way overkill. But he thought that was what he needed.

Over the years, Grayson and I could fix most of our equipment. We could repair most anything on the smaller choppers that we pulled with tractors. It wouldn't be pretty because we didn't have the right tools, but we could do it.

Self-propelled choppers are a much more complicated animal. Your annual spring tune-up on the chopping head alone can run $15,000. And today's computerized tractors are a whole different ballgame. When you're dealing with diesel engines and hydraulic systems and computers, you're better off leaving it to the people who know what they're doing.

When we came here in '68 we had three tractors, a 65, 75, and 50 horse. We bought the 65 and 75 after we started farming, and they were almost brand new. They were adequate and got us going. Then we bought the 85 in 1972 and then a four-row corn planter to replace our two-row planter. We thought we were really going uptown when we got the four row. And we bought some harrows, a couple forage wagons, and a windrower.

Everybody knows that raising a crop in Addison County clay is a whole different ball game from the Connecticut River Valley. Over there you couldn't go 10 feet without hitting 10 rocks. But it was a looser, loamier soil. You could plow in the morning, harrow it within a few days, and seed it. You couldn't do that here.

The first thing we learned was to plow your corn field in the fall and let the winter's freezing and thawing break up the clay. By the time your fields were dry enough in the spring to harrow, the clay would be so hard that you'd have a field full of hardballs when you harrowed it. We needed equipment like a cultipacker to smash up these hardballs to a powder so we could plant seed and get coverage.

Starting out we couldn't afford one. In the late 1980s we went to an auction and bought one secondhand for $1,800. Until then we had to rely on winter's freezing and thawing. Compared to most farmers, we didn't have a lot of equipment, but it was adequate for the land we planted. We didn't want to put a lot of money into something that we only used two weeks a year.

But some equipment, like a corn planter, is essential. When the field is ready to plant and you have your own planter, that is the best of all possible worlds. When you're sharing a planter or contracting the work out, you may have to wait until tomorrow or the next day or even longer.

With clay it doesn't take much more than a heavy dew to harden the surface, and then you have to rework it. It's like having

The daily 5-minute trips to the Drake Road feed bunk in the open cab bucket loader were brisk but bearably short.

skim in your paint can. The seed can be planted through the skim, but you want nice and loose soil so fertilizer and nutrients will leach down to the seedling's roots when it rains. Or it could be so wet that you might have to wait several days. Maybe it's five days before you have a chance to rework the surface again. You need to get that seed into the ground just as fast as you can. Seed doesn't grow much in the bag.

It's nothing to spend $15,000 for a four-row planter and $20,000 for a basic six-row, but I still wouldn't want to rely on borrowing a corn planter. It's the same when it comes to putting up your feed, whether you're chopping for silage or baling hay. You're going to need a mower, tedder, baler, dump wagons, trucks, and backup tractors. Every item is important.

If you hire a custom chopper, you're at the mercy of their schedule. When your name comes up on the list, they come. If the chopper doesn't let it dry enough, you can have problems with acidosis. Cows can get ulcers and have all sorts of problems from wet feed. And when you have as many stomachs as cows do, then you have problems. At the other extreme, you don't want grass that has dried too much. You put it in the bunk, and it heats up and all the feed's protein is burned up.

Spreading manure is about the only operation where you have a wider time window and can rely on custom spreaders.

For years, we dreamed of having a tractor with a cab. Many winters I spread manure morning and night with a tractor without a cab and would come back to the barn frozen through. It wasn't until the early 1970s that we finally got one, a Massey Ferguson 1135. This was the biggest tractor, 135 horsepower, that we had ever had. At that time tractors over

Winter is the cruelest season; it freezes men and snaps machinery. A broken chain in the feed mixing wagon, above, is one of a farmer's worst nightmares. Breaking on Christmas Eve is even worse. The Wymans made do with a backup for five days until they could get parts and Dan could reassemble the chain.

offered to buy it back from us for $22,000 to $23,000. We said, no, we'd hang on to it as long as we had it. As far as fuel, it cost less to run than our 85 because we could chop faster and more efficiently. The trick is to match your tractor to your equipment. You don't want to ask your tractor to pull a plow that is too big.

In the Midwest, crop farmers with hundreds and thousands of acres will use a tractor until the warranty is up and then trade. Their smaller tractors that are still in good condition are often resold here. For Midwestern farmers it's a cash and tax gimmick; they want the latest and most comfortable equipment, given all the time they spend in tractors. But this costs big bucks. A 150-horse tractor runs well into six figures today.

In the Northeast, most family farmers figure a tractor is good for 10 to 20 years and will hold on to it as a backup when it can't stand daily use. We ended up using the Massey right up until we stopped farming, not for plowing or chopping but to haul the feed mixer.

100 weren't that common. We felt we needed more power than our 85 to chop corn but were worried what fuel would cost us.

There were rumors that the price of tractors, especially those in the 100-to 150-horsepower range, which was becoming very popular, was going to increase dramatically in the next 12 months and that tires were going to cost a lot more. As it turned out, when we went to buy the tractor, all the major companies had tractors sitting in lots without tires because they couldn't make tires fast enough.

Our Fair Haven dealer found a tractor in Pennsylvania with tires and brought it back. We paid $13,000 for it. A year later he

Getting tractors with cabs was nice, but four-wheel drive, which took the frustration out of a lot of fieldwork, was the biggest change. You no longer had to be so concerned about getting hung up, particularly in the spring when you were working the fields or spreading manure. When you hit a wet spot with two-wheel drive your rear tires with their big bars would spin, and you'd dig yourself in deeper and deeper. Once those back wheels went down, you were there, and it was time to call someone with chains. Four-wheel drive gave you a constant pull over the land.

Cabs are great if you have to be out in all seasons. What farmers didn't realize, myself included, was how much it costs to repair a tractor with a cab. When you put in a new clutch, you have to take the cab off so you can split the tractor. That probably adds $1,000 to the repair.

We had three tractors with cabs at the end, the Massey and two Allis Chalmers, a 200 and 100 horse. You can say that's a real luxury. But in the fall, winter, and spring with a cold sharp wind it was awfully nice to close the doors. In the summer when it was blinking hot and the air conditioner wasn't working, you wished you could blow the cab off so you could get a little air.

Tractors are a lot better than they were 40 years ago, but don't believe those ads where a tractor is so smooth that a glass of water on the hood doesn't get spilled. They make our work easier, but driving a tractor all day is still dangerous and beats up your body. We all know of farmers who were in a hurry, were tired, took a shortcut, and lost a finger or arm or worse.

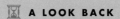

These Engines Were Tough

From 1918 until 1960, from the "Waterloo Boy" to the "new Generation of Power," all John Deere Waterloo Tractors shared three characteristics — the name; green and yellow paint; and 2-cylinder horizontal engines.

This was the four-decades-long era of the tractors called "2-lungers," "Poppin Johnnies," and a multitude of other nicknames born of affection and admiration. When that era ended, John Deere received rivers of tearful mail.

What was so remarkable about the 2-cylinder engine? Everything!

Two cylinders meant fewer moving parts than in engines with more cylinders. This meant fewer parts to wear, to require adjustment, repair, and eventual replacement. Each part could be larger, heavier, more rugged, able to stand up under long hours at full or three-quarters load. All of this translated into stamina, and it helped establish the John Deere reputation for dependability.

Simplicity also meant the engine was easier to understand, easier for a farmer-owner to service and repair himself. Parts were easily accessible and easy to handle because of their larger size.

These engines burned low-cost fuel — distillates and various fuel oils.

All of these factors added up to one important feature — economy. During the Great Depression, this was most important.

With all these advantages, why were these engines dropped?

Two-cylinder engines big enough to meet demands for increased power would require tractors with a physical size too large for working between rows. These engines were not suited for the shift-up, throttle-back, save-fuel operation desirable for the lighter work, which most tractors perform during more than half their working hours. In short, these great engines of the 20s to the 50s were simply not flexible enough for the 60s and 70s.

Company Booklet, *John Deere Tractors: 1918-1987*

Fix a broken chain in the field, above, a slipping belt, or loose harrow disk. Every farmer has a tool kit and knowledge for that. Working on today's computerized tractor engines is no longer possible for the jack-of-all-trades farmer, says Grayson.

Tractors Now Come With About Everything Imaginable

GRAYSON WYMAN: We didn't have a four-wheel drive until around 1990. When they first appeared in the 1960s, they were well beyond our means. A new four-wheel drive tractor back then could cost almost as much as what we paid for the farm. But if you have really heavy work, the peace of mind from four-wheel drive is well worth it and is a lot easier on your fields.

When you're pulling a chopper and a dump wagon, you can be pulling several tons. A four-wheel drive will drive through a damp spot. With two-wheel drive you can spin and chew up your field.

We got our first four-wheel drive tractor, the Allis 8070, by accident. Our Massey Ferguson, the 1135, which was our biggest tractor, needed a new engine. While the engine was being installed, the dealer loaned us the 8070, which was almost 200 horsepower. It was probably six to eight years old, and once we started using it— the tractor never went back. We paid $35,000 for it, which was probably less than half of buying new.

We have bought both new and used. It depended on our financial situation and what was available used. We always wanted to know a tractor's history and how it had been used or abused. Tractors are a major investment and unless you have hit the mother lode, you have to finance them through the dealer, manufacturer, or farm credit. We generally used farm credit or the manufacturer.

Some farmers buy new and trade when the warranty, generally two years, runs out because they don't want the cost of repairing them. A lot of Midwestern grain farmers buy a new tractor at the end of the warranty. So local dealers for many years would go there and buy two or three trailer loads of tractors that were the right size for here. They hadn't been abused and were in nice condition and you could buy them for a fraction of their cost. Our first four-wheel drive came from another farm in the county, but a lot have come from the Midwest.

Today's tractor comes with just about everything imaginable— stereos, headphones, air-conditioned cabs. Farmers in the Midwest can be in a tractor from sunup to sundown and want to be comfortable. It's almost impossible to buy a tractor today without all the bells and whistles. And so much of the tractor is computerized, which drives up the cost, especially with repairs.

You have a monitor that checks this and a monitor that checks that and something else. They all come with a price tag, and you can't say I don't want that because that's the way they're built.

It's unbelievable what they engineer into the tractor compared to the putt-putts that we started with. Today, computers are constantly adjusting the tractor's level and its engine performance. When you're chopping and the dump wagon gets heavier, the computer monitors the bite you're making into the soil so you have better traction.

In the Midwest they have GPS-guided tractors now. The GPS feeds coordinates into a computer, and the tractor is driven by the computer's information and plants the field. I don't know if Vermont has enough land that is flat and square and straight enough. Certainly conditions in the Midwest are different, but tractor companies must feel it has potential because they are putting a lot into it. They have even gotten into robotic tractors; experimental farms are using them.

We have never owned anything that sophisticated. We weren't big enough to afford that kind of fancy rig. Our first tractors had metal seats. It was like sitting in a dishpan. Then they added foam padding and vinyl covers. When cabs came in, seats became more plush with adjustable flotation. In newer tractors it's like sitting in an office chair that is "ergonomically correct."

Having a cab in the winter was awfully nice when we were spreading manure in a nor'easter, and it was 10 degrees and the wind was howling. First, you had to start the tractor, then free the frozen manure spreader. Then you had to find a place to spread it. If you had two feet of snow and didn't have four-wheel drive, that was a challenge.

You were pulling a heavy load and were spreading power over two pieces of equipment, and your traction might not be the best. You're doing all this without a cab. Many days you came back with cold face, fingers, and body. By the time we reached our fifties we had literally pounded ourselves to the nth degree.

To look at a farm tractor catalogue, one could believe that farmers spend their days in an air-conditioned, dust-free cabin with surround-sound stereo, cell phone, and a control panel worthy of a space shuttle. There is no need to get one's hands dirty or break a sweat. Some farmers may sit in ComfortCommand seats. The Wymans did not. Their tractors were strictly blue-collar. If they broke, they fixed them. If the air conditioning didn't work, they opened the window.

People who think driving a tractor is a cushy job ought to try it for eight hours. It's not easy on the body when you are not only listening to a tractor engine that is working hard but are pulling a chopper, which isn't one of the quietest things in the world. With a cab and AC, you have reduced some of the noise pollution, but driving a tractor is still very, very tiring, especially when the job has no margin for error.

And the concentration drains you. When you're pulling a chopper, you're not watching the birds fly by or checking to see if it's cloudy in the west. You have to keep your eye on what you're doing every second.

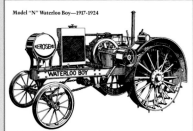

Onlookers Were Awed by This Giant

The first John Deere 4-Wheel Drive Tractor was the over 200-hp-8010 introduced in the autumn of 1959. The occasion was a John Deere field day. To say the 8010 was the star of that show is an understatement. Onlookers were awed by this giant. It stood 8 feet 2 inches tall to the top of its steering wheel, 8 feet wide, and 19 feet 7 inches from the grille to drawbar. It weighed 19,700 pounds (24,860 pounds with its 23.1-26 12-ply tires 3/4 full of ballast).

Four steps and a handhold were built onto each front fender to assist the operator in mounting to his spacious platform. A key and pushbutton, plus 24-volt electric system and fluid aid, provided fast starting in any weather. Articulated power steering and air brakes, both provided as regular equipment, kept the 8010 under easy control.

Performance? A 31-foot harrow and an 8-bottom plow were designed for the 8010. It pulled either at speeds up to 7 mph, and lifted the full integral plow high off the ground for turns at row ends.

A year after the 8010 came the 8020, with an 8-speed Syncro-Range transmission, an improved posture seat, oil-cooled clutch, and other advances.

Company Booklet, *John Deere Tractors: 1918-1987*

Dan's eye for an auction bargain is legendary. "I can remember one auction where there was an eight-foot head that would go on our grass chopper," Grayson recalls, "but Dan noticed that the augur had a big hole in it. We turned the augur over so bidders could see it, and the auctioneer mentioned it. It would have sold for $400 to $500; we bought it for $90. Dan welded a piece from another augur and we were in business."

I Could See a Diamond in the Rough

DAN KEHOE: I have always been able to fix anything. My father bought an arc welder from Montgomery Ward when I was in grade school, and I taught myself. If I knew then what I know now, we'd have been rich, but I could do basic stuff and bubblegum things together. I started rebuilding engines when I was in high school, but I'd been tinkering with tractors for a long time.

When I was in the 5th and 6th grades, I could do basic maintenance—change the oil, adjust the clutch, change wheel bearings. When I got older, my father would help me split tractors. We had a big walnut tree and would rig a chain on a big limb to pull engines. I really started repairing tractors after I took welding and ag and diesel mechanic courses at the vocational school.

I learned how to rebuild stuff there, but sometimes I don't even know where I learned what I know. All I can say is it's a God-given talent. It has always come natural, so that's why I think it is a gift from God.

When I got out of high school in the late 1970s you could buy a 100-horse tractor for $12,000. Two years later they were $30,000. It was just supply and demand. Now a 100-horse tractor is $60,000, $70,000; a 200-horse can be well over $100,000.

Big new tractors are nice, but they're not cost effective for this size farm. In the Midwest and West where you have thousands of acres and the tractors are going and going and going that's one thing. A GPS and row finder are for farmers who have fields that are straight for miles and miles. The average person can't stay awake in fields like that.

If I had a choice of a new or older tractor, I'd take a tractor from the 1970s and 1980s any day. I look at tractors from a mechanic's point of view. These new gadgets are nice, but it's a $5,000 repair bill when the computer dashboard goes. You have to replace the whole computer unit; you can't fix a gauge or speedometer for a few bucks.

I don't like paying a lot for machinery. But you have to shop around. In my repair work I'll buy old stuff that farmers don't want to fix or take it as a trade for other work.

Grayson and Larry liked to buy older stuff, too, but if you have to pay someone to fix it, then it wasn't always cost effective. I like to dicker, and when they saw the price I was getting stuff for at auctions they said, "Wow!" But it was all predicated on my ability to fix it.

I could always see a diamond in the rough. Jeanne would say when I brought equipment home that it wasn't a diamond in the rough. It wasn't even a lump of coal. But I could see it.

If you added all my tractors together they probably wouldn't cost as much as one new tractor, and I have nine tractors. My five Massey Fergusons range from 100 to 150 horsepower. They have to be 30 years old. They're cheap. They're easy to work on and get parts for. And they do the job.

Engines in the older tractors have heavy blocks, and you should get 7,000 to 10,000 hours out of them. Most of mine have 10,000 to 20,000 hours.

Today, tractor makers are after better gas mileage and are trying to get more horsepower out of a lighter engine. These engines and lighter tractors don't last as long and cost a lot more to fix.

A transmission job on newer tractors is 10 grand; an old tractor is three or four grand. You can buy them for a reasonable price, but they're not worth it because when something happens the repair bill is more than what the tractor is worth.

Farmers know how to fix things and, if they have the time, can repair a lot of their own machinery. They should be designing tractors and machinery because half the time they modify new equipment to make it work the right way. I see it because I'm out in the farms doing road service. Farmers will want me to add this or that. The dealer won't do it because of liability concerns.

Farm machinery is designed for thousands of hours of use. With the high cost of new equipment and low milk prices, 20- and 30-year-old tractors are kept running for daily use until they are put out to pasture as backups.

Farmers can tell you what the problem is, but that's just a start. I can weld a broken part in 10 minutes, but a good road-service man finds out what caused the problem and that can take hours to fix. If I just put on a band-aid, it will break again. Like bearings and shafts.

You can fix one bearing but the bearing on the other end is bad, too. Shafts go because the bushings are gone. In a four-wheel drive the joints go, but it may be that the bushings in the front end are worn and that has caused the problem.

When you're putting an older tractor together you have to throw the book away because specs don't consider the wear and tear on the rest of the parts. If the book says set the timing at 14 degrees top dead center, you may have to go 17 degrees to make it run right. That comes with experience and having an ear for the sound.

Everything is hydraulic today, and most times you can diagnose what's wrong before you open up an engine. Hydraulic flow meters can tell you where your leaks are. Different test points tell you if and where the clutch pack or power pack has gone bad.

Tractors of the future are only going to get more complicated with their electronics and hydraulics. I can work on them, but they're a nightmare. And with all the diagnostic equipment that's needed, dealers are gearing up to eliminate the little repairman like me.

But there is so much old stuff out there. By the time that is gone, I'll be retired. I have enough business so I don't need to work on the new tractors.

August 2004: Seven Inches of Rain

August was one of the wettest on record, but the corn was well established and "wet feet" did not damage the crop.

The barn and milking operation pass state inspection. There is no mention of whitewashing the interior, a welcome savings ($125) given the difficult summer. "Just brightens the barn, doesn't kill any bacteria," says Larry.

Jeanne's health and energy continued to seesaw. On good days, she has helped with barn chores for an hour. On the 26th, she milked for the first time since June, filling in for Dan while he hayed. With a bone marrow transplant scheduled for early September, there will be no more milkings or visits to a micro-toxin-filled barn with her compromised immune system. Doctor's orders.

The rainy summer continues with August's seven inches of rain, one of the wettest on record. Working around showers, Larry, Grayson, and Dan start the second cutting on the 6th and finish on the 18th.

The good news is that the protein content of the first cutting, feed company tests indicate, was not as low as expected. And with the delayed second cutting, the alfalfa has bloomed and has put its energy into deeper roots, which will strengthen the plant for winter's rigors.

The corn continues to do well but needs more sun to bring the ears to maturity.

Dan's availability to help with the upcoming, more time-consuming corn harvest is unclear. Monument Farms Dairy with its state-of-the-art corn chopper and a fleet of trucks will do the majority of the cutting in return for 10 heifer calves. A good deal for both farms.

Chapter 5

Miracle Corn

Push the Boundaries of Your Field's Potential With HybriForce-400

Every September, shortly after Labor Day, Bourdeau Brothers' Feed Supply, the largest feed dealer in central Vermont and the Wymans' longtime feed supplier, holds an open house and barbecue for farmers and its 20-plus suppliers. In the course of the day, several hundred members of the region's close-knit agricultural community will pass through the vendor's tent.

Opposite: Early settlers planted corn in mounds several feet apart with seven seeds to the hole: one for the blackbird, one for the crow, one for the cutworm, and four to let grow. By the end of July the Wymans' fields had become a cat's cradle of corn.

Today's hardy corn is resistant to bugs, drought, and heavy rains. But much can still go wrong—heavy frost or flooded fields can halve yields—and farmers sleep better when June's first sprouts are healthy and uniformly cover their fields.

Those expecting to come and kick the tires of the latest John Deere tractor, Knight 4-auger roughage mixer, or Claas round baler will be disappointed. Under the display tent are the banners of companies whose names would be foreign to many farmers of a generation ago: Alpharma, Syngenta, Farm Science Genetics, Forage Genetics, Mycogen, Alltech, Crystalyx, Callisto Plant Technology.

Bourdeau Brothers is in the business of seeds, food supplements, pesticides, drugs, and fertilizers. In today's agri-pharma world spreading the barnyard's manure in your fields and feeding Bessie a steady diet of hay with a few added minerals isn't good enough. If there is any doubt, read the suppliers' banners and brochures and discover a hostile world where the farmer's livelihood and pocketbook are threatened at every turn:

- Omnipresent gastrointestinal parasites will sap your cow's milk production.
- Waterhemp, lambsquarters, and redroot pigweed can clog your fields.
- Stem rot and corn borers can topple your corn.
- Production-stressed cows with "negative energy balances" are a step away from the slaughterhouse if their calcium, potassium, selenium, and methionine deficiencies are not addressed.

But don't despair. Read on and the brochures' spreadsheets, tables, pie charts, and synopses of research studies promise a safer, more profitable bovine world:

> Push the boundaries of your field's potential with HybriForce-400. The results of 1,949 on-farm strip-plot harvests across nine states in the past four years show HybriForce-400 averaged 15% higher yields than conventional alfalfas. On your top fields that equals one ton or more. With a hay value of $125 per ton and three production years, you're looking at $375 more per acre.
>
> • • •
>
> Cows fed MEGALAC®-R at optimal recommended levels of 1/4 pound per day experienced improved pregnancy rates by over 19%.
>
> • • •
>
> Research conducted in Canada with 400 cows across six herds showed FERMENTEN (rumen fermentation enhancer) led to a 4.9 pound increase in milk. IOFC equaled 56 cents in milk value to 34 cents in feed cows, a 22-cent daily net profit per cow.

Ag speak promotion aside, farmers can die a financial death from a thousand small cuts. Every farmer in the low-margin dairy business is constantly searching for ways to improve his herd's daily milk production, reduce vet bills, extend the milking life of his cows, and increase field fertility and crop yields.

Agribusiness is happy to oblige, at a price, with hybrid and genetically modified seeds for soil conditions, pest infestations, and drought-prone growing seasons; with feed supplements that enable farmers to squeeze the genetic potential from cows already bred to stuff themselves; with buffers, the equivalent of bovine Tums, to calm even the most sensitive stomachs; with head-to-toe drugs from pinkeye to hoof rot; with labor-saving but pricey around-the-clock robotic milking systems that transform a get-your-hands-dirty job into supervision of the computer printout; with GPS-guided tractors for most efficient field preparation, planting, and harvesting. The farmer who wants to "defend his bottom line," to ensure that his heifers are "potential profit generators," to turn "innovation into productivity" has, in short, lots of advice and help.

Seed companies have engineered stalks with a high ear placement to keep them out of reach of rodents. Deer, however, can trim the ears on the outside rows.

Jim Bushey, co-founder of the feed company, sums up how the business has changed in the past 40 years. "We used to have two or three different feeds and they fit everybody. Milk production was 11,000 to 12,000 pounds. Today it's closer to 20,000. Cows have to produce twice as much milk if the farmer is going to pay his bills because the price of milk hasn't changed."

This quest for greater agricultural productivity with less labor is nothing new. It is as old as our transition from hunter-gatherers to more settled agricultural societies. But plant and animal evolutionary changes, which were once largely driven by mutation and natural selection and stretched over generations and centuries, are now agribusiness driven and happen, if not literally overnight, many times within each farmer's lifetime.

The Wymans began farming in the late 1950s when the agribusiness revolution was in its relative infancy. They have seen their per cow milk production double and sometimes triple over the subsequent 40-plus years; their corn yields have doubled; their tractors and more specialized equipment prepare and harvest fields in a fraction of the time that it took their grandfather with his horses and mules.

They have been innovators, adopters, and lifelong students of how to get the most out of their cows and fields, and they have been show-me Yankee frugal and a step behind the technology and equipment of larger neighbors. Survival for them has meant, as it has for nearly all family farms, "get bigger or get out" and has led to the Catch-22 of contemporary dairy economics: greater efficiency and productivity create an oversupply of milk, which translates into lower and, at times, below-cost milk prices.

Like all farmers, the Wymans have been beneficiaries and victims of agriculture's success and its near geometric ability to produce more for less. Subsistence farmers of 1800 had little to sell after meeting their family's needs; diversified family farmers of 1900 could satisfy the needs of scores of consumers; specialized, megafarmers of today can feed hundreds. In 1910, producing 100 pounds of milk required 3.8 hours of a farmer's time, the U.S.

Department of Agriculture estimated. By the 1980s, that effort had been reduced to .2 of an hour. In 2005, the most labor efficient farmers were producing over 1.5 million pounds of milk (about 175,000 gallons) per worker, according to annual Northeast Dairy Farm Summary.

Navigating through this economic and technological minefield has been a constant challenge for the Wymans. As the following narratives of Larry and Grayson Wyman attest, their survival has always depended on how wisely they embraced, adapted to, and sometimes rejected technological developments.

In the 1970s, they were among the first in Addison County to install a manure pit, a low-tech solution to the disposal of a mature cow's daily production of 80 to 100 pounds of waste. Manure stored and spread efficiently is homegrown money in the bank, and the Wymans and their fields have now drawn interest for three decades.

Indian corn was a "miracle crop" for the first settlers, being far better suited to local growing conditions than the rye, barley, oats, and wheat brought from Europe. Corn plays a similarly vital role for the contemporary dairy farmer. A good crop is essential for a successful year. Today's high-tech corn, with its scores of varieties, has been bred to be drought, pest, wind, and frost resistant, to mature in 85 to 120 days, and to prosper in a range of soils. But its yield continues to depend, as it did when Native Americans first advised the Pilgrims, on the skills of the individual farmers, like the Wymans, who plant, harvest, and store it.

Every day about five tons of manure is stored in the 11-foot-deep, 150-foot-square manure pit. The several-inch-thick, weed-topped crust contains the smell and conceals the bubbling bacterial activity of the liquefied manure.

The Manure Pit Was Cutting Edge

LARRY WYMAN: When we first came to Vermont, you could build a 500-foot barn anywhere, do anything. There were no zoning regulations. As more and more people came in, there were those who said, "Hey, we need zoning regulations."

At first, you were very hesitant to support their thinking. But eventually you realized that as much as you hated it you had to have regulations. We all have vested interest in our properties and don't want them degraded by what someone across the road or down the road does to us. Down at Mt. Snow, developers desecrated the place with A-frames that they built willy-nilly with septic systems that weren't close to being adequate. You needed something of the magnitude of Act 250 to get a handle on it and control it.

Until the last few years, things on the farm were still pretty much wide open as long as you were in certain bounds. Some towns proposed distances from the road for your buildings, which was a good thing. But it was pretty easy to pass muster for those things. You didn't have to deviate too much from what you wanted to get approved.

It really hasn't been until water runoff became an issue as farms got bigger and bigger that Natural Resources and the Ag Department had to stick their nose in. They had to come up with regulations so the federal Clean Water Act could be complied with.

I'm 100% for it. But it creates more bureaucracy and more paperwork. You just don't wake up some morning and say, "I guess I'll go out and build a barn today," and start bulldozing. Sometimes by abiding by the regulations you end up with something that is better for you as well. It's not all negative.

The other stumbling block is financing. If lending institutions are going to loan you money, they want a sound investment for you and them. If you belly up and they have to move the farm, they want something with a market value.

We have 4,000 feet of frontage on Otter Creek with a lot of potential runoff. There is no reason why we can't manage that. It's not a pie-in-the-sky regulation. When we put in the manure pit in 1978, we were one of the first in the county. Our first consideration wasn't stream pollution; it was convenience. We did it so we wouldn't have to spread during the winter even though it was legal then.

We saw the value of not having to get the tractor and spreader out every day all winter long when it was 20 below. Before the pit, I'd spread two loads in the morning and then before afternoon milking I'd clean the cow barn again and spread it. You had to clean every bit of wet manure off the spreader. If you didn't it would freeze. When you started it up and put pressure to it, bang!, something would break and you'd have a major repair.

But we also wanted the value of the manure to go where it would do the most good and that was plowed under. You spread in the winter on frozen soil and in the spring it runs off and the phosphorus screws up the water in streams and lakes. I don't think farmers fully understood the concepts then and neither did we. Soil scientists were just beginning to tell us that nutrient content was better preserved in pits where your liquids and solids were together and covered. With manure piles and open storage you get a lot of nutrient evaporation and loss by the time you spread it in the spring.

Milking cows produce very watery waste. Dried-off cows and young heifers in the free stall and heifer wing eat and drink less and produce more solid waste. Their waste is stored in frozen piles until spring spreading.

In the early 1970s, John Stevenson, who was one of the county agents, would discuss manure storage and handling every morning he was on the local radio station. When my father died in '76, Grayson and I were doing everything ourselves without any help besides what our girls could give us after school. So when he started talking about manure storage and its time savings we had a very keen ear; manure storage could save us endless hours.

Addison County clay, he argued, was well adapted to pits because you could dig a hole and manure would stay there. It wasn't going to run all over the place. You didn't have to line the pit or do anything. John described how you could fill a 3,000-gallon tanker truck with liquid manure in a couple minutes with a pump run by your tractor. With a pile of dry manure, you needed a bucket loader to fill your spreader. You could fill a tanker, spread it, and come back for another load while you were still filling a spreader with your bucket loader.

Grayson and I looked at it and said, "We have to do this."

Soil conservation came up with a plan for the pit. And then we talked with Dan Heustis at Heustis Farm Supply about the systems and equipment. He said he had never put any in but he had to start somewhere. Badger made the tanks and spreaders and the ram pumps that pushed the manure from the end of the gutter cleaner into the pond and the pumps that pumped the liquid manure out of the pond and into the tankers. The Badger rep said he would work with them.

Soil conservation estimated a pit about 150 feet square, 11 feet deep in the center, would store two years' worth of manure from our 100 cows and another 50 or so heifers. The pit is shaped like an upside down pyramid so the top four feet are equivalent in volume to the bottom seven feet. You taper it that way so the pit doesn't freeze solid. The liquid enters at the bottom and constantly pushes the crusty or frozen surface up.

I think we spent around $2,500. Today, engineering and construction regulations are much more demanding, and a pit our size could cost you pretty close to $100,000. But $2,500 was a lot of money, and we had to think twice about where it was all coming from.

A 4,500-gallon tanker of liquid manure contains $50-plus worth of commercial fertilizer. Twelve tons of solid manure, a spreader's load, was worth about $80. In a morning, the Wymans could save $1,000 in commercial fertilizer expenses by spreading their own or hiring a custom spreader, above.

The manure pit has been virtually foolproof and as long as you keep water in the gutter cleaner your bedding sawdust, hay, and manure pass easily. Danny did some repair work on the ram pump the other day and that was the first major work since 1978.

It just took days of work and made nothing of it. When the weather breaks in the spring you can spread intensively for a couple days and plow it under before planting or you can spread it after you have taken the crop off in the fall and plow it in before the winter. Before, I could spend an entire morning in the winter cleaning those two barns plus the time it took me in the afternoon.

Now all I had to do was run the gutter cleaner chain each day. It eliminated all those hours and anxiety wondering whether the tractor was going to start or something was going to break down.

Manure is like having money in the bank. It's cheaper than fertilizer. And if you have a summer where fertilizer costs are really high and you can squeeze a little more out of the pit to put on your corn then you're way ahead. A two-year capacity gives you that option, although we may not have that much capacity anymore because we feed cows more.

As far as yields of the fields, they were better, all things considered. Instead of putting a chemical fertilizer on the field, like urea, we used more manure to get the nitrogen that corn needs. You could argue that if we put on more straight urea than we could have gotten a bigger yield. But we were utilizing what we had and were getting a pretty good yield and not having to take a lot of cash out of pocket to do it.

For most of our years, we did our own spreading. Only when Jeanne became sick and we were dealing with a million and one things did we subcontract a lot of the spreading. Perhaps I was reluctant earlier to see the advantage of having someone else do it. I can see now that subcontracting freed up time and equipment dollars for other things. Equipment that sat idle for many months of the year may not have been the best place to put your money.

The pit was cutting edge at that time. Some neighbors were very, very reluctant to admit that liquid manure was the wave of the future. But word got around and the county agent would bring people out by the busload from all over—New York and Quebec—to see it.

Other neighbors would say, "Ah, the smell. I knew you were spreading manure." There was a tradeoff. We could spread in a day what might have taken us a month, so yes there would be more smell. But if we plowed it under immediately it was much better for the land.

When we started, there were probably only a dozen farms out of hundreds in the county using pits. Some big farmers didn't jump on it, but it improved our situation, especially in the hours we saved. The manure pit was a decision we have never regretted.

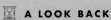

The Great Steam Engine
Which Drives the Vessel Forward

They (manures) are the strong moving power in agricultural operations. They are the great steam engine which drives the vessel forward. Good and clean cultivation is, indeed, all important; but it will avail little without a fertile soil; and this fertility must be created, or kept up, by a copious application of manures.

The great art, then, of saving and manufacturing manure, consists in retaining and applying to the best advantage, these soluble and gaseous portions. Probably more than one half of all the materials, which exist in the country, are lost, totally lost, by not attending to the drainage of stables and farmyards. This could be retained by a copious application of straw, by littering with sawdust.

The practice of many farmers shows how little they are aware of the hundreds they are every year losing by suffering this most valuable of their farm products to escape. Indeed, there are not a few who carefully, and very ingeniously, as they suppose, place their barns and cattle yards in such a manner on the sides of hills, that all the drainage from them may pass off out of the way into the neighboring streams; and some one mentioned the farmer, who, with pre-eminent shrewdness, built his hog-pen directly across a stream, that he might at once get the cleanings washed away, and prevent their accumulation.

He of course succeeded to his wish; but he might, with a most equal propriety, have built his granary across the stream, so as to shovel the wheat on the water when it increased on his hands.

Vermont Family Visitor, 1845

Few people are more eager for an early spring than farmers, who have been restricted to barn work for four months. At the start of March the land is still locked but field work is only weeks away.

You'd Like to See the Corn Jump Out of the Ground in Four to Seven Days

GRAYSON WYMAN: The evolution of corn has been just tremendous. Take the Pioneer catalogue and look up a variety and you can find its tolerance for drought, its resistance to this or that type of bug, fungus, or virus, whether the corn stands well after frost, its resistance to root worms and corn borers, its stalk-to-grain ratio. Today's seeds have become very specific. If the corn is being raised for silage, you can use seeds that produce taller stalks and smaller ears. If you're after more grain, you want bigger ears and shorter stalks.

We always looked for good silage, but we wanted as much grain as we could get. We looked for good drought tolerance because we knew what droughts can be like on clay soils. We wanted standability because we're in a windy spot. And we were always interested in stress emergence and tolerance.

You'd like to see that corn jump out of the ground in four to seven days. But if you have a very cold and wet spell and corn doesn't emerge for two weeks, then you start to worry whether it will germinate and if you'll have seed rot or mold and bacteria growth.

And we wanted a seed that was resistant to bugs and disease. An outbreak of army worms can eat a field of alfalfa or defoliate a corn field overnight. We only had a big problem one year when cut worms destroyed a corn field. The state entomologist looked at the field and said there were so many worms that the best thing was to harrow the whole field. The gulls and blackbirds came in and picked that field clean. We replanted with a quick maturing corn and got a crop. But we were lucky it happened early enough in the spring so we could replant.

Companies have produced genetically modified seeds that produce plants that will kill bugs if they eat the plant. Environmentalists have argued that there are unwanted side effects, like shooting a shotgun and having buckshot all over the place. You may end up killing something else because of the spread.

Seed catalogues will tell you the side effects. You have the choice to buy or not buy it. They ask you to notify your neighbors if you grow a GMO crop so if there is any cross-pollination it won't screw up someone else's field.

We used two GMO corn varieties the last year we planted and got a better yield because we didn't have any bug problems. GMO is a tool. How the tool is used is the question. You have the same argument with BST, which we never used. We were always opposed to using it, but you can turn around and say if you oppose BST why do you plant corn seed that is a GMO because you don't know what potential problems that may create. The argument is valid, but we all do things that we may some day find aren't beneficial.

In the past, seed companies went out in fields and selected hardy plants, took their seeds, and grew them in their fields and sold those seeds. We have a field off Drake Road where some alfalfa plants have been growing ever since we've been here. Usually if you can get four to six years out of an alfalfa field then you've got bragging rights. These plants are almost 40 years old and have something that has allowed them to survive, some form of genetic modification. Today they are doing all this in the lab.

Yields have just improved everywhere. Alfalfa used to have three leaves, which contain the protein, on a stem. Today, they have five and six. I can remember when the average yield in Addison County for corn was probably 12.5 to 13 tons per acre. We are getting well over 20 in some of our fields and some of our river bottom is up around 30.

When we started we planted 17,000 to 18,000 seeds per acre. Now it's 30,000 to 32,000. Corn leaves have been designed to be more vertical so you can tighten up your population. Vertical leaves also funnel rain down to the stalk and root system better. And we fertilize more precisely, whether it's commercial fertilizer or liquid manure, and that supports greater density. Up goes your yield.

You want your germination rates to be well over 95%, but so much is determined by air and soil temperature and the condition of the seed bed. Air temperature isn't as important as soil temperature, which you want to be at least 50. Even if corn is 2 inches to 3 inches high the growing point is still in the ground so you're protected from frost as long as the ground is warm.

Today's seed can take a lot more stress, but we still have to be concerned because we can have a frost at the end of May as easily as we have it at the end of April. When we started we seldom planted corn before June 1, because the seed wouldn't stand it. Several years

Addison County clays are relatively rock free, but years of winter freezes and thaws and spring plowings push and pull rocks, from softball size to half a bucket loader, to the surface. This boulder needed Grayson's helping hand.

Addison County's low-land farmers have roughly 150 frost-free growing days and several weeks at either end for fieldwork. The farmer's rule of thumb is get your 100-day corn in as early as possible and hope for a good start. If the crops fail, there may be time for replanting.

ago, my heavens and earth, we had our corn planted by the end of the first week in May. We worried more about an early killing frost in late summer. That can be a disaster for corn. One year we had a killing frost the last two days of August. The corn turned black and dried out so fast that it wouldn't ferment properly in the silo.

The other factor is your seed bed. If your clay soil still has lots of clumps, then your seed sits between them and won't germinate. So you want to make a seed bed with fine aggregate that will pack around the seed. Since we started using pulvimulchers and cultipackers our ability to break up clods and pulverize the soil has improved tremendously. When you're paying well over $100 for an 80,000-seed count bag (enough to cover about 2.5 acres), you want to make sure that you have a good bed.

A good bed starts after the fall harvest when you plow the corn stubble under for the winter. That helps to kill any borers by burying them and taking away their oxygen. When you plow clay, you get clumps, heavy pieces like cannon balls, and big long pieces. Spring thawing helps break up the clods.

The next step is to harrow the land when you start getting warm weather at the end of April. How many passes it takes to prepare the field depends on what the frost has done. Usually it takes a couple passes with a disk harrow, which does the rough work and breaks up the clods and fills in dips.

Then you'd run your field cultivator, which is like a big rake and produces a smoother seed bed. If you're having a hard time breaking up clods, then you run the cultipacker, which has sets of rollers and tines in between. This breaks up the clods, smoothes the ground, and packs it.

You want to start planting before the first week of May if you can, but you have to know your own land and what it will give you. You don't want corn going into a cold soil because it will just sit there and can rot.

My Seed Corn Cost Me Two and a Half Yards of Whitened Linen

When I came into Wolcott my farming tools consisted of one axe and an old hoe. The first year, I cleared about two acres, wholly without any team, and being short of provision was obliged to work the chief of the time till harvest with scarce a sufficiency to support nature. My work was chiefly by the river. When too faint to labour, for want of food, I used to take a fish from the river, broil it on the coals, and eat it without bread or salt, and then to my work again.

This was my common practice the first year till harvest. I could not get a single potato to plant the first season, so scarce was this article. I then thought if I could get enough of this valuable production to eat I would never complain. I rarely see this article cooked, but the thought strikes my mind; in fact to this day I have a great veneration for this precious root. I planted that which I cleared in season with corn; and an early frost ruined the crop, so that I raised nothing that first year; had again to buy my provision.

My seed corn, about eight quarts, cost me two and a half yards of whitened linen, yard wide, and this I had to go twenty miles after. Though this may be called extortion, it was a solitary instance of the kind; all were friendly and ready to assist me in my known distress, as far as they had ability.

Being destitute of team for four or five years, and without farming tools, I had to labor under great embarrassments: my grain I hoed in the first three years. After I raised a sufficiency for my family, I had to carry it twelve miles to mill on my back, for the three first years: this I had constantly to do once a week. My common load was one bushel, and generally carried it eight miles before I stopped to rest. My family necessities once obliged me to carry a moose hide thirty miles on my back, and sell it for a bushel of corn.

Narratives of the Sufferings of Seth Hubbell & Family,
1789

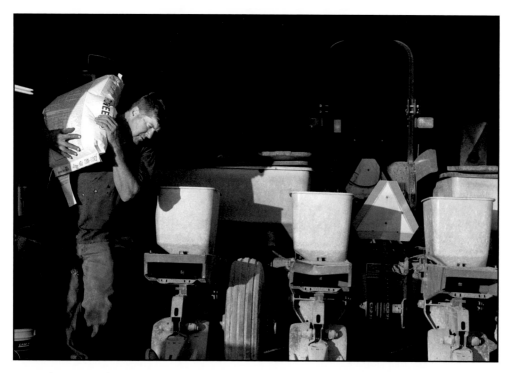

Farmers have scores of seed choices that allow them to customize corn for their soil and growing conditions. The Wymans selected seed with tolerance for wind, drought, bugs, and early season cold and with a good grain yield. An 80,000-seed bag that Dan is loading into the Wymans' four-row planter covers about 2.5 acres. Corn planting expenses have more than doubled in recent years with increases in fuel, fertilizer, and seed.

process. A chain can break on the planter or one of your drops can clog with clay. Today we have electronic monitors with an eye on each of the drops with a tractor readout, but you still have to watch it every minute.

We tried to spread planting out so fields didn't all mature the same day. Most corn maturities today around here are in the 90- to 105-day range. One year we planted 75-day corn because we were running short and needed feed by Labor Day. The tradeoff was a lower yield.

Basically you plant what nature deals you. If a field is ready, you plant it. We generally planted along the creek first because that had the sandiest soil and best drainage. We planted longer-term corn there because we wanted better yields. If we got into a rainy spell in the fall, we knew we could still get in there.

The rule of thumb is the earlier you can plant in the spring, the earlier you can get to it in the fall. And in the fall you can have heavy, hurricane-influenced rains. When clay gets wet, you just churn up ruts and it's a mess. I can remember many falls where there was so much mud that we couldn't do anything.

One of the worst was the fall of 1976, the year my father died. He died the 15th of November, and we weren't done cutting corn because one field was still wet. We finally said we would have to wait until the ground froze. Steve James had just gotten Monument Farms' first four-wheel-drive tractor. We opened up the piece, and he finished it for us. A lot of the leaves had been shed and we lost a lot of tonnage, but it had a high grain-to-stalk ratio, which makes for powerful feed.

With today's equipment, if all goes well and the field isn't too rough, we could prepare a 20-acre field one day and plant it the next. But it usually took longer because we had to sandwich field work in between milkings and other chores. And if we were spreading manure that would add a day or two to the planting.

You can fudge a little bit on tractor speed when you're harrowing and running the field cultivator. But when you're planting seed, you can't rush. Planting corn is a finesse operation and you have to keep your speed consistent so the seed flow is accurate. You want to make darn sure you're doing it right because that is the last step in the

We always pushed our land harder than we did our cows because we were short on the acreage we needed for our cows. The alternative was to rent land, which was against our philosophy. And corn is an expensive crop to grow with your seed and fertilizer costs, all your tractor expenses, and your time, so you have to get good yields to justify the expense. Some farmers buy all their corn, but that can put you in a real bind if there is a short crop and you have to pay a long price when milk prices are down.

But even with all the work I always enjoyed planting. Once you hitched up the harrow, the work never stopped until November. When planting was finished, you had to get ready to make hay or chop grass and alfalfa. Once you started there was hardly a week when you didn't have something going on—first cut, second cut, third cut, baling hay.

There wasn't much relief. You couldn't kick back and say first cutting is done. Usually by the time the first cutting was done, some of the first fields were coming back. You might have a week or two break but then you were right at it again. ⚘

The 35-acre Drake Road piece produced nearly half the Wymans' corn crop. It wasn't as productive as better soils closer to the Otter Creek, but its rectangular shape made for efficient planting and harvesting.

The Wymans' tractor-pulled, no-frills corn chopper—the two-row head is being greased here—is suitable for smaller fields and tight corners. It doesn't have a cob processor like today's self-propelled machines that chop the cob fine enough for even the most finicky cows, or auto contour to adjust the cutting level to ruts, slopes, and sodden ground, or auto pilot or a full-stop metal detector or auto lube. The price tag for all these features on a six-row chopper? $200,000 plus.

You Want to Cut Between Dough and Dent

GRAYSON WYMAN: We always sprayed for weeds right after the corn was planted and before it emerged. We hired a spray truck with a long boom that sprayed close to the ground so there was little or no drift. Once in awhile we would spray for insects, but over the years we didn't have a lot of insect problems with corn. When you rotate crops and have corn for a year or two and then alfalfa for three or four or five you break the insect cycle. That and cold winters kill a lot of insects.

We wanted to see corn knee high or better by the fourth of July and wanted tassels showing by the first of August. Once your tassels emerge, it's a matter of watching your ear development. Then you start watching the color of the silk on the ear. After the silks were brown for 10 days or two weeks, we'd strip an ear and check for the moisture in the kernels.

You took your thumbnail and pushed against the kernel. If it pops and is milky it's in the dough stage and too early to cut. If you chop now and pack it in a bunk, all that liquid runs away and your goodness goes down the drain. When the corn gets dry enough, it dents with a puck mark at the end of the kernel. That's a sign that it has dried. You want to cut between dough and dent. We used to wait for full dent, but with today's new varieties you can cut when it's a little greener.

The goal is to have your moisture within a range to get maximum feed value. Seed companies have developed a plant with potential; it's your job to harvest it at the right point. It's like breeding cows where you create a genetic base and it's your responsibility to feed them right.

It takes a bit of luck with your weather and soil conditions to get out in the fields at the optimum time. If your corn is ready and it's constantly raining then you can't chop. Corn quality doesn't fall off as fast as your grasses because it's a much bigger plant, but you do lose some quality in the ears.

Over the years as seed quality changed our maturity dates changed as well. Generally we'd start chopping around Labor Day. Longer-term corn and fields that were late being planted could be chopped in October. If you were raising corn for grain, you wanted the ears to dry down well and that would take you into October and November.

A lot depended on what you wanted the corn for and how you were storing it. With a bunk, you need some moisture to hold it together when you're packing it. Having your machinery set up right is important when you're chopping for silage. You want your knives to be sharp and your aggregate to be a quarter to half an inch so it packs well and you can exclude as much oxygen as possible.

If you cut it too fine and it's too dry, it just pops back after you drive over it. If you pack it when it's moist, it sticks together and the oxygen is pushed out; then you have a better ensiling process. You need the right moisture, especially when you're going to put it in a bunk and pack it mechanically. If it's going into an upright, like a Harvestore silo, its own weight will pack it.

The tractors we use today to pack do a good job, especially if the material is cut right. With tractors, the amount of tire surface is more important than weight. When we first started using bunker silos way, way, way back, a lot of guys tried packing with Caterpillar tractors because the weight was distributed over long cleat tracks. But they didn't pack as well as wheel tractors, where all the weight is concentrated on four spots.

Every time that surface is contacted at those four points, you're getting a lot of

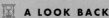 **A LOOK BACK**

Not a Single Crop Came to Maturity

The growth of the county (Orleans) experienced another severe check in 1816. That year was memorable as one of extraordinary privations and sufferings. An unusually early spring had created expectations of a fruitful season and an abundant harvest, but on the morning of June 9th there occurred a frost of almost unprecedented severity, followed by a fall of snow, which covered the earth to the depth of nearly a foot, and was blown into drifts 2 or 3 feet deep. All the growing crops were cut down. Even the foliage was destroyed, and so completely as respected the beeches, that they did not put forth leaves again that year.

No hope or possibility of a harvest remained, and the settlers had before them the gloomy prospect of extreme scarcity, if not of actual famine. Their forebodings were more than realized. Not a single crop came to maturity.

Wheat alone progressed so far that by harvesting it while yet in the milk, and drying it in the oven, it might be mashed into dough and baked, or boiled like rice. There was neither corn nor rye except what was brought from abroad, sometimes from a great distance, and at an expense of $3.00 a bushel, and sometimes more. Provisions of every kind were very scarce, and very high. Fresh fish and vegetables of every kind that could possibly be used as food were converted to that purpose. There was extreme sufferings through the summer and fall, and still greater distress during the winter: but it is not known that any one perished by starvation.

Abby Hemenway,
Vermont Historical Gazetteer, Volume II, 1871

pressure to force the oxygen out so that you get anaerobic bacteria going to work, which ferments the silage. You can tell how good the packing is by how much you bounce. If you walk over it and don't make much of a footprint, you have done a pretty good job. But if there's a lot of bounce there's something wrong.

You can also tell from the way the tracks look. If you're leaving a lot of ridges and see big depressions, you know you have more work to do.

The key in packing was keeping everything in synch. Corn can come from the field so fast that the tractor doesn't have time to adequately pack it. You end up with poor compaction, which makes for poor feed, which comes back to what you get at the milk pail.

You have to learn how many tractors and dump wagons you need in the field and how many tractors you need at the bunk. Too often, the attitude, especially on your mid-sized farms where you might not have the right balance of equipment, is let's get it done. Get it done but have something worth feeding when it is done.

For us sizing our equipment was never that exact a science. It was more what could we move for the cost of energy expended. Diesel fuel costs, at the end, were getting to be a large consideration, and if you could manage a little more with each load, that was a big help as long as you didn't bury the guy who was trying to pack it at the bunk.

Circa 1920

A Short Crop of Hay

We are to have a short crop of hay," is the cry of nearly all. And most farmers are in danger of making the crop less valuable than they might, by cutting too late. They will put off the cutting till the grass has lost much of its saccharine matter, to get a little more, and what they do cut will be little better than so much straw. The lighter the crop the more need of cutting it in the best time and making it in the best manner.

Cut when the seed is in the milk—cure with as little sun as possible; but cure well in the cock. Open to the air about two hours before carting in. Put on very little salt if any. Preserve as far as possible all the aroma, and the fresh green color, and though you have less hay, you will have a better quality, and it will spend much better than an equal amount cut from ground that yielded twice as much.

Don't be frightened about a short crop. Providence is all always better to us than our fears—and what is lost in one way may be gained in another.

Vermont Family Visitor, 1845

We wanted our bunk as long and as wide as possible so there were different areas where we could pile feed as it was coming from the field. We had one area that was packed and was ready for another load while we were working on the other side.

Some years we had one tractor packing; other years we had two, depending on how fast the feed was coming. With two tractors, one would level the load and the other would pack. The tractor that was spreading was also packing, though that wasn't its primary function. Then you'd switch sides with the tractors and the second tractor would fully pack it.

A long and relatively narrow bunk is easier to fill, but it is also more practical when you take the feed out. You want to minimize the amount of face that is exposed so you don't have a lot of spoiled silage. During the winter, spoilage is not that much of a factor, but the rest of the year when you have a warm day or rain you can have a lot of mold on an exposed face. That's bad news.

We know more and more about molds today and that a lot of them cause problems with the cows. We used additives and preservatives at the end when we chopped to try to reduce mold and quicken the ensiling process. As the corn or grass went through the chopper, it tripped a valve so the additive went right into the blower. By the time the chop hit the wagon, the preservative was already in it.

But it doesn't take long for the mold to develop. Silage is just a golden environment for mold. Spores are everywhere—in the soil, in the air, in the silage. If we knew how many passed through our lungs, we'd probably be staggered.

One thing we never knew was how long the harvest would take. Hard and fast rules don't apply in harvesting. There are just too many variables. One year we could chop the corn on our 30-acre piece and pack the bunk in two and a half days. The next year the field could be muddy and you'd get stuck or it would be rock hard and rutty and you couldn't drive as fast.

Our sandy loam piece by the creek is our best corn land and dries fast, but it can flood. One year we had a flash flood in August and the field had four feet of water. When the water receded the corn leaves were full of silt. We'd chop a loop or two or three and then have to stop and sharpen the knives. It took us almost a week that year to cut 11 acres.

The fingernail test for harvesting readiness: puncture a kernel, if it's milky it's not ready. This firm kernel, in the dent stage in early September, is ready. Geneticists have developed corn varieties with tighter husks but not tight enough to stop this bird damage.

2,000 Tons of Corn: A Good Year's Feed

The old harvesting adage, "Make hay while the sun shines," could be applied to nearly every farming operation. In 2004, a perfect spring was followed by a record-wet August and a sunny early September. When harvesting began on September 6, early corn was well above tractor-cab high, albeit "wicked green." But the Wymans, running low on feed, couldn't wait to start the three-week long process—chopping, packing, and fermentation—that would turn corn in the field to silage in front of their cows.

By the 18th, the Wymans, with the help of Monument Farms Dairy's five-person crew, had cleared 80-plus acres of corn, over a year's worth of feed. Some farmers believe they save time, money, and equipment by buying all their corn silage. The Wymans have always sought to be self-sufficient in silage, fearing that a short corn crop and higher feed costs coupled with poor milk prices could be the triple whammy that would put them out of business.

"You can't make a living growing corn unless someone is willing to pay you big bucks in a bad crop year. You get your money back when you feed it to cows and they turn it into milk," says Larry of their philosophy of raising their own feed.

The 2004 corn crop averaged 22 to 23 tons an acre yielding roughly 2,000 tons of feed for the coming year, an entrée worth about $50,000. A good year.

A record-wet August was followed by a sunny September, bringing the Wymans' 93- and 108-day corn to maturity in early and mid-September. Only a handful of stalks escaped the chopper in the two-week-long harvest.

The Wyman corn was cab high and more when they began harvesting in early September. The Wymans plant right to the edge of their fields, and the first outer pass has corn on the right and windshield-brushing sumac on the left.

2,000 Tons of Corn

Ears should be mature, but not too mature, for maximum nutrition. Stalks should have some moisture, but not too much moisture, for optimal packing and fermentation. The corn was wetter and greener than ideal—"wicked green," said Dan when they began cutting on September 6.

The Wymans hired neighboring Monument Farms Dairy with its state-of-the-art, six-row corn chopper to cut most of the farm's corn. The dairy's full-time crew can cut in two to three days fields that took the Wymans, working between milkings, two weeks.

Above: Good silage requires proper cutting and good packing. Chop grass or corn at optimal nutritional level and before it is too dry. Then squeeze excess oxygen out of the bunk to limit fermentation with repeated passes of a six-ton tractor. Feed covered tightly in plastic will last for several years.

Custom choppers can get into trouble when they don't know the day-to-day quirks of a farmer's fields. A rainy August turned this wet spot into a September sinkhole. Monument Farms' corn chopper, with the help of a neighbor's backhoe and the dairy's biggest tractor, was back in business in an hour.

Feed bunks have replaced silos for many farmers. The Wymans have found that bunks can be filled
and emptied faster and are cheaper to build and maintain than silos.

September 2004: A Very Big Pile!

Every day is a workday for farmers, and the Wymans begin the corn harvest on Labor Day, the 6th. Monument Farms Dairy, as planned, chops most of the corn, and on September 18 the bunks are brimful with more than a year's feed. A "very big pile!!," roughly 2,000 tons, Larry reports in his DayMinder.

Succumbing to harvesting's hectic pace, the drive of the 20-year-old Allis Chalmers tractor gives out while packing silage. A new front end will cost $8,000, more than it's worth. "She gave her all," says Dan. "Little John," the smaller John Deere backup, will complete the packing.

The third cutting of hay is on hold until killing frosts stop the alfalfa's growth for the year.

On September 16, after a week of preparatory radiation treatments, Jeanne has a bone marrow transplant—her brother is the donor. Larry's notes in his DayMinder chronicle her four-week recovery in Boston.

September 17: Jeanne & Dan called at 9:30 a.m.—she sounds great—like she was ready to come home!!—but she will go down before she comes up—next 8 days will be bad.

September 20: Talked to Jeanne & Dan 10:30 a.m. Jeanne has pericarditis—inflammation around the heart that is causing her pain and breathing prob—much morphine—will last 2 or 3 days.

September 27: Jeanne had a bad day—called 4 p.m.—was worse at 9 a.m. and noon when Danny talked to her—she wants to come home!

Dan called at 8 p.m. said he was going down (to Boston) tomorrow overnight—she had a partial collapse of left lung as well as pneumonia.

October 1: Jeanne called the barn at 6:15 a.m. & talked to all of us since she was wide-awake early. She called the house at 9:30—MD's had just been in—her white cell count was up to 7400—will continue to remove IV's—the light at the end of the tunnel grows brighter.

Harvest's end after a long spring and summer brings out schoolboy playfulness in Dan with a 25-foot-long slide down the season's wrapped corn silage.

Chapter 6

Pamper the Cow

Pamper Your Cows From Dawn to Dusk

Try this quiz for 4-H'ers, "What's your dairy IQ?" in the Young Dairymen section of *Hoard's Dairyman: The National Dairy Farm Magazine*.

Feeding and Nutrition

1. DCAD is a relatively new way to evaluate rations for transition cows. What do the letters DCAD stand for?
A. days calving after due, B. dietary cation-anion difference, C. dietary calculation as delivered, D. days culled after delivery

Herd Health

16. A cow's milk fat test that is lower than her milk protein test may be a sign of what?
A. acidosis, B. fatty liver disease, C. displaced abomasums, D. mastitis

Dairy Facts

28. Which state is home to the most certified organic dairies?
A. Minnesota, B. Vermont, C. Oregon, D. Maine

Genetics and Reproduction

41. Semen should be thawed in a warm water bath at about what temperature?
A. 64 degrees, B. 72 degrees, C. 96 degrees, D. 105 degrees

Cow Comfort

53. At what temperature do cows generally start experiencing heat stress?
A. 64 degrees, B. 78 degrees, C. 82 degrees, D. 94 degrees

55. Cows housed on what bedding surface are the most efficient and produce the most milk?
A. concrete, B. mattresses, C. sand, D. sawdust

Milking Procedure

56. An older cow that has a somatic cell count on the first test of her lactation was probably infected when?
A. calving, B. dry period, C. late last lactation, D. as a heifer

(**The answers:** 1.B; 16.A; 28.B; 41.C; 53.B; 55.C; 56.B) Fifty-five correct out of 60 is excellent; 40 or more is good; below 30, try again next year.

• • •

Low-scoring 4-H'ers and Future Farmers of America are urged to review the questions, which are keyed to past articles. And to prepare for next year's quiz by reading the magazine, which provides readers of all ages a healthy dose of dairy science and business management 20 issues a year.

"Grayson knew his cows. Ninety-nine times out of a hundred if he said a cow was ready to be bred, she was," says vet Walt Goodale of Grayson's encyclopedic knowledge of the herd's history. For 30-plus years, he relied on a very low-tech filing system, a clipboard and black notebook.

Farmers try to spread calving, about 280 days after insemination, throughout the year to maintain a constant flow of milk. Grayson tracked due dates and family lineage. Grayson, Larry, and Dan also monitored cows daily to catch them coming into heat.

The center of all this attention is the Holstein, the black-and-white cow that is featured—grazing in a field of clover, being milked in the latest parlor, being fed in a football field-length free stall—on nearly every magazine cover. And well she should be. Ninety percent of the country's 9 million dairy cows are Holsteins; Holsteins are the predominant milking breed worldwide—2,000 years of selective evolution having made them the most productive of the half dozen major breeds.

Inside, magazine articles have a profit-provoking hook: "Amino Acid Balancing Can Improve Your Milk Check"; "Can Carbon Credits Be a New Revenue Source for Your Farm?"; "The Real Drivers of Feed Efficiency"; "Don't Be Buffaloed by Today's Grain Prices." But readers will not find a silver bullet to profitability.

Rather, issue after issue they will hear a common refrain: pamper your cows from dawn to dusk. Better yet, keep lights on longer during winter to encourage cows to spend more of those quiet hours doing what they do best—eating, digesting, and chewing their cud.

Nothing is too small to be overlooked, the magazine stresses, in the care of the prima donnas of the barn. Are they comfortable, for example, in their stalls? Some studies (see background story on Question 55) suggest that sand-based stalls are a key factor in improving income over feed costs. In one limited study, cows housed in sand-based stalls ate 3.1 pounds more dry matter, produced 6.1 more pounds of milk, and generated 71 cents more income over feed costs each day over the course of a year.

Why? Seven or eight inches of sand can be squished around for a comfortable bed. Unlike sawdust, another popular bedding, sand is not a good host for growth of bacteria. Less bacterial growth leads to fewer udder infections and more milking days.

In a time of constant technological change, dairy farmers will find little enthusiasm in the magazine for the next new thing until it is peer reviewed and farm tested. "Stick to proven strategies and stay away from quick fixes" is the recommendation on Question 53, Heat Stress.

Dairy cows like it cool, 50 to 60 degrees, for optimal milk production. A heat-stressed cow drinks more, eats less dry matter, and chews her cud less, which can lead to rumen acidosis. Solution?

Add fat to the diet, increase mineral concentration, use feed additives, and increase soluble fiber levels. In addition to fans, keep the cow cool with stalls that are kept dry and fountains that refill quickly—cows can drink 30 gallons a day. And minimize the time spent "bunching"—1,500-pound Holsteins generate lots of body heat while waiting to be milked in a parlor or seeking shade from direct sunlight.

In 1885, the magazine's founding year, founder H.D. Hoard cited the availability of high-producing cows, then 4,000 pounds of milk a year, that boded well for the future. Today's magazine routinely runs articles on family farms with annual herd averages of 25,000 to 30,000 pounds per cow and on the current generation of super cows that have produced over 70,000 pounds (about 8,500 gallons) in a year.

In Hoard's day, cows spent much of the day on the move, from morning milking to pasture and back to the barn for evening milking. Newborn calves drank mother's milk. No more.

Today's cows get a balanced diet of hay, haylage, and corn silage, and mineral supplements delivered to them, either in constantly replenished bunks in free stalls or in front of their individual stalls in stanchion barns. Holsteins grazing on green hillsides make good photographs but are bad economics for dairy farmers trying to squeeze every pound of milk from their herd. Pastured cows very simply do not have a sufficiently varied diet, if not fed supplements, or drink enough to produce to their genetic potential.

Those cows we do see grazing? They are on a milking holiday prior to calving and no longer need a high-protein, high-energy diet. Indeed, such a diet could add unwanted weight, potentially complicating pregnancy and delivery.

In a cow's year, she will, if all goes well, be milked for 305 days, a standard lactation, and then have 60 days to rest prior to calving and resumption of milking. Once they have freshened (given birth), cows have a ski-slope production curve—it's all downhill after a strong start. At the end of the lactation when she is carrying a rapidly growing calf, her production may be half what it was six months earlier and barely offset her feed and vet costs.

In the bottom-line economics of dairying that means there is no time for Mom to suckle her calf at a time of peak production. After a day off when her initial antibody rich milk is not suitable for sale, she goes to work and her calf is bottle fed. Dan and Jeanne Kehoe, who fed the heifers, are imprinted as Mom.

Ideally, the Holstein, according to the Holstein-Friesian Association, the breed's trade organization, should be "large of barrel, high of udder, sturdy and shapely of leg, straight of back, with an all-around 'dairy-type' face." She should have a ravenous appetite and aggressive eating habits—cows in a free stall compete for food in a bunk. The ideal Holstein should be neither bossy nor submissive, accept close quarters with fellow cows, and be easily approachable by farm workers.

Sires who consistently outperform fellow sires by transmitting these characteristics and above-average milk production can, like Hanoverhill Starbuck, become a legend in their own time. Starbuck through sales of his frozen semen sired roughly 200,000 calves in 45 countries in his nearly 20-year lifetime.

The Wymans never used Starbuck as a sire. But a good sire requires a good dam, and the Wymans had a good dam, Laura. In the following narrative, Grayson recalls how Laura produced healthy, long-lived heifer calves year after year. Dairy genealogists estimate that many of the world's Holsteins are related to Starbuck; at one time, over half the cows in the Wyman barn were offspring of Laura, her daughters, granddaughters, and great granddaughters. Larry discusses how tending cows, a complicated piece of machinery, is a 24-hour-a-day responsibility and why the old way—let the barnyard bull do it—can't compete with artificial insemination and semen from the best bulls in the country. ❧

Over the past 50 years, artificial insemination using proven bulls has been a major factor in the doubling of milk production. Breeding technician Paul Barrett worked with Grayson and Larry in their herd improvement program.

The Herd That Laura Built

GRAYSON WYMAN: When we lived in Brownsville we had a neighbor in his mid-70s who still farmed the way his father had many, many years before. He never bred a cow to freshen before she was four years old. His cows would weigh 1,600 pounds, which is 400 to 500 pounds more than today's cows when they freshen. He pastured everything and didn't have big feed costs, so he could afford to wait that long.

Our goal was to grow our heifers, breed them, and have them freshen at 30, 31, 32 months. He thought we were crazy for breeding that early. When we stopped, our heifers were freshening at 21, 22, 23 months, which was a result of everything from the heifer's genetics to the quality of the feed. Our philosophy was the faster we got them milking, the quicker they started paying us back. The first year's milking is pretty much on the house; they're paying you back for raising them for 20-odd months.

Longevity in a cow is like a car. If you can drive it for 10 to 15 years, you have gotten a lot out of it. If you have to replace it every two to three years, then it's rather expensive. Today, people don't breed for longevity. Farmers push their cows for all they're worth, and when they're not productive, they're out the door. You beef her and put another in her place. That's not the way we farmed. We were looking for longevity in every heifer.

When we started we were flying by the seat of our pants and bought cows wherever we could. Some times we ended up with a good cow. Some times we didn't. One of our best, a first-time bred heifer, came from our Brownsville neighbor when we were trying to build our herd.

We chose the bull for her second calf, a heifer, and we milked that heifer, Laura, for 16 years. In those 16 years, she had 10 daughters. Of those 10 daughters only two of them milked for less than 12 years. Two milked for 14. You can't argue that longevity wasn't in Laura's genes. People weren't pushing cows the way they do today, but most farmers were still probably only getting five or six lactations, which was less than half of Laura's.

We never pushed for records, but Laura and probably two of her daughters were "Iron Grandmas." DHI (Dairy Herd Improvement Association) used to recognize all cows that gave over 200,000 pounds of milk during their lifetimes as "Iron Grandmas." Back in the 1960s and 1970s that was a lot of milk. Today, if you get 100,000 pounds over a lifetime you're doing well.

When she was 18, we had limited space in the barn and had to decide whether to breed her back or let her go. The risk of calving at her age meant that we could lose her, so we put her on the trailer and sent her to the commission sale. It was like losing an old friend. When the trailer pulled out of the yard, she was looking back, and you almost had the feeling that she was saying, "Hey, look what I've given you."

Laura gave us one heifer calf after another. Her daughters were the same way, giving us one heifer calf after another. A couple years after we shipped her, I went through the herd book and counted how many of her female descendants were in the barn. At that time, the barn held 102, and 50 of the animals were her direct female descendants, daughters, granddaughters, and great granddaughters.

Laura was the kind of animal that comes along once in a lifetime. She was the one that built the herd and put us over the top. She had good production, both milk and butterfat, and all her daughters were healthy and did not have breeding or mastitis problems.

Laura was short and wasn't long bodied, so we went for height and length in her daughters. She had daughters who stood a foot taller with a tremendous length of body. They could just pack in the feed. We used several different bulls with Laura and built very different daughters.

Like Laura's daughters, today's cow has been bred to be bigger. When we started there weren't milking parlors, and you milked the cows from the side. The teats were farther forward. Now with parlors and machines that you attach from the rear,

First-calf heifers now give milk like mature cows because of improved genetics and better feeding programs. Forty years ago, the Wymans' first-time milkers started at 40 pounds of milk a day; today they begin at 80 to 100 pounds and remain at higher levels longer.

the teats have moved farther back. With some of our cows we have to reach around their back legs to attach the machine. You also want a cow with tall legs so the udder will stay high. Cows are milked hard now, and the bag will drop over the years as muscles weaken. With some cows you almost have to lie on your stomach because the udder has dropped almost to the floor. So you want a cow with an udder that stays above the hock.

And I always wanted a bull with a mellow disposition to the extent that any bull is mellow. I can remember when we started, we were using the semen of a bull that came from the U.S. government herd at the Beltsville, Maryland, agricultural station. I called up the technician and asked him what the bull was like.

He said, "I'll put it this way. He'd never kill you because he hated you, but he might kill you playing with you." He wasn't mean. He was just so big that he was really difficult to handle when he was playful. Breeders are paying a lot more attention to the female line that produces the bull now because a lot of us squawked. Hopefully, the bull will pass on genes that reflect an easy-to-work-with factor of his female line.

When we started breeding cows in the 1960s, we got three insemination services for $6. If a cow had to be bred three times to get pregnant that was $6. Today, it's on a per-service basis. You pay an arm charge of $4 to $7 to the technician and the cost of the semen. You can start at the bottom and pay $5 to $6 for an unproven bull or spend hundreds of dollars.

We never went for the super-high-priced bulls. We tried to find something middle-of-the-road, in the $20 to $25 range, that would improve body-type traits and production. At the end it was probably costing us $30 for AI (artificial insemina-

Cows that give lots of milk can be forgiven many sins—ornery disposition, difficulty in breeding back, slow milking, occasional health problems. Culling the marginal producer is essential but was never easy for the Wymans, who sought to improve the herd through years of selective breeding.

tion) per cow. We might go $10 or $15 higher if we had a really good cow and found a good matchup with a bull. But most of the time we found we got the greatest gains by matching an excellent bull with a middle-range cow. Her offspring had the potential to show greater gains than the offspring of a cow that already was a good producer.

Years ago the trend was to have all the daughters of Bull X be bred by Bull Y. You were supposed to get more consistency in the herd by using the same bull. A certain bull was right for all the daughters. Today, you look at dams as individuals, certainly in a herd our size, and you have thousands of choices.

We used every bit of information we could get from farmers, vets, breeding technicians, catalogues, and breeding magazines. That meant that when the technician walked in the barn you didn't say, "Oh, I guess I'll use Old Harry today." You had to put a little forethought into it.

One of my peeves over the years was the farmer who complained about the price of milk but didn't pay attention to breeding. I was as aggravated as anyone about the price we got for milk because I think it was very unjust. But there were so many things, like artificial insemination, that people could do that would have given them a better income.

Why wouldn't you use a bull that is proven to throw a daughter that will be a better milker than her dam? Yet farmers would repeatedly let some old bull, "the best of the neighborhood," run with the cows and breed them. AI isn't an exact science, but it gives you a much better chance of improving your herd. Yet many farmers ignore AI because it is another monthly bill; the bull doesn't send a bill but the breeding technician does. It's another bill, but a more productive herd will pay you back more than a new set of harrows that you use for three days in the spring.

We raised all our own heifers once we got going and never bought a cow for 35 years. Today, on some big farms if a cow goes down, they go out and buy another heifer and put her in there. It's two totally different philosophies. If they need 10 or 12, they just buy them and don't know any more about them than the fact that the cow just freshened and can be milked. If she doesn't breed back, they beef her.

Walt Goodale (the Wymans' longtime vet) used to laugh—and I'm not tooting our horn—it's just telling it like it is. We might be doing checks for pregnancy, and he'd say, "This cow is open." And I'd say, "I'm not going to fool with her any more because her mother wasn't a good breeder and her grand dam wasn't either."

Walt would say, "Most places I go they can't even tell me who a cow's sire is, and I come here and you tell me not only who her sire is but who her dam was and who her grand dam was and who her great grand dam was." That is nothing more than when you live with them every day you get to know them. The better you know them, the better job you can do.

The one thing I always looked for in a cow was a desire to milk, almost a will to perform. Overachievers, if you will. This cow would stand and chew her cud totally relaxed while you milked her. She acted like she was thoroughly enjoying being relieved of her milk.

Laura and nearly all her daughters had this manner. You could do anything with them. Other cows had an attitude: I'm not giving you anything. You're taking it. You got rid of these "meaners" and tried to propagate those traits that made your day's work a lot easier.

Cows are no different than we are. When they get nervous or upset, the adrenaline begins to pump and they don't give as much milk. We always felt that a quiet barn was better than a barn with a lot of hooting and hollering and a blaring radio. But what's most important is cows like a routine. They sense if you're having a bad day or if one cow gets fired up she can upset the whole barn. That can make for a long milking day.

I was interested in breeding right from the start. Larry was, too, but when he went home after milking his interest was his family. I didn't get married until I was 38 and would go home and sit down with breeding magazines and store away information.

Over the years we had many good milkers, but none ever had Laura's longevity. We had others who we remember less fondly, like the ones who could kick the stars out of heaven when you tried to milk them.

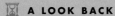

A LOOK BACK

An Animal Once Stunted Never Comes To Its Best State

A word about the care of animals: Nine out of ten men fail along this line—I refer particularly to the care and maintenance of high bred and valuable cattle, because they place people in charge of them who are unable to maintain the same standard of care and keeping that these animals were accustomed to, and they quickly deteriorate, and in a few generations they are worth no more than scrubs.

Unless you and I have high standards for the development of young stock in our herds we certainly will not make any money, no matter how priced the sires we may have. So, we must begin early; we must nourish the calves so they will come to maturity able to do the one thing we ask of them—simply to digest food; that is their main function; therefore, I want every calf that is raised on my farm to be kept continuously growing by a constantly increasing ration of good, digestible food, adapted to it. An animal once stunted never comes to its best state.

Prof. C.H. Royce
50th Annual Convention,
Vermont Dairymen's Association, 1920

When the Machine Came Off She Was Fully Milked

Milking was never a "foot race" to get out of the barn quickly for the Wymans. "We made darn well sure when the machine went on and came off that she was fully milked, that the milk that went into the tank was good milk, and that she was going to be all right for the next milking," says Larry Wyman of their slower-paced milking style.

Milking a cow for the first time is like breaking a horse, says Grayson. They learn that the machine relieves the pressure in their udder, but until then they may kick the milker off and trample it. Dan, applying "attitude adjustment" with his 190 pounds, pins this heifer to the stanchion to minimize her kicking. Some agitated first-time milkers require tranquilizers before letting their milk down.

Left and top right: Tails are effective fly swatters, but beware their whiplash. The Wymans tied their cows' tails to prevent injury during milking.

Bottom right: The use of milking machines, designed to mimic the sucking action of calves, did not become widespread until after World War II. Hand milking was possible with smaller herds. Limited electrification in rural areas also slowed the use of vacuum milkers.

When the Machine Came Off She Was Fully Milked

Left: Where does all the milk go? Cheese, not fluid milk, is now #1. Fluid milk consumption peaked in the 1940s and 1950s at 37 gallons per person and has dropped today to 24 gallons. Rising cheese consumption—it has nearly tripled since 1970—has made up the difference. Americans, thanks in part to fast food, now eat 32-plus pounds of cheese per person, the equivalent of 37 gallons of milk.

Below right: Struggling farmers have long argued that processors should pay for the cost of transporting milk that they own once it leaves the farm's bulk tank. This stop-and-hauling charge, roughly five percent of their milk check, is money they desperately need. In a tight-margin business, processors argue, they can't afford to pass this cost on to consumers.

Below left: In the early 1900s, the time of this photo, family farmers had hundreds of local creameries a short horse-and-buggy ride away. Much of this perishable milk was converted to butter and cheese, with Vermont leading the country in the production of butter per capita. By 1970 all milk handlers required that dairy farmers store their milk in refrigerated bulk tanks, forcing many small farms out of business.

"Bull calves are bigger, clumsier, and catch on a little slower. This one is dumber than a bag of rocks and doesn't want to suck," says Dan. "In the winter you have to warm them up so they want to drink. By tonight he'll be hungry."

You Reap What You Sow

LARRY WYMAN: When we started we had to buy animals to build the herd. We'd go to sales and be told that this cow was an outstanding cow, a registered Holstein. After she'd freshened, we'd find out that her teats were angled every which way and she wouldn't milk out easily. You can go to a sale and see animals that look perfect, but with a cow looks aren't everything. We have had some of the ugliest cows you'll ever see, but they were good milkers.

You can read the pedigrees and touch the goods, but that doesn't tell you about the things we ended up with. We were paying top dollar for a cow, bringing her home, and then finding out that we had bought a hunk of junk. By 1972-73 we had had our fill of buying damaged goods.

Grayson and I decided that if we were going to be buying junk, we'd rather raise our own junk. Our herd might not be the best in the world, but we would build on it. That's just what we did. For the past 30-odd years we have had a closed herd and haven't bought a cow. We have just tried to improve on what we had.

There is an art in breeding and Grayson has spent hours and hours matching bulls to our cows. It's a lot of work watching your cows to see when they come into heat and breeding them in that window of 24 to 36 hours. Some farmers don't want to take the time and put their cows out in the pasture and let the bull do it. But the bull can be the best bull that ever lived, and he can't service a herd with multiple problems—poor udders, poor feet, poor legs, bad back—to say nothing about production and butterfat and protein. One animal can't possibly correct all those things.

We always tried to breed to weakness. If we had a heifer with a narrow body, we bred her with a wide-bodied bull to give her room for a big rumen to pack with feed. There is no guarantee, but you're at least trying to move forward.

We didn't consciously work at improving the herd average. We tried to improve the structure of the animal and her longevity. We wanted to put good feet and legs under them. We wanted wide muzzles and rib spread and deep bodies so they could eat a lot. When you build a strong cow the other things come.

Trust to Nature and Good Nursing

In the absence of intelligent veterinarian skill, stock of all kinds are dosed and doctored too much, by ignorant and injudicious hands, and if all were to have good care and nursing, without one particle of medicine when sick, a larger proportion would get well than under the present practice.

I would not undervalue veterinarian skill. If one has access to such, it is best to take its advice and follow its counsel, but how intelligent, reading and thinking men can employ some old cow leach, who often cannot read and write, and knows no more of the powerful medicines he often uses than he does of metaphysics, I never could understand.

I have known such a one to kill a cow in double-quick time that nature would probably have cured, had she not been rudely and radically interfered with. Experience certainly teaches one thing: never to administer medicines of any kind that you are not certain are the right ones to be used at that time, and for that disease. It is far better to trust to nature and good nursing.

Raising and Managing Dairy Stock,
Albert Chapman, Esq., 1874

Farmers will give lip service to artificial insemination, but if they don't get results or quick conceptions, they'll jump ship and go back to letting the bull do it rather than trying to figure out what they're doing wrong. And so many farmers will use a beef bull, like an Angus or Hereford, that doesn't have dairy genetics, for a first breeding.

This supposedly results in a smaller calf and the dam will have fewer problems birthing. But you end up with a calf that is a mixed breed that most likely will be sent to the commission sale for beef.

A farmer committed to artificial breeding isn't wasting that first breeding and is using a good Holstein bull. If the dam freshens with a heifer calf, then you have another generation of milkers coming along.

Milk production per cow has been going up year after year, but I bet the increases would be significantly larger if you only took farmers who made conscientious breeding efforts. When we started, we were in awe of a cow that gave us 10,000 pounds a year. She would be shipped today.

Another advantage of a closed herd is that you get to know your cows and can take the time to try and straighten things out. Take a heifer that has just freshened and isn't giving much milk. We'd give her system a chance and fix her feed or whatever might be off. We'd often find in a week or two or three that she was giving milk like a geyser.

In some farms, cows are just numbers. The minute they don't produce, they get shipped. Grayson and I never wanted to work our cows so hard that they were just numbers. We wanted a herd size and productivity where we could pay our bills. We figured that if we paid our bills when they were due, then we'd be first in line for service when we called. That's the way we operated for 46 years.

But many farmers even today don't want to be bothered with artificial insemination, even with all the knowledge we have about it. Our feeling was always that you reap what you sow. ⟡

Cows returning to the stress of milking and more feed, especially acidic, high-energy grain, after calving can end up with a twisted stomach. Unless immediately corrected, here by vet Alan Clarisse, the condition is nearly always fatal. With a problem-free surgery and no use of penicillin, the cow can be milked again within 24 hours.

Cows Are Very Complicated Pieces of Machinery

LARRY WYMAN: Years ago we didn't push cows the way we do today. The steady producer that gave 35 to 40 pounds of milk would be beef today. We have cranked up their production through breeding, and they literally have to "overeat" to produce the milk we need to stay in business.

So we have created our own problems, many, like "milk fever," just after they have calved. With the onset of lactation, cows start losing a lot of calcium, and if the drop is sharp enough they can lose consciousness. So we always gave them a bottle of calcium right after birth. This charges them up and gets their system going.

Another concern is a retained placenta. That can cause infections if it is retained too long and deteriorates. You end up with lower milk production and decreased fertility.

Then you can have a DA (displaced abomasum) or what amounts to a twisted stomach. There are all kinds of reasons why it happens. A major one is that their feed gets out of balance. There are all kinds of theories and practices on how you change your mix of minerals, roughage, and grain as you change from a dried-off to a freshened cow.

You have an animal that hasn't given milk in roughly 60 days, has just gone through the stress of giving birth to a 100-pound calf, and has probably lost 100 pounds of fluid. Now the cow has the new stress of producing milk while we are pumping her with a different mix of feed.

Cows are very complicated pieces of machinery, and whoever designed their fourth stomach didn't do a good job. It's a little like a hammock. It can swing free, and sometimes it fills with gas and flips over and squeezes the intake and outtake tubes shut.

Sometimes it will flip back on its own. If it doesn't, the cow can't process its feed and stops eating. When it stops eating, pretty soon it has to start invading its body fat for energy. You can have the most beautiful looking cow and literally three or four days after she has calved she can be a bag of bones. She can be worth $2,000 before freshening and worthless in a couple days.

Sometimes it just seems to run in cycles. I remember one time, the vet came in did two DAs for us (untwisting the stomach and suturing it to the body wall so that it can't twist again). He had already done six that day and had three more to do that night. And they were in a lot of different herds. You ask them why and sometimes they'll joke, "Who knows, it must be the weather."

We have five cows freshening this month. Eleven next month. Nine the month after that. So there are plenty of opportunities for more problems. You just hold your breath and hope for the best.

Grayson and I farmed together for 46 years and knew what was going on with the cows, 24 hours a day, seven days a week. We had to.

If a cow was off her feed, we wanted to know why.

If her eyes were drooping, did she have a low-grade infection?

If she were bellowing, was she is in heat? Did she have enough feed? Was she getting the water she needs?

Dehorning of calves protects both farmer and fellow cows. Vet Don Hunt sedates the cranial nerve and then permanently destroys the nerve endings of the horn nodule with an electric iron in a smoky but painless procedure.

As I pelleted each cow before morning milking, I got a sense right off the bat if anything was off. Grain pellets are like feeding them candy. They love it and just dive right in.

When I'd come down the aisle, their juices would be flowing. Watching them react to the pellets was an early warning system, just like taking their temperature. If her temperature was 101.7 (normal is 101.5), you didn't get too excited. You'd give her overnight before you jumped in. But if she's off feed and her temperature is 104, you jump in a hurry.

If a cow spikes a fever to 104 to 105 and isn't eating, she needs to be chewing something. When a cow stops eating, everything gets out of synch in a hurry and she isn't going to get over that on her own.

We could check to see if she were ketotic from a urine litmus test. During milking we'd check her udder for problems. But if there was nothing wrong and she didn't touch her TMR (total mixed ration), which we fed after milking, we'd usually call the vet.

If she's not going to eat, she's not going to milk. It was better to bite the bullet than to deal with greater problems later on.

With a cow, there are dollars and cents attached to every decision. If milk is worth $100 a gallon, then you can afford all kinds of tests and procedures. If the price is only a couple bucks then you can't afford to put a lot of money into her.

Right now, young calves are worth a lot. I remember when you could buy a heifer calf for 10 bucks. Today, you can get over $500 for

"It was a real privilege to work with the Wymans," says vet Nate Heilman. "You go to some barns and there will be a note on the door, check cow 67. Larry and Grayson would be there to tell you the history of each cow."

We relied on old number 1. If we screwed up we had no one to blame but ourselves. It came out of our pockets. We were the first line of offense and defense.

Vets are essential when it comes to calving, lung infections, digestion problems, but their biggest role is dealing with a cow's reproductive system. Keeping your herd healthy and on schedule is the backbone of the dairy business.

The frequency with which cows conceive, drop a calf, and return to lactation drives the whole milk machine. If the bottom line of your checkbook looks bad, it may well be that you have a lot of cows that are going too long before they breed back.

We always worked with cows because we had an investment in them; that investment could run $1,000-plus in feed and vet costs before we even milked her the first time. From day one when we had 10 cows, we had vets do pregnancy checks within six weeks of artificial insemination. Were they open? Were they bred? And if they were still open, what stage were they in their heat cycle?

Then drugs came on the market, like Lutalyse, where you can short cycle them so you don't have to wait the full 21 days before they came into heat. You give her a shot of Lutalyse, and she would drop an egg again (in roughly four days) and you could breed her again.

Even 10 days or two weeks made a difference in how soon you got her back producing milk. For us, it was very important to keep calving intervals between 13 and 14 months. If she's open at the end of her lactation, she's not making much milk and she's costing you money.

day-old heifer calves and $250 to $300 for a bull calf. You still have to be very aware that a calf with pneumonia or a sickness of any consequence will often have serious health problems down the road. You really have to think about how much you'll spend on a sickly calf.

Pneumonia and scours (diarrhea) are your biggest concerns. Scours dehydrates them and can take a calf out in 24 to 48 hours. Jeanne worked with the heifers, and I don't believe she lost more than four or five out of hundreds. You put medicine into their feed and milk, but often when they're scouring they don't want to eat. So you have to force feed them with a tube through the mouth.

You can't jump the gun and throw antibiotics at them. You have to know the animal's history and give their system time to work it out.

With an experienced vet there is a common ground. We're on the same page. Vets who start out without an ag background can be really green. They know the symptoms from the pages of a book, but they have no practical experience. The older vets have lived it and walked it.

Good old farm boys used to go vet school. Now it's kids from the 'burbs and bunny huggers. I was talking with a vet the other day who was having a difficult time finding another bovine vet. He had called Cornell, and they told him that in a class of 60, 80% were women and they didn't want to go into dairy. They were interested in horses and pets.

But the biggest problem with many women is that they can't handle big cows and don't want to. But so far Addison County still has enough vets for the number of farms left.

You also have young vets who are very good. When we started out, nine out of ten cows that had displaced stomachs were shipped for slaughter. She either got better on her own or was shipped. That young vet just out of school knew how to operate on a displaced stomach, something the older vets didn't know. Fixing a stomach now is common with all vets and saves a good cow from slaughter.

Another change is farmers do many things today that only vets used to do. We don't do surgery, but we give most of the shots. Vets will give shots, but they won't give a shot of an antibiotic. They don't want the responsibility of antibiotics getting into the milk and having to pay for 60,000 pounds of contaminated milk in a tanker.

"We had a vet who came and looked at a cow that was off feed. She was diagnosed as having ulcers. Larry and I asked, 'What causes ulcers?' He looked at us and shrugged his shoulders and half smiled and said, 'I don't know, maybe she's worried about the price of milk.'"

When we started using more antibiotics in the 1970s, antibiotic residues could remain in the milk. We didn't know then how long it took for penicillin to clear from a cow's system; it wasn't even mentioned on the drug label.

Cheese and yogurt makers couldn't get a culture to live because the antibiotic residues were killing the yeast. That problem came together with the human health issue where some people are allergic to antibiotics. You don't want to give a cow antibiotics today unless you have to because it can be a couple days and more before you can ship her milk. We all carry contamination insurance today, but insurance is only good for one mistake a year.

Grayson and I have only had two trucks charged against us in 40 years. We had our doubts, but we had to pay. It was our word against theirs.

Vet bills are steep. The fewer times a vet comes through your door, the richer you are. They're not bashful about charging and have a thick pencil, but they are part of doing business. Our vet bills ran $800 to $1,000 a month at the end. Right now a vet charges $65 to $75 an hour plus their stop charge. It figures out $100 or more for a visit.

As far as surgeries, vets got very creative like the regular medical doctors. When we first did DAs back in the 1960s, it cost like $35. Now they charge by the hour, have a stop charge, charge for surgery kits. So you have to add up about 10 different things. DAs were up around $200 at the end.

A big monthly bill doesn't necessarily mean that you have lots of problems but that you're trying to prevent problems. Your worst nightmare is disease that spreads through the herd. That's where vaccinations are so important and why you have to keep them up to snuff. We had a closed herd so we didn't have to worry about animals coming in. But we had to protect the herd from vets and breeding technicians and salesmen who walked in barns all over the county and could bring stuff in on their boots.

Herd health is an ongoing battle. It's vaccinations. It's good air and ventilation. It's balanced feed. With experience you learn to look for things. I can remember when we were just starting out we had a cow that was acting funny, and we called the vet. He checked things and looked at the water bowl. It was the only bowl in the barn that wasn't working, and we hadn't picked up on it.

I'm not saying that you can go into a barn and figure out immediately why a herd isn't doing well, but you start checking off things that could be the problem and "bingo," you can find it.

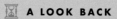

What Is Good Keeping?

What is good keeping? A dairy cow should never want for food suited to her age and condition, so that development of all her organs for secretion of milk, as well as of her size and constitution, may be at no time retarded.

Under the head of kindness, I would mention the great necessity of gentle treatment in breaking and training heifers. A heifer inclined to kick can generally be effectually cured by patient kindness, but if it's found necessary to use force, it should be some way of effectual confinement, not blows and loud scolding. Tone of voice will usually indicate the condition of the milker's temper, and is apt to inspire confidence and good will.

If a heifer or cow continues obdurate and a confirmed kicker, she should be disposed of. If she is too valuable to sacrifice, a place can very easily and cheaply be made, where she can always be confined and milked with comfort and safety.

If the treatment of cows and heifers is always considerate and gentle, in not only the management of the stables and in the milk yard, but in driving to and from the pasture, they will soon become gentle and docile, and with few exceptions quiet to milk and handle, but he who practices the contrary, or permits his dairy stock to be ill used by thoughtless boys, or ignorant, vicious help, must expect breachy, kicking, and bad tempered cows, not only unpleasant to handle and milk, but curtailed of their maximum capabilities for giving milk.

Under comfort, I would name good, well ventilated, but warm stables, with well sheltered yards, where, without long traveling through the snow, water could be taken at least twice a day. The stables should not only be well ventilated and warm, but dry, and where it will be impossible for cows to lay in their droppings. This can be accomplished by stanchions and platforms.

Raising and Managing Dairy Stock,
Albert Chapman, Esq., 1874

October 2004: We Get on a Treadmill in the Morning

In mid-October, the Wymans still had fields to be cut and corn fields to be plowed under, but winter's clock was ticking. By early morning, Canada geese were heading south after a night resting in the slack waters of the Otter.

DayMinder: *First frost, October 6. First sighting of geese heading south, October 11.*

If spring is a time full of promise when fields turn green and a high-noon sun warms the land, fall is the gradual closing down and locking up of the land. Corn fields, once a sea of green, are now bleached stubble. Lush waist-high pastures have been grazed down to roots, rocks, and Addison County clay.

The barn is not yet winter cold but brisk enough in the early morning hours for the cows' breath to create small vapor clouds a dozen times a minute. The river-bottom land exhales its summer warmth overnight, leaving ghostly morning fogs.

Machinery, too hot to touch in the July sun, is now frost covered and unforgiving to gloveless hands. Ridgelines begin to show their bony skeletons.

Canada geese that have gathered overnight in the slack water of the Otter form V's barely out of shotgun range as they pass over the barn. Turkey and deer sensing that they are not

November 2004: There Is Nothing Left

yet in season pause in open fields. The land will rest and so will the Wymans, who are counting the days until retirement.

"All I know is that next spring, Grayson and I will have farmed together for 46 years. Someone else will own the cows. Grayson and I won't," a bone-tired Larry says.

"I don't know what will happen, and I don't think Danny knows either. Right now we get on a treadmill in the morning and don't get off until night. Until Dan and Jeanne's situation evens out, that's the way it is going to be."

But there is still work to be done. Third cutting begins the last week in October and is completed on November 4. Like the previous two cuttings, all the fields are chopped for haylage, a less labor- and time-intensive process than baling.

The loft in the barn has several thousand bales from previous summers, enough to meet the needs of the coming year. Hay is in demand, and Dan bales on land he is renting, intending to sell it to horse ranches throughout New England.

Jeanne returns home on October 14. Weekly and then monthly day trips to Dana Farber for checkups will continue into the winter. Dan jokes he can now make the 4 a.m. drive to Boston with one eye closed. "There were times when all I can remember is leaving the hospital and driving in the yard four hours later," Dan would reflect later on the blur of those testing round trips. "All I can say is the good Lord was with me and He got me through it."

Larry's now infrequent DayMinder notes on Jeanne's recovery and weekly visits to Boston are brief, "good reports."

After a timely spring start and a topsy-turvy summer and early fall, the Wymans are now back on schedule with the completion of nearly all fieldwork by Thanksgiving. Spreading manure on corn fields is contracted out and is completed in early November.

The Otter Creek begins to skim over but the intermittent milder weather enables Grayson to plow under the manure and corn stubble. But the clay has stiffened in the cold, and the fall's plowing is the "roughest in years," Grayson observes one afternoon after watching the moldboard jump in and out of the field like a flying fish.

Eight months after it began, fieldwork ends with manure spreading and the plowing of the corn stubble.

** ALL PLOWING DONE FOR 2004!! a relieved Larry notes in his DayMinder on November 30.

"This is the worst year that we have ever had. Everyone is tired," Dan says at the end of the harvest. He can now begin to catch up with his repair backlog.

Milk production with the reduced herd continues to average about 4,000 pounds a day. Larry and Grayson have set a last day for milking, the morning of March 31, 2005.

"Grayson's legs are beat. There is nothing left," says Larry.

Chapter 7

The Business of Farming

An Operation Where We Could Pay Our Bills

In 1924, U.S. Secretary of Agriculture Henry C. Wallace, in analyzing the widespread "farm crisis" that followed the boom years of the previous decade, presented this cheerless thesis:

> In times such as these the problems of farm management on most farms are reduced to the simplest terms and can be stated very briefly.... Produce as much as you can and as cheaply as you can of what you can produce best; spend as little as you can; do without everything that you can; work as hard as you can; make your wife and your children work as hard as they can. Having done this, take what comfort you can in the thought that if you succeed in doing what you set out to do, and if most other farmers also succeed, you will have produced larger crops than can be sold at a profit and you will still be under the harrow.

Many family farmers would argue that little has changed since Wallace's assessment. Over the past century, dairy farmers have become marvels of productivity and built small businesses with six- and seven-figure assets. But the family farm's agricultural productivity has rarely been matched by a corresponding economic return.

In good years, the top quarter, or most productive farmers, will return a profit of 5% to 10% on the value of their farm equity. In bad years, farmers hope to break even or minimize their losses.

For the less successful, survival frequently depends on off-farm income, cattle sales, accommodating creditors, and doing without. And many farmers, about 5% a year, stop for a variety of reasons: high debt loads, inability to find help, below-production-cost milk prices, and retirement.

There are shelves full of *How to Survive* business plans in this environment, Dairy 101 if you will. The Vermont Agricultural Experiment Station offered this synopsis, "Secrets of a Successful Dairy Operation," in a 1966 bulletin on large dairy farms. "Who makes the highest income?" the report asked. "Not the farmer with the most cows—unless he combines efficient size with good milk production, high crop yields, and efficient use of labor and capital."

Successful Vermont farmers were not outstanding in any one factor but were above average in all factors. Those who lost money were only a little below average in each factor, the bulletin reported. In short, attention to every detail counts.

Nearly 40 years later, the *Northeast Dairy Farm Summary*, a report of four lending cooperatives, provided a similar analysis of the top quarter of its members. In its 2005 summary, the organization identified five management styles in 135 of its most profitable farms: great with cows, labor efficient, better milk price, tight with a buck, and balanced.

How many cows does it take to support one family, two families? How much acreage is needed to meet the herd's feed requirements? Should tractors be purchased new, used or leased? Answering these perennial questions requires constant evaluation of the farm's finances. Like his mother before him, Grayson used the kitchen table for last Friday-of-the-month bill paying.

The Wymans rejected many of the trends in agribusiness—the $100,000 tractor, growth hormones to increase milk production, ever increasing herd size. Know your cows and watch your debt. Be frugal but not inefficiently frugal. It's not how much you make, but how much you keep, the Wymans believed.

"The common theme among these management styles is that top profit farmers have reached a balance between milk production per cow and costs," the report concluded.

No magic bullet there. Good managers live within their means. Herein lies the rub. Given the volatility of milk prices—they may vary 20% to 30% and more over the course of a year—dairy farmers are never certain what their means will be. What farmers do know is that milk prices, when adjusted for inflation, have declined dramatically over the past 25 years. In 1980, farmers averaged $13 per 100 pounds of milk, roughly what they received in 2002 and 2003. But that price, if it had kept pace with inflation, would have been $28 to $29.

As hard-pressed farmers frequently point out, they are price takers, not price makers; they buy retail with embedded inflationary increases while selling wholesale without any inflationary adjustments. Only the most efficient and committed dairy farmers have been able to survive this combination of rising costs and volatile milk prices.

In Dairy 101 the Wymans are very little fish in a very big pond and have almost no control over the price they receive for their milk. Their milk checks are largely determined by federal policies and programs, national and global supply and demand for milk and dairy products, and deductions of cooperatives and buyers to cover expenses, like transportation and marketing.

Farmers have long sought to redress this imbalance of economic power, with mixed success at best. The first dairy cooperatives, in the late 1800s, were short-lived—victims of restraint of trade provisions in the Sherman Antitrust Act of 1890. The Clayton Act of 1914, which exempted non-profit dairy co-ops from antitrust legislation, 1916 state legislation permitting the formation of cooperatives, and a series of federal actions in the 1920s gave cooperatives a second life and farmers the right to bargain and market collectively.

While there was strength in numbers, Vermont dairy farmers were initially reluctant to cooperate fully in New England-wide bargaining efforts, arguing, in part, that Vermont's superior milk quality should receive a premium. But by the end of the 1920s, with continued low prices on the horizon, Vermont cooperatives and the Commissioner of Agriculture began working with their regional counterparts to secure higher prices. But like the individual farmer, all but the very largest cooperatives have relatively little ability today to affect prices in national and global dairy markets.

Fluid milk is a low-priced commodity—for some buyers the lower-priced the better—and that reality ruthlessly shapes dairy economics. Vermont milk, even if its promoters contend otherwise, is not appreciably different from milk from Wisconsin family farms or from multi-thousand cow dairies in Idaho, Texas, and California.

Transporting raw milk is expensive and presently limits the shipment of fluid milk from major milk exporters, such as Wisconsin, the country's second largest milk producer, to Vermont's traditional Boston market. But shipping cheese and other manufactured dairy products, the end uses of the majority of raw milk, is not so limited.

Cheesemakers, especially cheesemakers in states like Wisconsin where nearly 70% of all fluid milk is made into cheese, want cheap milk (a pound of cheese requires 10 pounds of milk). Wisconsin farmers, with more fertile soil and lower feed costs than their Vermont counterparts, can live with lower milk prices, enabling their cheesemakers to produce lower-priced cheeses. If New England milk prices are appreciably higher than other regions, local cheesemakers may lose market share to Midwestern and Western competition.

In short, higher-cost regions that ignore the fact that major dairy processors and cheese manufacturers seek the lowest-cost suppliers do so at their own economic peril. At the same time, buyers who ignore the financial squeeze facing the family farm may end up with fewer and fewer local farmers.

Since the Depression, when the dairy industry faced collapse, the federal government has formally recognized the importance of a stable and safe regional supply of milk and the need for farmers to receive a sustainable return. With the establishment of price support programs under the federal Agricultural Adjustment Act of 1933, the government first attempted to guarantee farmers a fair price for their milk. Support levels would be based on parity prices, which were set to restore the farmer's purchasing power to pre-World War I levels, a period of relative prosperity for farmers.

A LOOK BACK

What Shall Farmers Learn?

First, learn the peril of debt. You may think that with your present health and skill you can surely make your payments. This is a delusion. Sickness and misfortune, repairs and improvements, and the cost of living, will reduce your income.

The second requirement may be a knowledge of the greatest productiveness of soil. This includes a knowledge of how to make it produce. It is not all comprehended in the word manure: but includes its condition, its judicious application and its mixture with the soil.

Third, he ought to learn what are sure crops, doubtful crops and impossible crops. The sure crops here are grass, oats, potatoes, barley and certain garden vegetables. The doubtful crops are wheat, corn, rye, buckwheat, beans, peas, several garden vegetables, hops and apples.

Fourth, he ought to learn the total depravity of weeds. He can learn what great robbers they are by keeping a portion of the garden perfectly clear of weeds, and allowing them to have their way on a portion.

There ought to be a school and an experimental farm where many things about farming will be taught. Knowledge comes by experience, observation and instruction; and however highly we may regard experience, we must equally value the instruction of a competent teacher.

Z.E. Jameson,
Seventh Vermont Agricultural Report,
State Board of Agriculture, 1882

Since 1949, the government has been the buyer of last resort of surplus milk, purchasing the surplus in the form of manufactured dairy products such as cheese, butter, and powdered milk for free or subsidized domestic and international distribution. Not surprisingly, providing this safety net without encouraging overproduction has proven to be a challenge of Solomonic proportions.

In the early 1980s high support prices led to overproduction, and the Department of Agriculture had to purchase, at an annual cost of over $2 billion, as much as 17% of the country's manufactured dairy products. In response, the federal government disconnected milk price supports from parity pricing, which ultimately reduced the support price by about 30%.

In 1986, in a further effort to reduce the oversupply of milk—the goal was a 9% decrease—Congress authorized the U.S. Department of Agriculture to conduct a nationwide whole herd buyout program. Four hundred and fourteen Vermont dairy farms, about 13% of the state's total, submitted bids for a payment that would help them pay off bills and debts and retire or start a new business.

At a cost of $24 million, the department accepted the bids of 192 Vermont dairy farmers to stop producing milk. In return, farmers agreed to sell their cows for beef or export them and not return to dairying for five years. That one-time offer reduced the state's herd by 20,000 cows and milk production by 8%.

But this program, which eliminated 14,000 dairy farms nationwide, had little long-term impact as the remaining farmers, not bound by any quotas, increased production to replace the lost supply. Roller-coaster milk prices have continued through the 1990s and early 2000s, despite federal, regional, and state programs designed to offset these price swings and help farmers diversify and manage their farms better. Dairy history is clear. The "family farm crisis" stems not from a shortage of milk but a surplus. Dairy economists have a rule of thumb: a 2% surplus reduces milk prices 20%; a 2% deficit increases milk prices 20%. There is money to be made in value-added dairy products but little money in producing the milk itself.

In 1998, the USDA's National Commission on Small Farms summed up a century's progress and the challenge facing the contemporary farmer:

> Agricultural technologies have emerged that use ever greater levels of capital to enable fewer people to produce the Nation's food. As a result, income and opportunities have shifted from farms to the companies that produce and sell inputs to farmers. As farmers focused on producing undifferentiated raw commodities, food system profit and opportunities were shifted to the companies that process, package, and market food. Consequently, from 1910 to 1990 the share of the agricultural economy received by farmers dropped from 21 to 5 percent.

Larry and Grayson have understood from the outset that there is little room for mistakes in Dairy 101. Winter, as Larry recounts, reduces that margin even more and tests farmers as no other season does. As both note in the following narratives, the essence of successful farming is accepting what you can't control—from weather to the price of your milk—and attending to what you can control—the quality of your fields, crops, and cows and the size of your debt load.

"Grayson and I always wanted an operation where we could pay our bills when they were due," says Larry of their informal master plan. "Not everybody operates that way, but that's the way we operated for 46 years."

Call their management style Yankee frugal. ⚘

50 degrees on Thursday. 15 below on Saturday. Tractors won't start. Water pipes burst. Belts, pulleys, and chains snap. Calves born outside freeze to death. Milk production drops. Frosted windows are the least of a farmer's problems.

Winter Demands Your Total Vigilance

LARRY WYMAN: When we started farming in White River and Brownsville we didn't have much in the way of equipment and moving snow all winter was exhausting. The Connecticut River Valley gets lots more snow than we do here. If you have coastal storms, they dump on the eastern side of the Greens and miss the western side. Many storms from the west drop on the Adirondacks and then don't have much left for us. But in White River the snow just went on and on and on. A flurry here was a 12-inch snowstorm there. You were always ready to see spring come over there.

When we moved, the first two years here must have had record snowfalls because we could just see the roofs of the cars when they went by. The snow banks were that high. We didn't have a bucket loader then and did a lot of hand shoveling. When we got a tractor with a bucket loader it was much easier, but by then we didn't have as much snow.

The cold also used to be much, much deeper and more prolonged. During the winter of 1959-60 when we were in White River, it went below zero and never rose above zero even at noon for two weeks. After the 99th time, you figure out a few tricks to keep everything from freezing.

Our first diesel tractors were a dog to start in cold weather. When we were in Brownsville and spreading manure outdoors all winter, we pulled the nose of the tractor right up under the barn's exhaust fan each night. We put a canvas tarp over the hood of the fan, which was drawing relatively warm moist air from the cows, and over the engine of the tractor. It wasn't foolproof, but it helped.

Then we started using canned ether and engine heaters when they came along. The dipstick heater heated the oil. The best one circulated hot water through the radiator and engine. It used a lot of electricity and was expensive, but it did the trick.

In Weybridge, we learned early on that we couldn't keep the heifer barn warm enough during a sub-zero night to stop the pipes from freezing. We would shut the water off at night, give the cows hay, and make them drink enough so there wouldn't be any water in the pipes or water bowls. That saved us a lot of headaches in the morning.

We had a vet who used to say that he saw farmers at their worst in the winter. Everyone was up against it financially, and once you get behind in winter it takes a long time to catch up. Winter demands your total vigilance 24 hours a day. You have to be on the top of your game in ways that you never have to in the other three seasons.

You have cold, moist air in the barn and then you get pneumonia in the herd. You have stomach problems that go from zero to a hundred overnight because of molds or wet feed. You have winter scours (diarrhea). Every animal in the barn can get it, and it just has to run its course. Your pipes freeze and you lose water for a day. Without water cows can't make milk.

Someone gets careless and doesn't close the door or clean off the gutter chain or doesn't check it before starting up. It's caught somewhere and frozen. It snaps and breaks. And if you can't get it going for three days, what do you do with all the manure that is piling up?

All this affects your milk production.

There are just so many ongoing little things. When we left the barn at night we always had to know what cows were freshening and if they were outside in the free stall or inside in the holding pen. Sometimes we thought they were a week away and they suddenly calved. We went to the free stall in the morning and found a wet cold calf.

I don't know how many mornings Jeanne and I dragged calves into the milk house and gave them a hot bath to get their blood circulating. We'd towel them off and put them in front of a heater. We wanted them to drink mother's milk as soon as possible because it's full of antibodies. So we'd give them a bottle of colostrum and a shot to prevent pneumonia. Then we'd put them in the main barn with some hay bales around them to keep them warm.

It might take 45 minutes with two of us going at it. Milking just had to wait.

Calf mortality rates can be much higher in the winter, but they never were for us. Last winter, we didn't lose a single calf. Sometimes, we'd end up with a calf that had a funny looking ear where it had frozen to the cement over night. But we could generally bring them back.

Some farmers would say that they looked forward to winter as a bit of a break and a time to get out on their snow machines. Take some time after lunch and go out and tear around the countryside. If we had any down time, we cut wood. When we came to Weybridge, wood was our sole source of heat for the house. For about 15 years, I probably cut 25 to 30 cords of wood every winter on the ridge behind the house.

It was a good diversion and got me out of the barn. I enjoyed it as long as it wasn't snowing or storming. Grayson didn't cut as much. He'd stay down here and worked around the barn. If a breeding technician came he'd be there. I tried to keep a year's supply ahead. All of it might not be split, but it would be down here and I'd split it during the summer and get it under cover.

Extreme cold was worse than storms. You could deal with a foot of snow, especially when we had a bucket loader. We could remove snow in no time at all. That wasn't a big issue. But when we first started and were driving cans of milk to the creamery, snow was a different issue. Once we got to the point where we could deal with the snow, cold was the hardest thing to deal with. When we put in a manure storage pit in the late 1970s and didn't have to spread it through the winter, cold became less of an issue.

Since the mid-1980s we haven't had a lot of real cold winters. I don't know if that has anything to do with global warming, but it makes you think that it is more than a possibility. When we started we knew that each winter we'd have a half a dozen or more 30-below mornings. I'd bet I haven't seen a 30-below morning in 10 years. Ten or 15 below has been it.

You Figure Out a Few Tricks to Keep Everything From Freezing

Chimney feathers, frosted silage, and Arctic-level wind chills. Welcome to a January cold snap.
"I can't wait for spring," says Dan after loading the mixer wagon during a cold spell.

Everyone's metronome slows in the bone-chilling cold of January and February. Stressed cows give less milk. Non-essential outdoor projects are postponed. The body stiffens. Steps slow. Spring seems far away.

"I've got five sweatshirts and two coats on. If I ever fall down, Larry will have to pick me up with the payloader," says Dan of the challenge of working outside in 10-below mornings.

Vermont's snowy winters provide more than Currier and Ives views. They give the state a comparative advantage over their snow-poor midwestern competition. Dr. T. H. Hoskins, editor of *Vermont Farmer*, explained why in an 1872 presentation to the Board of Agriculture:

> Even in those rich, wooded States, like Missouri, most resembling Vermont in the character of the land, the absence of that very winter climate, against which so many object, and which so many urge as a reason for emigration from Vermont, is a great disadvantage. We do not reckon at its real value the coating of snow that lies every winter upon our fields and pastures; protecting the nutritious grasses, giving them the peculiar protection and support which brings them to the highest perfection as food for our domestic animals. There is much truth in the saying, that snow is the poor man's manure, and no stock-raising country that is without it can compete, in certain directions that are very profitable, with those that possess it.

Dr. Hoskins' sanguine assessment of the virtues of snowy winters would be shared by most farmers today. A foot of gentle snow to prevent deep freezing and winterkill is fine. Thaws, ice storms, weeklong cold snaps, and blizzards are not. Recent Vermont winters may be milder than their 19th century counterparts, but winter remains a time of short, testing days. But winters don't last forever. By Town Meeting Day, spring is just around the corner, sometimes several corners.

On cold mornings, Holsteins' body heat creates a ghostly barn fog. Visibility is about 75 feet with the mooing of hungry cows the barn's foghorns. Cows are susceptible to life-threatening pneumonia if fans don't pull bacteria-laden moisture out of the barn.

On January 1, 1975 Larry began recording daily farm events, monthly milk totals, and high points of the year in brown and black notebooks. Over the next 30 years, he never missed a day with his black ballpoint pen entries.

We Just Launched Into It

LARRY WYMAN: Grayson and I didn't have a long-term master plan when we started out. We just launched into it. Neither of us had gone to ag school or grown up on a farm, so we depended on our neighbors and sales personnel and field people from organizations like Agway and its predecessor Eastern States and H.P. Hood, which had people to help with your milk house and milking equipment. And we used the extension service and had cows on DHI (a dairy herd improvement program) for the first two or three years. But it was a big expense and the information was long coming. So we

stopped and went with our best judgment.

I'm sure we made our fair share of mistakes. Perhaps, if we had spent more time looking into it, we wouldn't have had to move so many times. But on the flip side, Dummerston was too small to even be a possibility. White River gave us a place to start. Brownsville with the combination of the two farms gave us the opportunity to increase the herd. Weybridge finally gave us the land and the barn we needed.

But you can only anticipate so many things. We never thought when we went from cans to our first bulk tank in the early 1960s that we would fill it and have our milk picked up every day. Those were all things that we just didn't give any thought to. I'm sure there are issues today where 10 years down the road people will be asking, "What were they thinking?" They should have done such and such.

I remember when we came here we put in a vacuum system for our milking that was supposed to be state-of-the-art and was built to UVM specs. Heavens, within a year and a half the dairy extension agent came into the barn and said, "A new setup like this and you put it in that small!" So there it was. In a year and a half's time, it was totally inadequate, according to new recommendations. But we used it to the last day that we milked, 36 years later, and never changed it.

We put money in, and we were going to get money out. A larger system was supposed to be easier on a cow's udder because it had a reserve and didn't have fluctuations in pressure. So in trying to avoid those potential problems they recommended a bigger pipe and volume of air. We just went ahead, and the cows got used to it.

There is nothing wrong in trying to shoot for a hundred in a spelling test, but you may get 98 or 94 or even 85 depending on what else is going on. The farmer has to translate textbook and theory into reality. That's what it's all about.

With just above everything in farming—crop work, feeding, breeding—you're constantly making adjustments as you go. Take feed quality. Dealers will analyze your feed and tell you it needs such and such protein level and dry matter and these minerals and vitamins. When you make your TMR (total mixed ration) in your mixer wagon, you're not working in a lab measuring everything to milligrams. You're using bucket loaders picking up 500 to 600 pounds of silage at a scoop from your bunk. One day it may be relatively dry. Another day it may be wet from a downpour.

How careful is the person operating the equipment? Your TMR calls for 100 pounds of supplemental minerals for roughly 4,000 pounds of silage. Some people weigh the supplements precisely. Others say three quarters of the pail weighed so much yesterday, I'll dump it in again today. It's a ballpark thing. Finesse isn't part of the recipe.

How often do you check your feed quality? You have different quality in your bunk or silo or haymow depending on the cutting and how well it was stored. Some farmers are constantly checking. Others check every six weeks or three months.

We probably checked every three months or when we were running out of one bunk and were transitioning to another bunk. If we neglected balancing, we might not notice it immediately because there are so many other factors that can affect your overall production, like the number of cows that have just freshened, but we'd notice it over time.

When it's all over, cows are probably getting a better balanced diet than we are. And they're perfectly happy to eat the same thing 365 days a year. The bacteria in their stomachs get used to it. That's what they want. Give me some more.

Another big change has been the use of computers. People starting today would just figure it was the accepted thing. They'd have the skills from school and wouldn't think of doing it any other way. We weren't a textbook operation by any stretch, but we had a handle on

What are the keys to success for the small family farm? Know your cows by feeding and milking them. How cows react to the morning's grain is an immediate indicator of their health, says Larry.

things by knowing the animals. Until Dan and Jeanne came, Grayson or I were there at milking time, morning and night, 365 days a year.

Jeanne came to us that first summer and said they were going to do something different the next night. They were going to do the milking. We just laughed and Jeanne said, "No, it's not funny. We're going to milk tomorrow night and you're both taking the night off." That was the first time both of us had missed a milking in 38 years, but I'd seen enough of them to know they'd do it right.

We never wanted to rely on others to relay information to us or have to read a computer printout. And we could keep in touch with each cow even when we were milking 125. If we had gone to 200 or more, perhaps we would have had to change. But it wasn't all in our heads. Grayson kept breeding records with due dates, heats, and family histories. I kept daily notes about the herd and general farm information.

One thing didn't change over the years. We never tried to come up with a master plan on December 31 or January 1 that would carry us through the coming year. There were just too many variables — weather, milk prices, growing season — that we couldn't control.

We could start out with a wet May and have a bone-dry July and August and then have a wet September when we were getting ready to harvest corn. We could seed down a 20-acre corn piece and see beautiful corn in June. Several days later the field could be as barren as a desert. The cut worms had cleaned it right down. You had to start all over, buy more seed, harrow the field, and replant. That's if there was enough time left in the growing season to start again.

And we had absolutely no impact on prices. It was all determined by supply and demand and what the market administrator set for a

Improved genetics and individualized and better balanced diets have been central to annual production increases. Supplemental grain, one of the costliest items in the farm's feed bill, is essential in sustaining high production.

price. If you belonged to a co-op, you got what they would pay you. If it was below what the market administrator said it was worth, you got what the co-op said was needed for them to survive.

Over the years Grayson and I made many of our decisions about day-to-day operations long and short term while we were milking. Some farmers milk alone, but Grayson and I always felt it was safer to have two in the barn during milking. Not only was it safer, but it was also a time when we could talk about crops and cows and problems and ideas that we thought might be worth trying. We wanted to have a handle on things before they became a problem. We wanted to know at all times what we needed to do and what we could put off for a day or week or month or year.

Grayson is an optimist by nature, and there were times when we didn't agree. Walt (Walt Goodale, their vet) would look at a cow and say, "It's 90% dead," and Grayson would say, "We're going to make it live."

Farming is a constant challenge. The way we saw it was that we both owned the farm, and we had to get along. He wasn't always wrong, and I wasn't always right. I needed him, and he needed me. What we thought the year might be like in January was often nothing like what it was come December. ∾

Lenders have rules of thumb. Start with the value of total farm assets—land, cows, equipment, barn. In well-managed Addison County farms, this will average $8,000 to $10,000 per cow. Good managers should be able to carry $3,000 to $4,000 debt per cow. Debt cautious, the Wymans carried a fraction of that.

What Was Best for Our Situation

GRAYSON WYMAN: In all the years we farmed, buying the Harvestore silos back in the late 1970s was probably the worst decision we made. Everyone was buying them, and you saw big blue silos all over the county. They were supposed to store and keep better feed, which meant we'd be getting more milk. And a higher protein feed from the silo would cut down on our grain and supplemental feed bill.

They did produce fantastic feed. The problem was that they were high maintenance and if something went wrong with the unloader all that feed might as well have belonged to someone up the road. You couldn't get it out. The cost of repairing the chains on those unloaders was unbelievable. You could be looking at a $2,000 bill and more. At that time, milk production and prices didn't pay for anything like that.

As time went on, service was farther and farther away. It started out in Middlebury, then the closest service was in the central part of the state. When we finally stopped using them and went back to bunks, the closest service was in central New York.

We put nearly $50,000 into two silos, and it would probably have been double that if we had bought them new. We have often wondered if we could have reaped more benefit from other options, like building a milking parlor.

Who knows what that would have done? A milking parlor would have been more convenient and faster, but we thought it was more of a luxury. Maybe if we had bought four-wheel drive tractors then we would have been better off. But we thought better feed would improve our bottom line more.

Over the years, we didn't want to be the first nor the last when it came to buying new things, whether it was from seed or tractor companies or in animal breeding. Let them be tried on someone else's farm first. What was the best for our situation? How would we use it? Most farming decisions are expensive. Once you have made them, right or wrong, you have to live with them.

Maybe we did some things the hard way, but we were able to turn a dollar when we needed to. Over the years what helped us most was limiting our debt so we weren't overwhelmed by low periods. Survival was a case of keeping debt under control and not doing something just because the neighbors did it or someone thought we ought to.

We never used the forms and spreadsheets that some farmers do or spent hours each day at a computer to make two cents more per hundred. But Larry or I always knew within a few dollars what we owed on this tractor or that piece of machinery or what the feed bill was going to be that month. We kept track of all those things on a daily basis.

Every month we sat down with our bills and established priorities and paid everything possible. If we had to let something ride, we hoped we could work something out. We couldn't fudge on some bills, like electricity. But most things that had to be put off were things we hoped to do. Hoping to do and facing reality when your milk check wasn't big enough were two different things.

Our two biggest expenses every month were the mortgage and feed. As far as the mortgage, depending on your credit, you could usually just pay interest for so many months to get over a rough spot. We had to pay the feed bill. Over 90 days and they will shut you right off. I've heard farmers say, "If I get shut off on one, I'll just go to another." Today, computers tie everything together. Information is shared. So everybody knows who is up to snuff and who isn't.

Our feed bill over the years has been as much as 50% of the milk check. I'd rather see it down around 30%. But some years when we had feed shortages and had to buy lots of

Franklin County, 1906

A Little Farm Well Tilled

The greatest obstacle to the improvement of agriculture in New England, is the propensity of the farmer—the mania, I might call it—to own more land than he can till to advantage. And it is thus that we see scattered over the country, large tracts of sterile, unproductive land, which under good cultivation, would yield bountiful and valuable crops.

The law is universal that the secret of success in agriculture consists in the thorough cultivation of a small piece of ground. In almost every part of New England, one capital error runs through the whole system of farming. A great deal of money is invested in land and a very little employed in its cultivation.

What a harassed unhappy being is usually the owner of such a farm! He has chalked out for himself a hard lot, and voluntarily entered on a state of servitude worse than Egyptian bondage. His work is never accomplished. His house is out of repair, his barn is dilapidated, his cattle poor, his pastures overrun with bushes, and acres of land, which, under proper cultivation might be made to yield rich harvests, are but little removed from barrenness.

Vermont Family Visitor, 1845

More cows are not always the road to survival says Ken Button, who has managed lending for Yankee Farm Credit in Addison County for the past 30 years. Doing all the little things right separates the successes from the failures.

month it was done. We walked up and down the line. This one hadn't bred back and was only making 30 pounds of milk. She'd bring $500 to $600 for beef so we'd sell her. That was added to your milk income, but it wasn't an easy decision.

There are several co-ops and a few independent buyers, but we didn't have much choice where we could sell our milk and had to make do with the price we got. Until the Milk Income Loss Contract (MILC) program came along in 2002 when milk prices were at record lows, we had very rarely been part of any federal support programs. In order to qualify you had to sign up for other federal programs, and we didn't want to do that.

When MILC was starting, federal Farm Service Agency representatives came to us and said, "You have a soil map for your farm, but our records show that you have never signed up for any soil conservation programs." One of our corn fields has a slope and there

supplements the feed bill was bigger. From 1990 until we quit were our best forage years. We were growing better crops because we had better seed and better information from our seed and fertilizer suppliers. We knew when to fertilize and what to use.

Fertilizer was the one place that we never cut. We always felt the return on that dollar was such that we couldn't ignore it. But if you don't have the dollar, it's hard to invest it. Most of the time that meant fudging someplace else because fertilizer and quality of the seed were always a priority.

The rest was left up to Mother Nature and good luck.

In tough times, your milk check wasn't your only option. We had the option of selling heifers and cows as a last resort and many a

was a question whether we were raising corn on erodable land. So they came out, checked the grade, and approved everything that we were doing.

For us the MILC check meant economic survival at a time when milk prices weren't covering our costs. The subsidy was based on a breakeven point determined by the Boston market price. Our MILC checks ran as high as $3,800 a month, but they varied enormously depending on milk prices. Some months the subsidies might be as little as two cents per hundred. Other months they were as high as $1.28. At first we had to wait months and months for the promised checks, but the program is geared to the small farmer and has helped. (The program stopped in 2007; Congress reauthorized it in 2008.)

Grayson's introduction to the lifelong financial and familial stresses of farming began during a college summer break when he worked for a young couple. "One morning it was obvious from their long faces that they had a pretty rocky time the night before talking about finances," he recalls. "At lunch she threw a copy of a farm journal on the table with a picture of a couple holding hands as they walked to the barn. 'Maybe this is why we're not being successful. We're not holding hands enough.'"

The Northeast Dairy Compact had helped us with higher milk prices for several years in the late 1990s, but milk processors, not the federal government, supported higher milk prices in that program. The idea was that a healthy dairy community was important to the New England economy and that Northeast dairy farmers got paid less for their milk than farmers in other regions.

Congress approved the compact in 1996, and our local representatives wanted the compact to continue when the Federal Farm bill came up for renewal in 2001. Well, Midwestern dairy states were against it because they said it gave the Northeast an unfair advantage, and big handlers and even some co-ops pushed for cancellation because they didn't want to pay the surcharge. Co-ops were supposed to be representing dairy farmers, but they were looking out for themselves first.

MILC is a reasonable substitute, but co-ops and handlers ought to be paying for it, not taxpayers. The minute the driver reads the measuring stick in the milk room and makes out the slip, that milk becomes their property. So if they own the milk, why in thunder shouldn't they be paying the cost of getting it from the farm to the plant?

The last of our milking we were paying $1.20 a hundred weight. Yes sir, when you're getting $10, $12, $14 a hundred weight for your milk, transportation is a big cost. We all know that the processor, not the farmer, is making all the money. If they want to keep us in business, they should be paying for transportation and the MILC program.

Over the years we got better at what we did, but we never got to the point where we felt that we knew it all. If you do, that's the time to quit. By the 1990s I felt that we had gotten a lot of problems under control and were more or less in cruise control. There weren't going to be any big expansions or investments from here until retirement.

It was a matter of getting rid of indebtedness and reaping the benefits from our first 30 years. ❧

Your Farm May Be Too Big If...

• If the fence rows are either gone or so clean you no longer hear the birds singing.

• If gullies appear on slopes and road ditches and are filled with muddy water after a rain.

• If the soil feels like pavement under your feet, or you don't like walking across it anymore.

• If the farm begins to look more like a sea or desert, rather than a patch work quilt.

• If your cows no longer have names and your children wouldn't know them if they did.

• If your animals never feel the sun, don't have room to walk, or never touch the dirt.

• If your farm no longer smells like a farm but stinks like a sewer or a factory.

• If it's no longer safe for anyone but an adult to work with your machinery or chemicals.

• If you work harder and harder, but it always seems there is more work to be done.

• If a bigger tractor, combine, or new pickup truck seems like it might solve your problems.

• If your banker or contractor owns more of your farm than you will ever own.

• If the farm is keeping the family apart, or tearing it apart, rather than bringing it together.

• If your children begin to dislike farm life and vow not to return to the farm.

• If you no longer feel good about asking your family to live on a farm.

• If you're too busy to bother with community affairs, and rarely go into town anymore.

• If you drive right through "your" town to buy things in the city, just to save a few dollars.

• If neighbors complain about dust, noise, or odors from your farm, and you don't care.

• If caring for the land no longer gives purpose and meaning to your life.

• If continuing the farming tradition feels more like a burden rather than a privilege.

• If you're too busy to notice changing seasons, to watch the sunset, or to feel the wind blow.

• If farming is no longer exciting, no longer fun, if it's hard to face a new season.

• If you have forgotten why you wanted to be a farmer in the first place.

• If very many of these things ring true, odds are your farm is too big.

Prof. John Ikerd, *Small Farm Today Conference*, 2002

December 2004: I Don't Even Want to Take Care of a Goldfish

December 3rd was picture-postcard perfect with the season's first snow, above. And less perfect the rest of the month, with snow, sleet, freezing rain, and rain. Temperatures sank to 8 below on the 21st and soared to 52 degrees on the 23rd.

December 3, first snow, 2 inches overnight.

The barn's 102 stalls have been filled for the winter, with the 65 to 70 milkers joined by heifers and dry cows from the free stall. With the start of single-digit temperatures, animal body heat is needed to keep the unheated barn's gutter cleaner and water pipes, as well as the water supply to the Kehoes' and Larry's home, which runs through the barn, from freezing.

December 21 is a harbinger of the locked-in months ahead with the first below-zero night, minus 8 degrees at 4 a.m. Water bowls and pipe are frozen near a drafty door. The chain on the feed mixer wagon snaps on Christmas Eve, requiring a week of improvisation before it is fixed.

The year's milk production, 2,004,391 pounds, is several hundred thousand pounds less than normal. Monthly production that had been averaging 205,000 pounds through May averages 130,000 pounds after the partial-herd selloff in June. Milk and cow prices have been strong, which has helped offset some of the production loss.

Fields are now rock hard, but, planning ahead, the spring's seed corn has been ordered and paid for. Dan has a yard and building full of winter rehabilitation projects—manure spreaders, tractor transmissions, feed wagons.

Jeanne's bone marrow transplant appears to be working. Tests in Boston indicate that the leukemia is in remission and that her white blood cell counts are good.

Larry has begun the countdown to March 31's last milking. Ninety days left. "It has come to the point where I just don't want the responsibility of caring for animals anymore. Not even one cow. I have done it for 45 years and I don't have to do it until I die. The responsibility is just never ending.

"Dan is always teasing me that I'll miss them and that I should keep a couple cows in the backyard. I've told Dan when the day comes and the herd is gone, I don't want to take care of anything. I don't even want to take care of a goldfish."

"The day in and day out gets to you. But my guess is that neither will completely give up farming on March 31," says Dan, who will need help with crop work in the spring.

January 2005: The Cold Just Takes the Energy 0ut of You

Farmers share the tourism business's aversion to January thaws. Temperatures in the 50s, rain, ruts, and soaked bunk feed followed by minus 15 turn the fields and barnyard into sheets of ice and send plant-killing frost deep into the ground. Mid-January produced such a weather mix, with Larry noting in his DayMinder, the need to "spread sand 'everywhere' all day job" and "bitter cold!!" in several of the month's eight sub-zero days.

"The cold catches up with you and just takes the energy out of you," says Dan of the siege.

Productive milkers and replacement heifers are a farmer's savings account, rainy-day fund, and IRA. Milk prices fluctuate, but good cows will always find buyers. Most cows calve successfully without any human intervention, but winter births require a heightened awareness so that the dam can be moved from the open free stall to a warmer enclosed birthing area. Calves born outside during the night may be frostbitten by morning but generally can be warmed and revived without permanent damage.

Early January is a good birthing spell with three calves, desired heifers. A fourth, a very large bull calf, is a problem. A breech birth, the calf suffocates despite the Wymans' efforts to pull him out while dam #556 pushed. Later in the month, twins, as often happens, are born dead. They'll be covered in the manure pile and burned and buried in the spring.

"Grayson can't milk every day. His knees won't take it. Larry's knees aren't good, and he's in pain most of the time from a wrist and shoulder that bother him. He really shouldn't be milking now. The only thing that keeps them going is that they want to see the farm continue," says Dan of a long and at times bitter cold January.

Larry milks 51 of January's 62 milkings; Dan, 42; and Grayson, 27. David Kehoe milks twice, filling in for Dan.

Jeanne's recovery is now being monitored by Porter and Fletcher Allen hospital doctors. She has gastrointestinal problems and spends four days in Porter for observation and tests at the start of the month but has no major problems after that.

A 1,500-pound Holstein exhales about 25 pounds of water vapor a day in a 40-degree barn. Fans draw out the moisture and adjacent trees become a winter wonderland. "Without good fans, a barn is like a cold sauna in the winter," says Larry. "Your clothes are sopping wet and just hang on you."

Chapter 8

Family Life

Free Time Was An Almost Unknown Concept

The family farm, Ronald Jager observes in his wide-ranging history, *The Fate of Family Farming: Variations on an American Idea*, has always been a revered way of life but a difficult way to make a living.

For Thomas Jefferson, the family farm was the moral backbone of the nation:

> Cultivators of the earth are the most valuable citizens. They are the most vigorous, the most independent, the most virtuous, and they are tied to their country and wedded to its liberty and interests, by the most lasting bonds.

A century later, President Theodore Roosevelt shared Jefferson's faith in those who tilled the soil:

> Nothing is more important to this country than the perpetuation of our system of medium-sized farms worked by their owners. We do not want to see our farmers sink to the conditions of the peasants of the old world, barely able to live on their small holdings, nor do we want to see their places taken by wealthy men owning enormous estates which they work purely by tenants and hired servants.

Fast forward to the start of the 21st century; the family farm is still the most prevalent family enterprise in the country. But in the inexorable economics that govern farming, only one to two percent of Americans now live on farms, compared to over 90% in Jefferson's day.

Family farmers' independent spirit has shaped the American character but often at enormous personal cost— a life of unrelenting work and scant financial return. Tom Wessels describes this commitment in *Reading the Forested Landscape: A Natural History of New England*:

> Free time was an almost unknown concept to the early settlers. If all the day's chores were completed, there was always more land to be cleared, more stumps to be pulled, and more rocks to be removed from fields. These early settlers worked hard from sunrise to sunset. Without the Sabbath, which forbade work one day a week, they might have worked themselves to death.

Thoreau would write in his journal, only half facetiously, of the toll of the still labor-intensive farm life in the 1850s:

> Consider the farmer, who is commonly regarded as the healthiest man. He may be the toughest, but he is not the healthiest. He has lost his elasticity; he can neither run nor jump. Health is the free use and command of all our faculties, and equal development. His is the health of the ox, an overworked buffalo. His joints are stiff.... It would do him good to be thoroughly shampooed to make him supple.

Farming with its long hours and touch-and-go finances constantly tests families. Fern Wyman grew up on a farm and knew what to expect— there is plenty of work to go around and the farm comes first.

For years, Larry and Grayson routinely worked 100-hour weeks, starting with a temperature check and morning milkng at 4 a.m.

Americans no longer care how or where they get their food as long as it is "firm, fresh and cheap." In a society of ease and abundance "the last generation of American farmers have become foreign to their countrymen, who were once as they." Hanson further observes in *The Land Was Everything: Letters from an American Farmer*:

> Farmers see things as others do not. Their age-old knowledge is more than the practical experience that comes from the art of growing food or from the independence of rural living. It involves a radically different—often tragic—view of human nature itself that slowly grows through the difficult struggle to work and survive from the land.

For tourists and second-home owners from urban, industrialized states, Vermont may seem like a contemporary Arcadia, "A Place Apart" as the state's marketers would have it.

Family farmers like the Wymans know better, as the following narratives attest. For those who have not grown up on a farm and even for those who have, the farming lifestyle, where the farm comes first, can be a difficult adjustment, observes Fern Wyman, Larry's wife.

Neither Grayson nor Larry regret that they chose to farm, but the farming life, they acknowledge, is all consuming and requires understanding wives and children.

There were some unwritten rules, Beverly Wyman, Larry's daughter, notes in her recollection of growing up on the farm. First and foremost, there shall be no idleness. ✿

One hundred and fifty years later, Victor Hanson, a classics scholar and part-time fruit farmer, would despair in *Fields Without Dreams: Defending the Agrarian Idea* that economic forces have irrevocably changed American agriculture.

One percent of the country's farms, the largest farms and agribusinesses that benefit disproportionately from government policies and subsidies and university and corporate research, now account for more than half of all farm income. Ninety percent of all farms in the 1990s had a net income of less than $20,000 a year.

"When Grayson and I were younger we could run all day," Larry recalls. "If we were doing one job, we were always thinking about the next. It was just a go-go proposition. We didn't stand around the way we do now."

For 46 years, Grayson and Larry kept the herd small enough to enable them to do nearly all of the milking and field work. Grayson's 3,492 consecutive milkings in the 1960s and 1970s is not in the *Guinness Book of Records*, but it is testament to his and Larry's hands-on management style.

3,492 Milkings Without a Break

GRAYSON WYMAN: Both Beth (Grayson's wife) and Fern had grown up on farms and that it made it easier for them to understand why we weren't at home on time or why we had to get up in the middle of the night to go to the barn to meet the vet. Things like that that might have been a little more difficult to explain to somebody without a farming background.

Both always worked off the farm, except for a short time in the early 1980s when Beth would help me and Fern would help Larry when we were swapping chores for two milkings on the weekend. Both had been around cows, and we didn't have to say this is the front end and this is the back.

Their milking lasted less than a year because we knew we were getting to the point where we needed help. In 1982, we hired our first help, and he stayed with us for six years. Farmers are usually ambivalent about their wives working on the farm. They might enjoy that their wives are part of the farm, and some women really enjoy farm work. But there is always some doubt.

I can remember a Brownsville neighbor who had a small farm where his uncle took care of the cows during the day while he ran a farm machinery business. He said that his uncle was getting old and he might not be able to keep his cows, but he definitely didn't want his wife working in the barn. "You know I've got nothing against women working," he said, "but as far as doing a man's work on the farm is concerned when I get in the bed at night, I don't want to think I'm crawling in beside the hired man."

That's the way a lot of farmers felt.

Fern enjoyed what she was doing at Geiger (a high-end clothing manufacturer), and Beth (a registered nurse) enjoyed her work. We certainly weren't about to ask them to change. They had their routine, five days a week.

We tried to do as little as possible on the weekend so we had time together. It certainly wasn't a case where Fern and Beth felt that every time they had a minute off they had to be over helping us. They had other things to do. We always raised a big garden. And on weekends they were canning or freezing or making pickles.

We raised our own turkeys and broilers for many years. We would have a day and clean out the hen house. We always had our own eggs. We had as many as 70 sheep in another barn behind the house in the '70s and '80s. We used them for wool and sold lambs. My father would sit in the back of the house and watch the coyotes try and pry the barn door open with their feet. They never got in, but they tried.

We divided the work up. Larry's girls took care of pigs and sheep. We had pigs in a pen on the north side of the barn and would buy three piglets in the spring and butcher them in the fall. We weren't self-sufficient, but we grew a lot of our own food.

The hardest part was vacations. I couldn't take time off in the summer, because that was our busiest time. Beth would say, "I have two weeks vacation coming this summer. Can't we do something?"

During the 1980s, we had a camp on Lake Champlain. We bought it in 1981 and held it until 1987. We couldn't get up there very often and were building a new house so we sold it. We took a few vacations, but we didn't travel much in the summer. Beth grew up in Mississippi. I wasn't used to the heat and humidity of the South, and she was happy to get away from it.

She was working in doctors' offices, and we took time off at other times. During the '90s, we took a couple weeks off and went to Mississippi at Christmas time. We used to try and go every other year, but it has been some time since we have visited.

At one time, Bev (Larry's daughter) figured that I had worked 3,492 milkings without a break. That would been from the day Larry and I started in Weybridge in 1968 to the day I got married in 1977. Larry worked almost that many consecutive milkings but missed a couple for family picnics and mountain climbs.

With a small operation like ours you can't trust your business to anyone. You have to be on top of your operation every minute because so many things can go wrong. I know one farmer who took a week's vacation. He brought in a man and worked with him for two weeks and figured that the farm would be all right. He called in every day. On the third morning, the man said the unloader on the

"I don't know how many million knee bends I have done in my life, but I've done a few," says Grayson of a dairy farmer's occupational hazard, bad knees. A portable milking stool helps some.

155

silo had broken, and he couldn't get feed out. The next day he said that the repair person couldn't get parts. When he got back the herd production was totally shot. It took him a year to get back to where he was.

What they say about farming is true; it is a great place to have a work ethic. There is always enough work around. ✒

"Grayson and I have been business partners all these years, but when we left the barn he had his life and I had mine. You need that separation to make it work," says Larry of a lifetime working together.

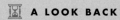

Is the Farmer Duly Appreciated?

In no occupation within the range of human employments, does success depend more on the judgment and discretion of the operative than that of the agriculturist. In the business of the mechanic and artizan (sic), an uniformity in every movement and act and in fashioning the object of his labor, is the height of skill, and results in the best and most finished article. It is not so with the farmer. His operation must be varied, to meet an almost endless variety of circumstances of soil, climate, weather, and so forth.

Now, in view of all these facts, in all candor and soberness, I ask the question, is the importance of a thorough scientific and practical knowledge of the business of the farmer duly appreciated?

The farmer, in debt for his farm and struggling to meet the daily expenses of his family, cannot be expected to devote his time and means to the experiments and investigation required to make important advances in science. But when the tone of the public mind shall have become right, he will, in this matter, gladly adopt the suggestions of his neighbor, whose greater leisure and learning have permitted and qualified him to engage in and carry out systematic and successful experiments, for the improvement of our domestic animals, the enriching of our soils, the increase of our crops, or the introduction of new varieties, either from the animal or vegetable kingdom, calculated to add to the sustenance of the human race.

Silas H. Jenison, President,
Addison County Agricultural Society, 1844

"Larry's father saved everything. We have pails and pails of nails. We must have paint scrapers by the hundreds. I didn't know there could be so many square pieces of metal that don't appear to have any purpose in life," says Fern, here cleaning the storage barn with daughter Bev, of the family's frugality.

There Will Be No Idleness

BEV WYMAN: * There are some unwritten rules or guidelines for behavior in our farm family.

First, there will be no idleness. Around the "must" jobs we sandwich "need-to-be-done" jobs, and this is where rule number two comes in. We try to do as much housework as possible for Mom's sake, and for Dad and Grayson we do as many of their daily chores as we can.

Rules three and four follow. Perhaps the more important is keeping out of the way. There is nothing worse than a helper who, however good his intentions, slows you down or creates more work for you. Most of all, you learn not to not help.

The fourth rule Carin, Sandy (Sam), and I also learned at an early age—never admit that you can't do something or ask for help; instead, figure out how to do it yourself. Every so often we would run into something that would just stump us. In these cases, we would ask Mom for help before we would bother the men.

Each person's familial role has changed over the sixteen years we have been on Our Farm (1968-84). The first family included my parents, grandparents, my Uncle Grayson, my sisters and myself. The second family emerged after Grampa passed away (1976). Included in this present family is my Aunt Beth.

The earlier form of our family I remember as "the good ol' days." My parents and uncle were young, strong and tireless; my grandparents were healthy; my sisters and I enjoyed growing up on a farm.

Dad and Grayson were the primary farm workers in our family's first form. From the day he set foot on Our Farm in April of 1968 Grayson did not take a day off until he was married in October of 1977. In that time, Dad—only because he had a family—took a few days off.

Grampa was their official helper. He fed the calves twice a day, washed the bulk tanks every other day, fed the cows at night. He ren-

---

*Excerpts from "The Biography of Our Farm," Honors Thesis, American Studies, Amherst College, 1984

ovated and wired most of the house, built a new porch, did plumbing, electrical, and carpentry repairs.

Gramma's official capacity was as bookkeeper for the farm—no easy task. During the first couple of years when the men were baling hay she used to help unload wagons with the rest of us. When Grampa didn't feel well, she used to go to the barn to help him sweep back.

Mom was in charge of keeping three girls out of mischief, maintained a large garden on her own, and held a few part-time jobs at the Weybridge Elementary School. All this in addition to keeping our house and doing her part of yard work, not to mention an occasional stint in the barn.

Carin, Sam, and myself did very little barn work in those days but helped with the lawn and garden. Mostly, we were busy being farm children—playing with the animals and roaming the land on foot, bicycle, skis, skates, and sleds.

My favorite projects were when the men were cutting corn, and we would ride back and forth to the cornfield in the wagons. Or, when the men were fixing fence we would go along to carry the staple pail or unroll the wire. I also loved to help bring calves in when they were born in the pasture or to move the cows across the road.

In the summer we would help Mom shell peas, cut beans and husk corn when she was freezing vegetables; in the fall we would pick apples. We had some responsibilities like taking care of our dog and our horse, but for the most part we were free to go anywhere we wanted to on the farm as long as we let someone know where we were going.

Needless to say, Grampa's shoes were hard to fill. After his death, Carin, Sam, and I tried to take up some of the slack. I fed calves, Sam swept, and Carin helped with heavier jobs like milking and feeding.

Dad and Grayson still do almost all of the farm work. They are older now; farming has taken its toll on their bodies. They get tired faster. Gramma continues to do the farm's bookkeeping. She does light yard work and housework. The rest of the day she bakes for all of us, and she walks to improve her health.

My mother's role has both changed and intensified. She works essentially three full-time jobs. She continues to keep the house but has decreased the size of her garden. This, her first job, also includes mowing half of the lawn. Her second occupation is as farm worker. She works semi-monthly shifts at the barn on Grayson's weekend off. Every day she takes care of the chickens, ducks and dog.

Her third job is off the farm. She is a shipping clerk for Geiger of Austria, receiving all the merchandise from Austria and sending out orders to the Geiger accounts all over this country.

It is a high-pressure job. Mom is so burned out by the time she gets home at night that it is hard for her to face cooking a meal, doing the grocery shopping, washing, or working in the garden.

I think my life's greatest frustration is that I, who am so used to helping my family, cannot help Mom at Geiger. All I can do is lighten the amount of housework and barn work that she must do.

I never realized what a tough job it was just to help Dad keep working. The very first eight-hour day that Mom worked (at Geiger), Dad picked me up at the bus stop after school. His hand was all bloody. It seems that the chain saw nicked his hand that day. I bandaged his hand for him.

He was gone for half an hour, and then he was right back. This time he was covered from head to toe with hot oil. The gasket had blown out on a tractor and all the oil sprayed out. I got him some clean clothes and rebandaged his hand. I was glad to see Mom home soon after.

Beth's work and family responsibilities are much like Mom's. She works as a nurse in a family practitioner's office in town. Beth does less housework than Mom, since Gramma helps her. She keeps a big garden, though, and does her half of the lawn. Beth has all the chores to think about when she gets home, too. She also sings in the church choir in New Haven.

Beth was at a disadvantage when she married into the family and moved onto the farm. She had to begin where I had begun at birth to pick up and assimilate the mysterious forces that drive our family.

"When we were kids, Dad used to have us clean the windows in the barn. The cows would see their reflections and jump. It wasn't until I was an adult that I realized it was just a way to keep us busy," says Bev.

Perhaps the hardest thing she had to deal with was our memory of Grampa. We had all left Grampa's work unchanged whether it needed to be or not. Beth, not knowing who had done what, ran into our sentimental walls by no fault of her own.

After six and a half years she has figured out most of our idiosyncrasies and unwritten rules. We couldn't help her very much because we know them only subconsciously ourselves. She works well in the family now. She pulls her own weight.

Carin, Sam and I together took over Grampa's position as full-time helper as best we could. During summers we did most of the morning chores except milking. In the afternoons we worked on some needed project that probably wouldn't be done if we didn't do it, like clapboarding the end of the porch, tarpapering a roof on the shed, scraping and painting the corn planter, touch-up painting on buildings, tearing down the horse barn, insulating the attic.

The summer we cleaned out the old barn and made it into a heifer barn, Sam and I wheeled twenty-seven tons of crushed stone in our wheelbarrow from outside the barn onto the floor of the heifer barn in preparation for cement. We kept at it until it was done.

We managed rather nicely through high school, but each of us has, in turn, gone off to college. When we go home we work as if we had never gone: doing, helping, keeping out of the way, and being stubborn.

There is a security that grows from the earth, a sort of confidence and reinforcement. My family will support me, unquestioningly, in whatever I choose to do; they have a confidence in me that is the result of years of working together.

I am so secure in my farm family that my "family" now extends to include animals and the people I meet. On the farm we treat our animals with a respect that some people don't have for another human being. Growing up on a farm has given me a respect for all living things. Even at Amherst I play by the basic rules of my family—doing, helping, not bothering others, not accepting defeat—and I am better off for it.

Some say that with the disappearance of the American farm family, the United States will crumble; maybe, they are right. ⌀

Such Unceasing Toil

We do not know whether it is a proved fact, that the atmosphere surrounding a farm necessarily changes the female sex into iron machines or whether when a farmer takes to himself a wife, he considers that he is only securing another domestic beast of burden; to rank in point of utility with his horse and ox; but we do know that in too many instances he lives and acts as if prompted by such principles.

I do not intend by these expressions, any disparagement whatever to farming, as an occupation, for I consider it the noblest employment a man can engage in, the most healthful, the most conducive to morality and expansion of intellect, and when properly conducted, best calculated to ensure the greatest amount of happiness to his wife and children. But it must be confessed, it is sad as well as amusing, to look over the various agricultural periodicals and mark how multifarious the labors which a farmer's wife is bound in duty to perform; labors, which if imposed upon the wives of any other class of men, would be stigmatized as outrageous and absurd.

Then, it is argued that nothing can prosper unless performed under her immediate supervision, and every thing in the house, cooking, baking, washing, ironing, sweeping, scouring, dusting, with all the other thousand *ings* require her presence. All the clothing she must make and keep in repair; and it is hinted that it would be a fine thing if farmers' wives could spin and manufacture cloth.

They must, of course, make sausages, cure the hams, and dry the herbs; while her husband is advised that if he gives the poultry yard into her care, he will be much more likely to secure a good stock of chickens, as well as more eggs for market.

And last, she is urged to cultivate her mind; and it is enforced as the highest duty, that she considers the education of her children entrusted to her charge.

Now I would ask, where is the most willingly disposed woman to find time for all these things, setting aside the health and strength necessarily required for such unceasing toil.

Vermont Family Visitor, 1845

Haying technology has changed enormously, but the attraction of the haymow for visiting grandchildren remains the same. It's still dark and spooky and full of smells found nowhere else.

They Stuck With Me Through Thick and Thin

LARRY WYMAN: Farming is a good life. It's too bad that the way many people farm today on the megafarms is not the way we farmed. An old stanchion barn like ours was an extension of the house. It was a place for our kids and kids from the neighborhood to hang out. During the summer our kids would ride their bicycles in the barn. The rule was once we got past the crosswalk they could ride the feed alleys on the other side. They'd do it by the hour.

When we were getting hay in our kids wanted to be on the wagons and be up in the mow. It kept their minds occupied, and they had a good time. We always had chickens and turkeys and pigs and sheep when they were growing up, which is an experience they probably wouldn't have had any other way.

And I'm sure they remember sitting on the porch cutting beans from the garden with my mother. Growing up on a farm is a different set of experiences—the kind city kids don't have and that aren't often repeated in adult life.

I never pushed our kids to do farm work. That was my life and responsibility. Their responsibility was to grow up and have a good time along the way and take every advantage of school that they possibly could. The farm was a big part of their life, but I wanted them to have the same opportunities as everyone else.

I don't think the scope of farm life restricted them. They knew they could stand toe-to-toe with the best of Middlebury. Two were top in their high school class and one was second. One went to Wesleyan (Sandy), another to Amherst (Bev), and the third to Williams (Carin). They have had the chance to rub elbows with kids of all kinds of backgrounds. So they didn't do too bad.

I've always been annoyed by city people who think farms only produce idiots. I can recall getting a call from a person urging me to support a vote on the high school. This person said it was important for people in the surrounding towns to vote because all the farmers were going to be against it because it was going to raise their taxes. This was the kind of attitude that irritated me.

I don't think I would have felt any different if we had sons. They would not have fared any worse than my daughters because I would have wanted them to have the same opportunities.

What the girls did around the farm, they did voluntarily. They helped out a lot, especially after my father passed away and Grayson

In the increasingly mechanized world of dairy farming, there are fewer and fewer hands-on opportunities for kids. Unrolling the plastic wrap for the feed bunk is one of them. Jordan Kehoe, 4, helped, albeit briefly, his father, Jay, grandfather, Dan, and Larry.

and I were basically hoofing it alone. We'd get through milking at night, and they'd hear the vacuum pump go off. They'd bail out of the house and all three would be over here. One would help in the milk house. One would scrape the platform and bed the cows. Another would get the feed out and help feed the cows for the last time. They were a big help, and we had a lot of fun together.

Their coming over at the tail end of the day really helped us the most. When you get to the end of the day my father would say your sled is dragging a little hard. So we appreciated their help that much more, and the girls always said they had some of their best times growing up coming over here after school. It was also good for Grayson, who thinks the world of them, because he didn't have any kids. He was so close to them that they were just like his own.

I adopted the philosophy early on in farming that when I went to the barn in the morning I would put everything I had into it until I got ready to shut the lights off whatever hour that was. But when I went home what was over there, stayed over there.

I could be so tired that I could just about crawl, but I'd walk through that door and I'd see those three kids bouncing and jouncing and full of life and the fatigue just went out the window.

I didn't worry about what was over there. The best thing I could do was to get a good night's sleep and go back with a fresh mind and approach. That was my attitude the entire time I farmed.

There was a spell when the girls were in junior high and high school when we worked our schedule so that Grayson and I came over and ate and then went back and milked. That was the best therapy in the world; it was worth the price of admission to hear their school stories.

Growing up has become so completely different today with the expectations and lifestyles of parents and children. Running a family farm and keeping up with all the things that are going on would be difficult. It would take a better person than me to make it all work.

Both Fern and Beth grew up on farms and understood how farms worked and how important it was that we get things done when they needed to be done. And there were many times when everything could have gone downhill in a hurry, especially when Grayson and I worked seven days a week for nine years and hardly took a day off. Other wives might have not been quite as understanding.

Except for a year or so when they alternated weekends and helped us with milking, they never did farm work. They kept the gardens and mowed the lawns. Fern ran a million errands for us over the years until she went to work when we moved here. Taking care of three kids—two of the kids were only 14 months apart—was a full-time job without worrying about milking.

Working off the farm was a necessity. There is no doubt that what both Fern and Beth earned was a major contribution. It gave us a flexibility and stability that we wouldn't have had. Grayson and I could put everything we made back into the farm and didn't have to worry about setting aside money for family expenses. That outside income was a blessing.

Fern's job allowed our kids to have things they never would have been able to have. They had a lot of college bills that would have taken a long time to pay off. What they would have contributed by working on the farm was nowhere near what they contributed by working off the farm.

Fern didn't have any problem with country living. She liked the gardens and being out in the fields. That was the way she grew up. But it was still probably hard at first for her to move here. We had just built a new house in Brownsville in '65. The house here was a wreck, and we didn't have the money to fix it. If we put the money into the farm, there was none left for the house.

It was cold and hard to heat. There was door in the living room and if you sat half a dozen feet away, your teeth would be chattering. There was a "storm door," but this place was like a sieve. The kids laugh about how cold the house was. They put up with it and Fern did, too. They put up with a lot of things. Those first years were rugged, but they stuck with me through thick and thin. ⚘

Fern always worked off the farm, with the exception of the early 1980s when she and her sister-in-law provided weekend milking relief. Twenty-plus years later, her philosophy unchanged—help when needed—she returned to the barn to feed the heifers.

Your Life Really Comes in Second to the Life of the Farm

FERN WYMAN: I grew up on a small farm right after World War II. My father had gone to M.I.T. and was a textile designer in the mills in Lawrence, Massachusetts, for 10 years before he married and moved to Vermont in the late '30s. He married late and was in his forties when he started farming. My mother's family lived in New Haven (Vt.), and his was in Boston.

Everybody had a little farm, a dozen to 30 cows, and all your social life was in the school and church. Our farm was about 150 acres— not a big dairy farm, more of a subsistence farm. We had bees and fruit trees and a big garden. We had about 15 cows and sold eggs and made butter, which went to Boston.

My brother and I did everything. We cut wood with cross-cut saws, cared for the chickens, milked the cows, spread manure, and hayed. My father converted an old pickup truck into a tractor, which we loved to drive. The "tractor" pulled a sickle bar mowing machine and dump rake. Our city cousins from Boston would help with the haying, and they loved it, too.

Subsistence farming was enough for quite a while, and then times changed and family farms like ours started disappearing around Guilford and Brattleboro. You needed to get bigger, and we didn't have the land. My father wasn't well, and my mother, who had a degree in teaching from UVM, went back to teaching. My brother farmed for a while, but then he went into carpentry. He still lives on the farm and sells hay and his daughter keeps horses.

Farming was just more fun in those days and wasn't as pressured. With Larry, everything was on a bigger scale. Even with more machinery, there was always more to do, and it was more labor intensive. It was just work, work, work.

Years ago just about everyone had some connection to farming, and there didn't seem to be the division between city and rural people. You knew everyone and everyone came to school Halloween and Christmas parties. Now nobody knows anybody.

Today, a farmer's wife is the butt of all kinds of jokes. We're looked down on. People just think farmers shovel manure and ride a tractor and the farmer's wife milks the cows, which I never did. When I worked off the farm, I never told anybody that I was from a farm.

I enjoyed the work and growing up on a farm, and I think my daughters did, too. They had chores and worked hard, but no one ever had to get after them to do them. I think it was a respite for their minds to come home from school and do some mindless things like feeding calves and then come in and hit the books.

They were able to hang right in there as far as grades. Two were valedictorians and one was salutatorian, and all went on to college. In later years, they'd comment, which I never heard when they were growing up, about attitudes toward "dumb" farm kids. But more than anything else, I think they have carried over the feeling that other people don't know how to work. Beverly (a computer systems developer) will say people don't get to their jobs until 9 o'clock and want to go home at 4. She thinks of a day's work as 12 hours a day. Her sisters (an environmental impact consultant and printing firm administrator) are the same way.

Many people say, "I could never work the hours of a farmer." Well, farmers get tired of the long hours, too. As farms have gotten bigger and more and more demanding, farming has become a grind. That's the way I looked at it. When I was a growing up you had to get the hay in on a nice day, but somehow you worked in that trip to the swimming hole.

If Larry had allowed himself some vacations, it would have been better for everyone. But Larry and Grayson were so disciplined and didn't feel that anyone could do the farm work when they were gone. Their mother was deeply involved in the farm for many years and had that same discipline, too.

Every once in a while Larry would realize that he never saw his children and would try and do something with them. When the kids were little we went to New York City a couple times but never for more than two days. Never. Even in later years when we would visit our daughter in Washington, Larry would have to call home every night to see if everything was OK. He just couldn't get away from it.

It's really only been since retirement that he's taken time off. But Larry did pretty well most of the time in leaving problems in the barn when he was home. He would be interested in what the girls were doing, their schoolwork and teachers. But still the farm was always in the back of his mind.

I was a stay-at-home mom until the girls were in junior and senior high school. Larry and Grayson and their parents were into the farm far more than I was, and I decided I would do something on my own and see what the outside world was like. And the outside income would help with the bills and college.

I filled in first at the Weybridge Elementary School, helping the cook. That was less than a year. Then I worked at Simmonds (an aerospace company 20 minutes away) in the late 1970s. That was an eye opener. I had never been in a factory. I worked in the stockroom and learned lots of new words about jet engine parts.

After four or five years, I said I can't do this anymore and went to work at Geiger (an Austrian manufacturer of high-end clothing with a distribution center in Middlebury), which was high pressure but a pleasanter place to work. I worked there for 19 years, shipping their clothing around the country, until I retired in 2000.

Larry wasn't supportive of my working off the farm at first. He liked to have me here for his meals, and the kids had a lot of comings and goings at school. He didn't have time to help with that. But when I started working, Carin had her driver's license—so the girls weren't restricted in their after-school activities.

What it comes down to is if you're a farmer's wife, your life really comes in second to the life of the farm. That was hard, and I voiced my objections occasionally, "Why does your life always have priority over anything that I want to do?" Then I'd feel bad that I had. Larry wouldn't see it that way. It's a good thing I had a little background in farming. I never would have stuck it out, if I didn't realize that that's the way farm life is.

I really never had the feeling that we were over the hump and could relax. But I also never worried that we were just barely hanging on. When you're younger you feel if it doesn't work, you'll just do something else.

When the Kehoes came in 1997 and did more of the work that made a difference. By then it was way past due for Larry to get help and to retire. They had tried to get help, but the help wouldn't show up. Bev's husband worked with them (1988-95), but he couldn't take the long hours. He never saw his kids and didn't like that. When he went to work as a plumber, he said it felt like he was on vacation.

By the late '90s, Larry was exhausted. He'd come in for dinner. The next thing I knew he had fallen asleep in his chair. He didn't need any urging to retire. He was ready long before it happened.

We put the farm in the Land Trust so the Kehoes could afford to buy it. And we all wanted to keep the land open. I have gone for walks on Drake Road and the ridge for years and didn't want to look across the fields and see them all full of houses.

When Jeanne got sick, Larry saw his plans disintegrate. He thought that Dan wouldn't want to milk cows, but he hoped the farm would stay intact and he still does. I don't think it will ever be a dairy farm again, but it will be some kind of a farm, even if it's just selling crops.

Wood, 25 to 30 cords, used to heat the homestead. Today, a smaller wood pile shares the heating load with an oil furnace. Larry chops and splits. Fern transports.

We both feel that we are in a transition period and anything could happen. We are just going to take it as it comes along. I knew there would be an adjustment in retirement, but it has worked out all right.

Larry misses his routine more than the actual barn work. For so many years, he did something at a certain time, something else at a certain time. He helps Dan in the fields, cleans the barn, and helps with the loading and unloading of hay, but Dan doesn't go by such-and-such a time. It just happens. They are way different that way, but it has worked out. Larry has mellowed.

He still needs a little structure, but he has so much to do. We were going to paint the house this summer but didn't get to it. That will have to be our goal for next summer. We have only gone out West to visit our daughter once but probably will in the spring. We seem to be too busy.

One nice thing about retirement is the weather. You don't have to worry that it's going to rain on your hay or stop your planting. Dan has to so we haven't gotten completely away from worrying. I don't know how many times Larry has said this fall that he's glad he didn't have to cut the corn and plow the fields under. The fields have just been mud, and there's nothing you can do about it.

One thing you learn about family farming is to expect the unexpected and to accept the long hours. That's hard for a lot of people who don't know what they're getting into. But if you think it over, I'd say go for it. It's a good life. It's a chosen alternate lifestyle.

That's what it is. People should respect those who choose to live differently. Way different. Many people need to have a new car, the latest style in clothes. We don't have the income to keep up with the Joneses and just don't care. Larry said he had enough of that in New Jersey.

Everyone has their ups and downs. We had our share. But we hung in there. Farming was most satisfying for me when the girls were growing up, and we all worked together in the garden and barn and with the animals. I think the girls enjoyed it, too—at least they never complained. ⠦

February 2005: Are You Going to Miss Milking?

No one likes a snowy winter more than farmers. Deep cover prevents the deep freeze that leave alfalfa fields full of winter kill in the spring. But short days and icy going make for long months.

Few people look forward to spring more than farmers. By the end of February, the cold snaps that glaze barn windows, frost the bunk's silage, and freeze a mixing wagon's 4,000 pounds of feed when left outside are largely over. Tractors now start with little coaxing, and Larry, Grayson, and Dan lose their hunched postures and appear 30 pounds lighter as they shed layers and feed caps replace fur hats and face masks.

Sunny 49 degrees!!, Larry writes on February 6. A February tease as this would be the warmest reading that Larry will report for the month.

The Wymans have had another good run of calves, with nine heifers in ten births.

With outdoors work still months away, Dan fixes stanchions and water troughs in the heifer barn. Larry washes the outsides of pipelines and cleans cobwebs, a losing battle, in the main barn. Grayson in a warm spell is able to scrape layers of frozen manure from the free stall with the skid steer (a small, maneuverable tractor with a bucket loader).

Barn, equipment, cows, procedures and sanitation conditions pass the state inspector's muster, and the Department of Agriculture renews the farm's annual license to sell milk.

Jeanne's recovery continues to progress with only one DayMinder entry—a trip to Fletcher Allen for a CT scan—to remind everyone that her remission is not a sure thing.

Dan has all but decided that he won't be milking cows in the future. Jeanne had tired of milking even before her leukemia. Finding reliable help and uncertain milk prices are also discouraging. Selling hay, leasing barn space and raising heifers for other farmers, and tending to his repair business appear to be a better business model.

"Are you going to miss milking?" a visitor asks.

"You mean getting up every day at 3?" Dan replies.

Two buyers look at the herd. The herd, valued for its quality and the Wymans' detailed breeding records, will be sold on a take-all-or-none basis.

Dan's teasing about Larry and Grayson's impending retirement continues.

"Don't look for much activity from me on April 1. I'll be sleeping in," says Larry.

"This summer I want to find out what summer is all about. It's been 1957 since I haven't worked a summer. It's been a long haul," says Grayson.

"I can see it now. They'll be coming over and saying, 'I'm bored, can I help with the chores?'" Dan predicts.

"Never happen," Larry replies.

Chapter 9

Retirement

Somebody Will Have Their Day After Us

Daytime farming concerns rarely kept Larry and Grayson up at night. They were simply too tired for middle-of-the-night second-guessing. But in the mid-1990s, they were facing the one issue that can give older farmers sleepless nights: What to do with the farm when the spirit is flagging, the body is nearly spent, and there are no family members to continue this all-consuming way of life?

In 1995, Larry's son-in-law, Joe Miller, left, after working on the farm for eight years, to join his brother in the plumbing business. For the next two years they relied on a local farm worker service to provide help.

By early 1997, Larry, in his early sixties and Grayson, in his late fifties, were seriously considering retirement; they could no longer manage the farm workload alone and their temporary help was not reliable. Their dilemma, finding help, historians would point out is nothing new; it is as old as the family farm.

The solution has long been known: shorter days and better pay. In 1872, E.R. Towle suggested such in a presentation, "How to Make Farm Life Pleasant," at a meeting of the newly established Vermont Board of Agriculture:

> The labor of the day should always be brought to an early close. There can be no reasonable excuse for continuing this until into the night. Nothing will tend more perhaps to discourage farmers' sons, to say nothing of "hired help," and bring the occupation into disrepute than this practice. Then we say, to assist in making farm life pleasant, let everything be done in season and in order.

Easier said than ever done. In the past dozen years, farmers, unable to find local help, have increasingly hired migrant workers, mainly Mexicans, to help with milking. The Vermont Agency of Agriculture estimates that there are now 2,500 migrant workers working on dairy farms, with an estimated 500 working on Addison County farms. These workers, representing roughly a third of farming's full-time labor force, are involved in the production of about half the state's milk.

In the winter of 1997, Larry and Grayson found what would unexpectedly become a long-term solution to their labor problem, Dan and Jeanne Kehoe. Both Kehoes were in their thirties, had grown up on small dairy farms, knew cows, and had the energy the Wymans once had. The Kehoes, who began by helping with milking, would solve the immediate problem, keeping the farm going until it could be sold.

Selling the farm, when and to whom, was the next question. Developers and bankers, indeed anyone concerned about the character of our communities, must consider the highest and best use of land. Hill farms with their rocky soils

Dairy farming's physical demands make it a young man's game— the average age of Vermont's dairy farmers is 54. After 40-plus years of farming, the Wymans accepted the inevitable, sold the herd, and leased the farm to Dan Kehoe.

169

The Wymans sold development rights to the Vermont Land Trust, ensuring that their prime farm land could only be used for agricultural purposes in the future. The Land Trust has conserved over 180 farms and nearly 50,000 acres, about 12% of Addison County's acreage, and over 600 farms and 160,000 acres statewide.

commercial and residential development. But land-use theory may not always dovetail with marketplace realities.

Developers can almost without exception afford to pay far more for a 5- or 10- or 20-acre building lot than farmers can justify paying for its use as pasture or crop land. In the 1980s this spread increased as land values skyrocketed and farmers faced challenging conditions— increasing fuel costs and more volatile milk prices, a result in part from lower government support prices.

In short, farmers, seeking a return on a lifetime of work, found that the highest value, if not the best use, of their land was for house lots, or less frequently, for commercial development. The result? Thousands of acres of prime agricultural land were being lost, not only in Vermont but also throughout the nation, to residential and commercial development.

For years, the Wymans have been steadfast; their land with commanding views was not for sale for residential development. "I don't have fingers and hands to count the number of times we could have sold land off Drake Road. We have never wanted to split the place up, although I'm sure we could have turned the place into a fortune," Larry says of the many overtures.

"To use a cliché, farmers are stewards of the land," says Grayson of their shared philosophy. "We had our day and somebody had their day before us and hopefully somebody will have their day after us. That was what we wanted to ensure."

But it wasn't until 1987, when Governor Madeleine Kunin and the state legislature created the Vermont Housing and Conservation

and higher operating costs were marginal for dairying but ideal for house lots. They were the first to go under, and very few exist today. Land-use analysts point out that about 20% of Vermont's land is devoted to agriculture today, less than a third of the acreage it once occupied. But this percentage roughly mirrors the soil acreage considered most suitable for farming.

Addison County has much of the state's prime farmland; agriculture is the highest and best use of the county's poorly percolating clays soils, which generally do not meet septic tank regulations for

Board (VHCB), that state funding for farmland conservation became available. The board's mandate, funded by a tax on the sale of property, was to create affordable housing and to conserve critical farmland, important natural areas, recreational lands, and historic properties.

VHCB in partnership with conservation nonprofits, such as the Vermont Land Trust, subsequently developed additional sources of support, most notably from the private, nonprofit Freeman Foundation. This funding gave farmers the ability to recoup the difference between the farm's value as agricultural land and house lots or commercial development.

Vermont, largely through public, private, and foundation partnerships coordinated by VHCB and the Vermont Land Trust, has since become one of the country's leaders in preserving agricultural land by buying development rights from farmers. In return for selling development rights, which generally range from $1,000 to $2,000 an acre, the farmer must agree that the land can only be sold and used for agricultural purposes and never be subdivided for homes.

Since 1989, when the Vermont Land Trust bought its first development rights or conservation easement in Addison County—a 194-acre farm in Shoreham—the organization has conserved, either through purchase or donation, nearly 50,000 acres of dairy farmland, about 12% of the county's total acreage. Statewide, about 160,000 acres of agricultural land had been conserved by 2009.

In the fall of 1999, the Wymans, preparing for retirement, began discussing the sale of development rights with the Vermont Land Trust. Allen Karnatz, regional co-director who annually oversees the acquisition of development rights to 10 to 20 Champlain Valley farms, recalls the negotiations over land that was eminently suited for development.

"My initial question was could we come up with enough funding to make this work. Weybridge is a higher-priced real estate market than a lot of other areas in the Champlain Valley. That didn't concern them that much. Their attachment to the land was key

to their decision. That's true of most farmers. In many cases the money is important, especially when many of these farms are heavily mortgaged.

"But with the Wymans it was less about the money. I can remember Larry saying, 'We have already decided. The only thing that is going to change our mind is if the Land Trust really screws things up.'"

In his funding request to the VHCB, Karnatz laid out the land trust's rationale for buying the farm's development rights:

> Weybridge has changed a lot in the 40 years since Larry and Grayson were eager young farmers. Back then Weybridge was losing population. Now the population has taken an about face and practically all the land is at risk from development. Weybridge building lots are fetching high prices (>$50,000) and the Wyman farm is especially vulnerable; it's only 4 miles from Middlebury, has over 2 miles of road frontage and beautiful rural views in all directions. If not conserved, it will almost surely be lost to development.

The Weybridge town plan, he noted, urges the town to "protect and encourage the maintenance of agricultural lands for the production of food and other agricultural products," "plan public investments to minimize development pressure on agricultural and forest land," and "(concentrate) growth in designated areas while simultaneously conserving open space in the surrounding countryside."

In October of 2001, the Wymans sold development rights to the land trust for $301,000, ensuring that 274 acres of prime land would be preserved for agricultural use in perpetuity. The Conservation Board contributed $296,000. Weybridge contributed $5,000 from the town's Conservation Fund.

In the following narratives, Larry and Grayson discuss their last years of farming, the impact of Dan and Jeanne Kehoe, and their hopes for the farm's future. Dan describes growing up on a family farm, Jeanne's and his years working with the Wymans, and the possibility that some day the farm will be known as the Kehoe Farm. ⋅⋀⋅

The hiring of Jeanne and Dan Kehoe in 1997 solved a longstanding problem for the Wyman farm—finding reliable help. Their youthful energy enabled Larry and Grayson to continue farming for another eight years.

Dan and Jeanne Were Rare Finds

GRAYSON WYMAN: In 1997, we would have been through if it hadn't been for Dan and Jeanne. We were at a point where the farm was more than we could handle. After Joe (Larry's son-in-law) left in 1995, help was catch-as-catch-can. A local man had a business where he trained young men to milk; we probably had five or six of his people help with morning and night milkings. One was reliable, but with most it was a 50-50 proposition whether they would show up.

One night Larry was supposed to have the night off, and the help was supposed to milk with me. He never showed on time, which was typical. Larry and I had started milking and were as far as the crosswalk (half the herd) when Larry said, "This is ridiculous. Absolutely crazy. If they're not going to be reliable, I'd just as soon milk the cows myself." When he finally came, I wrote him a check and said, "That's your last one. We don't need you anymore."

We went about two weeks without help when Dan walked in the barn one night. That would have been January of 1997. He had bred some cows for us a few times, and we knew who he was. He said he'd heard from a mutual friend that we were looking for milking help and that his farm machinery repair business was really slow and that he could give us a few nights during the week to spell us if we were interested. We said we were.

And he said his wife also wanted to work. He said he wouldn't let her work anywhere, but that he knew us well enough to know that she would be treated right. It's all history from there. He helped us a few nights a week so one of us could have a night off until Jeanne came in February. Dan continued with night milkings four times a week so Larry and I could have two nights off a week. Jeanne worked five mornings a week so I could do the feeding.

Dan would also come in the morning and see if we had a breakdown to be fixed or needed help. It got to the point where he was helping more and more. Then he started helping with the morning feeding, and we put him on the payroll.

Dan and Jeanne were rare finds. We had the same kind of work ethic and had all learned the hard way. They had grown up on small farms and knew what it was to put in a day's work. Larry and I didn't grow up on a farm, but we struggled when we started out and learned by trial and error.

Until Dan and Jeanne came we had never delegated much of the responsibility for the operation. Larry or I were always on top of whatever was being done. But it was obvious they had enough experience. Jeanne took over the heifers and calves. Dan repaired all the machinery.

We didn't want to expand the milking herd because that meant we would have to build an addition to the barn, which we didn't want to do at our age. What changed was that with four of us, even with the two of them part-time, we had the manpower to do things faster and the way they should be done. If we had five or six calves in a week, we could absorb the extra work. We got newer and bigger equipment and were able to maintain it better.

In the winter of 1998, I was looking at a knee replacement and three months rehab. Nine out of 10 times, you'd have to hire somebody to work for three months. While I was out, three people did four people's work. When Jeanne had back surgery, three people did four people's work. When Larry fell out of the haymow, we all filled in. And when Jeanne got sick, we shared the workload for 14 months.

It worked, but it takes its toll. I give them the credit for sticking it out. They didn't have the attitude, "What's in it for me? When's my next day off?" None of those things. They appreciated what they had and their opportunities.

If you were to ask Dan right now, he'd tell you honestly that what we did together set us all up. It was a godsend for us. I wasn't ready to retire. It kept the business going and the land in use. It gave us the opportunity to put the farm into the land trust. And it provided them with a home. We paid for everything that was on the outside—the foundation, septic system, and water—and they bought the house and put it on the foundation.

Dan would say that's the best house they've ever lived in. Dan has his repair business, and we built the shop for him. He rents the shop and the farm. The day will come when he wants to buy the farm. That will be easy to do because the farm is in the land trust, and the barn and his house are all on one side of the road. Larry's house is separate. It won't be difficult to divide.

Keeping the farm going also gave us a place for our mother. This had been her home for many, many years, and we knew that we could never set her up in any other place where she would be as happy. She had lived in 14 different places and had a rough start. She lost her father when she was 11 and her mother when she was 14 and then grew up with a foster family (the Fanchers). She lived here from 1968 to 2004. This was home.

The biggest disappointment was losing Jeanne. She had worked hard for everything they had and died when she and Dan were getting to the point where they could finally appreciate it. ◌

Dan Kehoe and Larry and Grayson were a good fit. They were workaholics, frugal, and fussy about getting cows and crops right.

Jeanne's illness turned family and barn schedules upside down. Her daughter's birthday was celebrated two weeks early on September 6 with a barbecue. On September 8 she left for Boston for her bone marrow transplant and a month-long hospital stay.

For seven years Jeanne milked and cleaned equipment with Larry. "You learn how a person is wired," says Larry of the bond that develops from working side by side for three hours each morning.

It Feels Like I've Almost Had a Fourth Daughter

LARRY WYMAN: Grayson and I started in 1960 and until the 1980s it was just the two of us. My father and three daughters helped, but it was on a catch-as-catch-can basis. If something was going to get done, Grayson and I did it. That was the way we wanted it. It wasn't until around 1983 that we had our first paid help, Francis Sumner; he never milked but just helped around the barn and fields.

It wasn't until Joe (Joe Miller, Larry's son-in-law) came in 1987 after Grayson had knee surgery and was laid up that we had regular full-time help. Joe left in 1995 to work with his brother in the plumbing business. Grayson and I were of the generation where the farm and barn were your life. There wasn't the money to hire anyone. You had to do it. He wanted a more traditional lifestyle where you had weekends off, benefits, and paid vacation.

For the next two years we scrambled for help, using young kids in their late teens and early twenties from a farm worker temp service. They all left, and the manager was left holding the bag. He was also helping us with milking, but he was milking three times a day and wanted to cut back, and he left, too.

Roger Stowe (a New Haven farmer) was buying some heifer calves from us at the time. Roger came down one morning and said, "I hear your help is all done. Are you looking for someone to milk cows?"

A couple days later I was washing the bulk tank and a man walked in and said, "Hi, I'm Danny Kehoe. I understand that you're looking for someone to milk cows." I said, "Yes, I guess we are. Grayson and I will be getting out of the business, but we will probably continue to milk through this year, get things cleaned up, and then get out."

At that point, we were going to get rid of the cows. We couldn't do all the work—the milking and fieldwork—that needed to be done. Grayson's legs were bad and mine were getting worse by the day.

Danny said his wife milked cows and she was interested in morning milking. Would we be interested in someone helping with just morning milking? I said it would be nice if Grayson and I could have a couple of milkings off a week.

So a couple days later, he stopped in again and asked if his wife had stopped by.

I said, "No." He said he'd talk to her again and asked if it would be any help if he milked four nights every week, Monday, Tuesday, Thursday and Friday. I said that would give Grayson and me two nights a week off and would be quite a help.

The next night, I was graining the cows and a stranger walked in and said, "Hello, are you Mr. Wyman?" And I laid eyes on Jeanne Kehoe for the first time in my life. We talked and we decided to give it a shot. Basically, she would milk with me in the morning. She had to be done by 8 o'clock in order to get her kids off to school and so Dan could start making farm calls. I said, "If you have to be home by 8 and we get to 20 of 8 and we're not done, then I'll just finish up. We start at 5 o'clock."

She said, "OK," and we started in milking. That was February 3, 1997. They both milked that spring and into the summer. We were still thinking of going out of business, and Grayson and I started selling machinery. Danny helped us sell some of it with contacts he had from his machinery repair business.

"Jeanne went from feeling the best she had in two weeks at morning milking on June 7 to getting lab results that afternoon and being told to see the doctor immediately. They said she had a very fast-acting form of leukemia and sent her to Fletcher Allen that afternoon. They started chemo that night," Larry recalls of Jeanne's illness. "She probably put off going to see a doctor longer than she should have. We just didn't make the connection that something was wrong because we're all tired and pushing the limit all the time." Here, three days before her diagnosis she was putting in a full day in the barn.

Then we started selling heifer calves, and we got to September and suddenly our market for calves dried up. If we sold them for beef, all we could get was $35 or $40. So I said to Grayson, "If we send them off to the butcher, all those years of breeding will just go down the drain. We should at least sell them to someone who is going to raise them and can benefit from them."

So we talked about it, and I said, "Why don't we ask Dan and Jeanne if they're interested? If they're interested, we can fix a place in the heifer barn. Maybe we can work a deal so they can own some of the animals." We talked to them, and they came back the next day and said, "I thought you were going out of business." I said, "Let's see what happens."

We went ahead and come spring things were going great. We had not lost any heifers and had started a good bunch of animals. They were willing to work and were young legs. The first thing we knew, instead of going out of business, we were buying back machinery.

"Jeanne enjoyed milking with Larry because they both liked to talk. The back and forth was constant and about everything under the sun. Larry probably spent more time talking with Jeanne than I did because of all that milking time," says Dan, an engaging storyteller himself.

"Jeanne was unbelievable in her faith. A psychiatrist in Boston kept asking her if she wasn't bitter or mad. She said, 'No, I know where I'm going. If the Lord wants to take me that's his choice,'" says Dan of his wife's 14-month-long illness. "Even in her condition she always looked on the bright side."

So we were able to go on until 2004. By then I wanted to get out. It was getting to the point where I had had it. It had been four years since I had fallen out of the haymow and broken four ribs and a collarbone. I was laid up for six weeks and never recovered to what I was.

Grayson and I were both slowing down. We didn't need a stopwatch to tell us that. In the past, I could get a night's sleep and come back refreshed in the morning. As I got older the problem wasn't getting up early but the hours you put in the rest of the day and the next day and the next day.

My plan was to stop in April of 2004. But I decided to stay another year until Grayson was 65, when he would stop. I told Grayson that I'd get through the winter and then I'd be done.

We brought in a younger man because we needed a younger body to do those things we couldn't do. We tried to bend so he could work at his pace, but I'm sure we used to annoy Dan a little bit when we didn't run quite so fast. But there were plenty of days when all I did was run all day. I didn't walk from the house to the barn, I ran. When I went from the front of the barn to the back, I ran. That was the way you got things done. But when you work hard like that and take things from your body, you can never get them back.

I have to laugh now. Just as soon as Danny stops he stiffens right up, and he's only 46. He's not like he was either.

We were in good shape until Jeanne had her problem (June 2004). After that nothing was on schedule. Things just happened and we were like corks bobbing in the ocean. But even before Jeanne was

We couldn't pay Dan and Jeanne enough out of the milk check ($1,000 a month each), so we started cutting more and more deals. They were living in East Middlebury when they started, and it was a long trip over here. Their kids would come here after school and it would be a while before they could get home. So Danny and I worked out a deal where we would help them build a house next to the barn.

Then we helped Dan set up his repair business here. We put up the garage. In return, he contributed morning help for free, and we got first dibs on his repair time. This was a lot easier for Dan. He could walk from his house to the barn to his repair shop, which saved a lot of time.

diagnosed with leukemia they had gotten to the point where neither wanted to milk cows. Jeanne was tired from years of milking cows. She was much more interested in raising heifers.

And she would say that if they milked, Danny would always have something more important to do. "You know who will be milking the cows? Me. I'm not going to get myself in that position." I have laughed many times about that little bit of wisdom. She could see the handwriting on the wall.

When Jeanne came she said she had a reputation for talking non-stop. If she talked too much, I was to tell her. I said, "Don't worry. I can hold up my own when it comes to talking." We milked mornings together for seven years, and you could probably put the mornings we missed on one calendar's page. When you milk together, you talk about everything. Over time your whole self comes out. As they say today, you find out how the other person is wired.

With Jeanne, it feels like I've almost had a fourth daughter.

Looking back, it has worked out very well for both of us. Grayson and I kept going for another seven or eight years that we probably couldn't have done otherwise. Dan and Jeanne never had the resources to have a farm of their own. We created a way for them to get started by owning some of the animals and building up equity in the farm. By selling development rights to the Vermont Land Trust we paid off some debts and got some money for our retirement, reduced the value of the farm, and made it easier for them if they eventually wanted to buy the farm.

It was all leading that way. The only thing that changed was Jeanne's leukemia and the fact that they had gotten to the point where neither wanted to milk cows anymore.

Dan and I have spent a lot of time together since Grayson and I retired. He's made tremendous strides. He's in a position to do well selling crops, with his repair business, and with the heifers he and others are raising in the barn. They will all work together, and he won't be relying on one source of income, a milk check.

He will probably need one full-time person and probably two or three part-time people to make it all work. I have no problem believing that he will be very successful. That's really the satisfaction of these past years, seeing the farm continue.

"I used to tease Jeanne about cutting her long hair. When she'd go out, she'd have to wash and wash and wash it to get the barn smell out," Larry recalls. "She had it cut short when she was in Fletcher Allen, and at the end of chemo when her hair was falling out in clumps she had it shaved. Her hair is gone, but I told her she had the same smile."

The Spring Was Very Cold and Backward

In the 1880s, the diversified Vermont family farm was still several generations away from its specialization in dairying. Marshall Carpenter and his son Henry jointly farmed 150 acres in northern Vermont until Henry, his wife, and four children moved to the Dakota Territories in the spring of 1882. Marshall, unable to manage the farm alone, then leased the farm to Charles Hinman and his young family.

About half the acreage was hilly woodland and pasture with the rest suitable for tillage and mowing. Stock consisted of 3 horses, 13 milk cows, 10 cattle, 35 sheep, 5 hogs, and 39 chickens. The farm provided meat, milk, eggs, wheat, corn, apples, and vegetables for home consumption and butter, wool, maple sugar, and potatoes for market.

While there is no record of why the Carpenters moved, one can assume that they were attracted, like thousands of Vermonters, by the prospect of more prosperous farming in the West. In the following excerpts from a letter to his grandchildren, Marshall laments their moving before describing the news of the town and the farm.

The full letter is available in *While the Sun Shines: Making Hay in Vermont, 1789-1990* by Allen Yale, Jr.

My Dear Grand Children,

It is so long since I have written a letter that I hardly know where to begin. Now dear children do not think that in the multitude of business I have been forgetful of you, no, no, not so; not a day nor scarce a single hour passes but something brings to mind some of you and then by association all of you, I do not see your father, Frankie, and Eddie in the field, Harry about the house, or Eunice about her work. To say that we are lonesome falls far short of properly expressing our feelings....

The winter was probably the hardest one for the grass crop of any for many years. Our repeated snows, thaws, and bare ground killed almost the whole of the clover of every variety, the Red, Alsike and White all went together. We had no clover on the farm this year except on the hill where we raised Oats and Rye last year, and that was greatly injured. There is no white clover growing this year. I do not think I have seen a hundred blossoms this year in highway or pasture....

The spring was very cold and backward, and up to past the middle of June it seemed that our Hay would be a failure. But after the weather became warmer grass began to grow and thicken up, and when it was time to cut it was the handsomest crop of grass I ever saw standing. It was thick and remarkably tall and free from weeds....

Our barns were never so full before, I certainly think three or four tons more than last year. Although farmers were complaining and predicting a failure of all crops, I think the cold backward spring was our salvation, for it kept the crops from growing except by getting thoroughly rooted, and the roots well spred; whereas, if it had been dry and warm, the grass would have grown in stalks instead of root, and instead of a broad setting, would have thrown up stalk or two for seed only.

Family farm, Royalton, Vermont, 1909

Our Oat crop is of very heavy growth, and bid fair to equal that of last year. Barley a very fair but not remarkably heavy crop. Our Wheat we think extra good. Corn light, and late, will require a week or ten days to get it fairly in the milk.

We prepared the ground well and phosphated as usual. The wire worms have worked upon it as bad as they did last year. It has been the general complaint, that the worms were eating corn badly. All in all corn is doubtless a failure, so far as I can learn all through Northern Vermont, at least east of the Green Mountains and in Canada. Potatoes are looking finely but are late, tops are fresh and green, and no appearance of rust. Tubers of Early Rose and other early varieties are of fair size and beginning to cook dry and break in boiling. On account of the high prices last Spring large fields were planted. As is usual on the farm the Turnip crop bids fair now to be large. Beans and Peas are late. Peas just hardening and Beans half grown in the pod.

Apples an almost entire failure, this is emphatically an off year. All small fruits and berries scarce and poor. Strawberries some, Raspberries next to none. Our Pumpkins and Squash just in blossom, will require much warm weather to ripen them.

Now after telling you about the crops....

Our Calves are very good, I think they are very promising. They are speckled some Red and White. We have not sold our Lambs or Wool yet, Have been offered but $3.25 for our male Lambs, the Ewes we shall keep. In July we were offered 23 cts for wool, we can get but 21 or 2 for it now. Shall probably hold it till next season, Mr. Hinman likes the Cows very well, they have had plenty of feed this summer, and are in good flesh.

"Old Gray" is in very good flesh and travels better than she did last year. She has been worked quite a good deal on the harrow and has done the tedding and raking this summer and has been driven to mill and of errands more or less all summer, and has run in the pasture since about the middle of June.

The Pigs we bought of Mr. Thatcher last fall do not prove very good ones. We have fed them well but they will not weight as much by 75 to 100 lbs. as ours did last year. Now I have told you a long story, and mostly about affairs of the farm hoping you will all be interested.

Kiss Harry for Grandmother and for me, and tell him something of us, and of the farm so that he may retain something in his memory of his babyhood home.

Your Affectionate Grandfather,

M. Carpenter

Few farmers ever completely sever connections to their life's work. The Wymans were no different in their retirement and have continued to help Dan during critical planting and harvesting seasons.

This Is Our Little Piece of Vermont

GRAYSON WYMAN: Philosophers over the years have tried to define beauty. For me, looking out at a field of corn that is green and lush and growing can be the most beautiful thing in the world. You can look at a pen full of 18-month-old heifers that are all bred and think there's a beautiful pen of heifers. They're like money in the bank.

You can be chopping in the fall and look back at all that corn piling up in the wagon, and you can say when that field is all done, "Boy, that field is all chopped." It all comes back to one thing— accomplishment. In farming, there are so many ways that you can say, "I have done something. I have made an impact today."

Both Larry and I wanted to have our own little unit. This is our little piece of Vermont that we are going to manage until the next guy comes along. We wanted the independence to farm the way we wanted and to accept the results whatever they might be. That meant raising our own crops, taking care of our animals, and having a life with our families in the time that was left.

I don't want to convey that we did everything right or our way was the only way. You could put 10 people on our farm, and they would go about it 10 different ways. This was the way we did it. Heaven knows we made mistakes along the way.

I'm sure if I had a family I might have looked at our commitment differently. I know there were many times it was difficult for Larry.

He had three girls involved in school activities, and he had to give up many opportunities to see them. It wasn't until after our father died that he had much opportunity to spend time with them and that was often when they came over to the barn to help.

Once they got into college Larry had more free time than when they were at home. During those grade school and high school years, we were plugging away trying to make advances. We were young and vigorous and hoped that down the road we could reap the benefits, hire help, and have some time off. I realized all along that Larry and his family made a sacrifice. That's the truth of it. I didn't have to because I didn't have a family.

I'd be a fool to say I never had second thoughts about farming. Everybody has their days. We had days when we absolutely hit bottom and wondered if we were ever going to make it back up. There were nights when we sat down for supper and asked, "What in thunderation did we do today? We got absolutely nothing done. This broke and that broke and that went wrong."

I couldn't say I ever tossed and turned much at night. Usually by that time I was so dead tired that I was lucky if I got by supper without falling asleep. But you wouldn't be human if things didn't play on you. Basically, we tried to get back to where we were. If we did that by the end of the day, that in itself was an accomplishment.

Then there were days when we finished milking and went to the house and could say, "I can't believe the amount we accomplished today. Everything went right." I appreciated that sense of accomplishment, even when I was flat worn out, more than anything else. You knew that at the end of the year you had all winter to get your stamina built up for another season.

It used to be that people farmed longer. When we were in Brownsville we had a neighbor who was 73 or 74. He was very frail and had to go into the hospital for a gall bladder operation, but he didn't want to sell his herd. He asked if we would milk them for him. So we moved his cows into our barn and our heifers into his barn and milked his herd from November to March.

People don't hold on like that today, primarily because the business has changed. He had a little bitty herd, probably 12 to 15 cows, and it was more something to do.

"What do you want to do? You're the boss," Dan would ask at the end of field and cow deliberations. But decisions increasingly became consensus decisions, as the Kehoes prepared to take over the farm.

When your stamina runs out and farming is more than your body can stand, then it is time to call it quits. At the end, Larry and I felt that we were more than 50% dependent on others. When you can't put at least 50% into it, then it is time to stop. ❧

"Dan liked to line up the rows by eye when he planted, and he was good at it. When you harvested the rows, they would be right on with no overlap," Grayson recalls of Dan's low-tech approach to corn planting. The only drawback was a very stiff neck.

I Don't Know What the Next Step Is Going to Be

DAN KEHOE: When Jeanne and I got married in 1982, we figured if there was ever an opportunity to get back into farming we would. We needed a situation where somebody needed help and they worked you into the business. There was no way we could start on our own. We had been looking for years and meeting Larry and Grayson just kind of happened. If we hadn't met them, we probably wouldn't be in farming.

Both Jeanne and I had grown up on dairy farms. She grew up milking and doing chores on a Bridport farm, where they milked 80 or 90 cows. It's organic now, and her parents still run it. I grew up on a farm in Shoreham. We had 80 tillable acres of good corn land and rented another 200 acres. We milked about 70 and had about 140 head altogether.

My older brother died of cancer when he was 19, and I started doing a lot of the chores when he was in the hospital. I was in the 2nd grade then and my sister was in the 5th. We milked the cows and cleaned the barn while my parents were at the hospital. We machine milked into buckets and carried them into the milk room. We did that for a year and a half while my brother was sick, and then we just kept on.

We got up at 4 a.m for chores and got on the bus at 7:45. At night we'd get home from school at 3:30 and it'd be 8:30 to 9 before we were through. Being in the barn was nothing new. I'd been helping out since I was 4 or 5 when I'd sweep the feed back to the cows with a broom. My dad had farmer's lung, and by the time I was in junior high, he couldn't do much. From then on, my sister and I basically ran the farm.

When my younger brother David got old enough to help with milking, I stopped milking and did all the fieldwork. I'd feed the cows in the afternoon and then would work in the fields into the night. Usually I'd harrow at night and plant during the day. Sometimes it would be 1:00 or 2:00 before I quit. I'd get a couple hours of sleep and then start planting.

I loved driving tractors. When you're working a big piece in the middle of night and it's dark all around, it's just very peaceful. I was 16, 17 then and figured I couldn't afford to go to college, so I took lots of ag classes at the vocational center in Middlebury. I slept a lot during class, but I pulled off an A average. Ag courses just came easy to me. I had enough credits to graduate from high school in January of 1978 and began running the farm full time then with my sister and younger brother.

We grew up to be workaholics and had no idea if we were underworked or overworked. I had nothing to compare it to; we just thought that was the way life was. Looking back, we never had a childhood. We had to grow up fast because of my brother and were thrown into the adult world.

But we had fun. When we were putting up hay, we would have contests to see who could stack the most layers of hay on the flatbed trucks and get it to the barn without any bales falling off. We'd stack the bales like a set of stairs and just kept adding more until we had 10 to 12 layers. If you tell people that's your idea of fun, they think you're nuts. But that was fun to us.

Our big day out was on Memorial Day when we brought flowers to the family cemetery in Rutland. We'd stop and get a foot-long hot dog with a six-inch long bun. It was no great deal, but to us it was a big treat.

We made a living, but it wasn't anything to brag about. We weren't making enough to hire someone. I stayed on the farm until just before I got married, when I left to work on a small dairy farm in Shoreham because I needed money to get my own place.

My sister and I were supporting my father, and the farm just couldn't generate enough income to support another family. I was only getting paid $25 every two weeks. I was living at home and never went anywhere, so it didn't make any difference.

My younger brother was old enough then to help, but about two years after I left they ended up selling the farm. Milk prices were bad, and they got to a point where farming wasn't worth it anymore. My sister got married and farmed with her husband in Castleton. The farm was sold to a sheep farmer, and he sold three or four building lots. A neighboring farm rents the land now.

I didn't meet Jeanne until she was 19. We were buying feed from one of her neighbors, and our tractor got stuck. We borrowed their four-wheel-drive tractor, and after that the farmer's son set us up on a blind date. So we went roller skating. I'd never been roller skating in my life. I had never even been on a date. Girls were the furthest thing from my mind. But we went out and hit it off. On our first date, we talked about barn cleaners and having your hands smell for

"When you go into farming, you'll have good years and bad years and you're going to have to ride out the whole thing. If you think short-term, you'll lose your shirt," says Dan of the roller-coaster economics of dairying.

days before you could eat a sandwich and not have it taste of barn cleaner. She could relate to that.

After we got married I worked for Wood Brothers Orchards for seven years. This was Jeanne's grandfather's business. I went that route because they had health insurance. It was still farming, but it wasn't dairy farming. It was apples.

In 1989, I went out on my own, working on my farm machinery repair business. I'd been working at the orchard during the day and was building my farm machinery repair business at night. I probably worked four years on the side and built up a clientele of 20 to 25 farms before I left the orchard. Back then I was working for $5 an hour, which was good money, but I thought I could make more money on my own.

Jeanne worked in the orchard and farm stand in the fall. And we always had milking jobs on weekends, relief milking. So for those seven years, I was working at the orchard, doing my repair business at night, and milking on weekends. I was probably working 18 hours a day because I was trying to build the business. Some days I wouldn't get home until 2 in the morning.

In the early 1990s, I went to work for Roger Stowe at his New Haven dairy farm. It got to the point where farmers couldn't pay me for my repair work. It was the same old story. It's not that they didn't want to but that the price of milk was down and they couldn't. At Roger's I did his field and shop work and had my road service business on the side. I also did his breeding and worked with his feed program.

One summer I worked 120 hours a week for him for six weeks when he had lost two men. My shortest week was 118 hours and longest, 126. He was short of help and had extra land that needed to be cropped. That's like working two and a half jobs, but I was getting paid $10 an hour so I made a lot of money. I tell my kids about those days, and they don't believe it.

In 1993, I wanted to go back on my own, and Jeanne and I moved to Bridport where we did morning chores for a dairy farmer in return for the use of a house. I still did a lot of Roger's repair work and learned about Larry and Grayson needing help from him.

I stopped in and Larry was washing the bulk tank. I told him my wife was looking for work. Larry rolled his eyes. Up to that point, they hadn't had very good help. They'd offer help $50 extra just to show up for four milkings in a row. And they wouldn't.

They thought that they had scraped the bottom of the barrel and were about to cash in. We came along and said if you want to milk for another year, we would help you get through. We really didn't think about what would develop when we started. It just felt like the right thing to do. We never had anything in writing. It was just a handshake.

When we started, I milked in the afternoon with Larry or Grayson and Jeanne milked in the morning with Larry. At the start one of them was always milking or doing chores with one of us. It was probably a couple years before they felt comfortable leaving us alone so both could take the same day off. I can understand that because this was their whole livelihood. But we always treated the farm as if it were our own. That was the way we worked. We didn't say when the cat's away the mice will play.

We commuted from East Middlebury for the first year, and then they came to us and said things were working out and would we be interested in staying. Their debts were low and financially they could keep on, but they didn't have the physical energy to keep the farm going. They couldn't afford to pay both Jeanne and me a lot from the milk check, but would we be interested in raising heifers on halves? We'd each own half of the new heifers, which would help us build some equity in the farm. So we started raising heifers on halves.

Then they advanced us $4,000 for the down payment on our house, which we paid off weekly, so we didn't have to commute. Then they put up the garage for my repair business. The garage is 42 by 60 and 18 high and cost $45,000. In return I did morning chores for seven years. The shop paid for itself on the repairs I did on their equipment and worked out well for me. I still did road service but unlike when we were in East Middlebury I now had a garage, too.

The Kehoes brought young legs to the physical demands of dairying. Dan also brought his jack-of-all-trades skills—
feeding, field work, milking, machinery repair, and welding, here a new water trough in the heifer barn.

After we had been here a couple years, it felt like we had been here half our life. It felt like home right from the start. We all had the same goal, to get the most out of the cows. We all knew what needed to be done and picked up the slack.

Sometimes we got frustrated with each other. They were getting ready to stop and didn't want to spend a lot of money. We had to stay within a certain budget and work around it, but we never let it get in the way of what needed to be done. It was like dealing with your father all over again, except having two of them. To get an idea across, you had to prove it to them. But they were open.

I see a lot of different farms in my road service. What works for one farm won't work for another. Each farm is its own situation.

"If my boy joins me, I'll probably keep milking," Dan once thought, here hitching a hay wagon with son Jay. "Right now he's making pretty good money working construction but that can be seasonal. A milk check is steady."

The barn is different. The land is different. The cattle are different. When I came they didn't have a mixing wagon with a scale. They had a superior herd, and I thought we could get more out of the cows if we were more precise in how much hay and corn silage and grain we were giving them. Cows are creatures of habit and don't like change. If you give them what they like and balance it for what they need in their lactation cycle, you can get more milk.

We needed another mixing wagon, so I bought one with money I made from the shop. That was the way we went at it. When we needed something, like trucks to haul feed or our second manure spreader, I bought them. It was investment for me, building equity in the farm, and it helped them.

If Jeanne were still here, I think we'd be milking cows but only 50 or 60. Jeanne could handle that comfortably. She would do all the milking. I'd do all the feeding. We'd talked about taking the east end of the barn and turning it into a milking parlor. We would have farmed it totally different. I would have run the repair business, and the milk check would be a side business.

It's taken me a little time to regroup from Jeanne's death, and I'm taking it one year at a time. Right now, I have five or six different ways to make money. I'm leasing the farm and rent out the calf barn to a fellow who helps me with chores for the rent. We're raising veal and beef and have our own label, Run Free Meats of Weybridge. I'm raising replacement dairy heifers, have the shop, and am cropping the land and selling what I don't need. If I had to depend on a milk check, I'd be out of farming. There's not enough money in it.

If I didn't farm, I could concentrate on repair work and make a good living. But farming gets in your blood. Part of it is the variety. If I worked just on machinery, I'd get sick of that. If I worked just with cows, I'd get sick of them. But when you mix it all together, you're an electrician one day, a plumber the next; you're a vet, a feed analyst, and a mechanic.

Every day is a challenge. Every spring is a new beginning. After a rough winter, you have another opportunity to put up better feed and make more milk if you hustle.

But when I get a little older I might not feel that way. Larry and Grayson probably thought it was challenging when they were younger, but when they got older it wasn't so much fun. I'm getting to the age when it's not going to be as much fun. I still enjoy farming, but we all have our days and wonder whether it's worth it.

On a megafarm you can work a little longer because you're doing more managing and not as much physical labor. But you have to milk 200 to 300 cows to afford someone just to milk, someone to do just fieldwork. Do-it-all farmers like the Wymans with 100 to 150 cows are a dying breed. Younger people aren't going to put in their hours because they can make a better living doing something else.

A lot of younger farmers don't realize that farming is like a roller coaster. You have good years and bad years, and you're going to have to ride out the whole thing. We're going through some tough times now. The smart farmers who survive will be the ones who will be around for a long time. You're not going to get rich, but if you push your pencil you can make a good living and build some equity.

Working with the Wymans was the "slickest thing I have ever seen" was Dan's assessment of the seven years that he and Jeanne milked with Larry and Grayson. "We were all pulling in the same direction."

But sooner or later you'll have to sell and pay Uncle Sam.

I'm not in a position now where I can buy the farm. The way the economy is, I don't know if that's a good idea anyway. But this is a good farm in a good location with a lot of road frontage. It's not way off in God's country.

We haven't really haven't talked about it that much. Larry and Grayson have said they're happy with the way things are going and are in no rush. ✺

Expiration Date

"My plan is to have no plans," Larry reflected on the freedom that began with retirement. After 46 years of days defined by morning and afternoon milkings, Larry closed the milk house door the morning of the 31st with a simple farewell, "It's history."

Thursday, March 31, 2005, "expiration date" as Larry calls it, is little different from the routine of the Wymans' roughly 16,000 other morning milkings. Muck the stalls, milk the cows, spread the day's feed, clean the milking equipment. Over the past two days, Dan has come up with a temporary fix for the mixing wagon whose augur had broken on Monday. Just before morning feeding, Dan, Grayson, and Jay push a conveyor belt system, worthy of Rube Goldberg, across the road.

Sam DeVries will drop off a load of their feed, a slight modification of the Wymans' mixture, as the DeVries will begin milking the herd that afternoon. In the afternoon, Dan will unload 600 bales from the haymow; a Maine feed dealer has several horse ranches that need resupplying, and the Wymans, with no herd now to feed, have more than they need.

A typical day. There will be no hoopla. No gold watches. No end-of-era speeches.

For the first time in seven months, Jeanne visits the barn. No one suggests that she leave.

"They don't remember me, but I remember them," says Jeanne, walking the aisles, her baseball cap covering reddish hair that has begun to grow back and is now curly short rather than straight long. A painter's mask covers chipmunk-chubby cheeks, swollen by steroids.

Much like farm kids in the 4-H barn at the annual summer fair, Jeanne has a throwaway camera. There's a shot of Dan milking. Not quite his last. He will milk with Sam and Dave DeVries in the afternoon and give them a rundown on the herd's milking quirks.

There are shots of Larry and Grayson and shots of Bunker and a handful of other favorite cows. And there is a stream of comments as she moves up and down the center aisle. If cows were vain, they would be puffed up with vanity.

"You're absolutely gorgeous."

"Larry, they look beautiful."

"You look so much bigger than the last time I saw you."

And if they were sensitive, there would be a lot of hurt feelings.

"Remember 550?" Grayson asks.

"Oh, yes."

"She's just as pokey milking out as ever."

"Remember the one with the glass udder? We shipped her to Cabot."

"How's her quarter?"

"Still a problem."

"Remember me? You look a little bigger than the last time I saw you." Seven months after her last milking, Jeanne said hello and goodbye to a barn full of milkers.

"The first time I washed the tank was in April of 1962. We have washed it every day except for two in 1968 when we moved the herd to Weybridge," says Larry. "It was a year old when we bought it, so I'd say we've gotten our money's worth."

"We came this close to shipping Matthew. We had thrown the book at her to get her healthy. Finally we said she'd either have to sink or swim. She came back and bred on time. We shipped Continental this week. She had a hard time getting up and down," says Grayson.

"This one wanted to snuggle. She pinned me to the wall in the free stall, and I had to holler for you and Larry."

"There's no sense of looking in the calf barn now, I wouldn't know any of them," says Jeanne, acknowledging her long absence.

"Larry, how'd last night's milking go with Grayson?"

"Fine. I asked him if he was going to write in his diary, 'I've done my last milking.' He didn't even crack a smile that's how much I impressed him."

"I suppose if this were the movies, I'd ride off into the sunset," Grayson had quipped the previous evening upon leaving the barn.

Larry did not ride off into the sunset either, but he did record March 31 events in his DayMinder. *Weather data*—35 at 4 a.m., sunny 50s with a south wind. *Milk production*—5,343 pounds. *Chores*—clean feed alleys, wash two bulk milk tanks, clean heifer barn. There were notes on Jeanne's barn visit, the sale of a tractor trailer's load of hay out of the mow, and a farmer's visit to look at Dan's open heifers.

There was no indication after months of anticipation that this was their final milking.

"Bev here with a hug after milking," ends the Day-Minder listing.

Expiration Date

"What a relief," Bev Wyman emailed to distant family on the last day of milking. "I guess I didn't know how worried I was that the cows would outlast them. I stopped at the barn on my way to work, and Dad was just coming through the milkroom. He had milked his last cow, and he was walking out. Better than any action movie with the hero walking out of the flames. I gave him a big hug, and we both cried. I found Grayson pouring milk on a giant bowl of cereal. He had milked his last cow last night. He's already smiling."

March 2005: You Don't See a Light in the Morning

Every farmer hopes to cash out when demand is strong and prices are good, but many are forced to sell at distress prices. With the mad cow disease outbreak in Canada cutting off imports and strong demand from the booming Western dairying states and Vermont megafarms, the Wymans will be selling their herd in good times.

The DeVries, a father-son operation in neighboring Bridport, had asked for first dibs and had offered the highest bid and will be taking all the cows and heifers. Like the Wymans, the DeVries have a breed-your-own-cows philosophy and know the herd well—the Wymans' breeding technician, Paul Barrett, milks cows for them. In a by-the-numbers business with little room for sentiment, the Wymans will not sell

Barn smells linger. "One of the first things I'll do is take the truck to the car wash and really clean and vacuum it," said Grayson of his immediate retirement plans. "Then I'll take the vinyl off the front seat. I'll tell you I won't miss sitting on cold vinyl in the winter."

one cow. Bunker, the first heifer that Jeanne raised and that Arrin, their daughter, had shown at 4-H, is now 9 years old, Methuselah-age by today's standards. After freshening in June, she will be dried off and put out to pasture. That is unless Larry wants to continue milking her, Dan teases.

"Bunker will be a pet, an expensive pet," says Dan.

Dan, who has been building equity in the farm, will also not sell his half share of the farm's heifers. They are a good cash crop, and he will sell them at peak value, when they are ready to freshen. Unlike the ups and downs of previous months, Jeanne has had a largely uneventful March. With barn work prohibited, she is considering a home occupation, possibly custom sewing.

Farming can be a solitary business. The contract manure spreader, vet, or milk pick-up man, however harried and behind schedule, is expected to tarry for at least a few words of community farm intelligence. Who's selling out? Who's getting bigger? How long will milk prices stay up or down? Who has their corn in? Who's finished their second cutting? What's hay selling for?

Farmers can be famously taciturn with strangers. Yups and nopes is the image. How do you explain a life that is so foreign to those with limited first-hand knowledge of what it takes to produce a gallon of milk? How do you explain the in-your-bones attraction of near-constant 16-hour days, 365-days-a-year labor to neighbors who work 37.5 hours a week with paid vacations and benefits? And how do you explain the brutal economics of the family farm and the toll that a lifetime of physical work takes on knees, backs, and every joint?

April 2005:
I Do What Strikes My Fancy

For the most part, farmers don't bother. There is too much to explain.

With colleagues, there is no need to explain. Many have grown up or worked on a farm. In this like-minded community, much can be conveyed without saying much. With the end of milking in sight, vendors are tarrying longer than normal and summing up, albeit in understated fashion, relationships that go back decades.

Vet Don Hunt started practicing in Addison County in 1964 and has known the Wymans for many of those years. At the end of March, after a final pregnancy check of several bred cows and the dehorning of seven heifers, a final reminisce with Grayson is in order.

Don: When I started out I might visit 20 farms in a day. That first year in practice, I put 75,000 miles on my car. The IRS couldn't believe it when I depreciated it. Today, I might visit two farms in a day. I see just as many cows. I just don't travel as much.

Grayson: I can remember the IRS asking us how many hours a day we worked. I said 16 to 17 hours. They said you can't be serious. They should have asked how many hours we didn't work.

Grayson: I can remember driving up 22A early in the morning to Burlington and seeing lights on all these little farms. Now you don't see a light in the morning.

Don: Each of those farms supported a family. It may not have been a great income, but a lot of good kids grew up on those farms.

Stories are legion about the difficult transition that dairy farmers—defined by a lifetime of seven-day work weeks—have in adjusting to retirement. Grayson has house and spring barn cleanup—spreading four months of manure—on his immediate list. Fishing starts May 1, lots of it, he hopes.

Larry doesn't see idleness as a problem. "My schedules are all over. In the past, the cows always came first. Now, I do what strikes my fancy. If I want to go to an auction with Dan, I can go. If I want to go to my grandson's lacrosse game, I can go. If I want to work in the garden, I do."

And with rest Larry hopes that his knees will have a few bends left. "My dream of hiking the Appalachian Trail from Maine to Georgia probably isn't in the cards, but I should be able to get up Mt. Abe and Camel's Hump and Mansfield." But extensive hiking, fishing, and traveling will have to wait.

Both Larry and Grayson, as expected, have not severed all ties to the farm. They will help Dan with the fieldwork and planting. While heifers do not require as much feed as milkers, Dan will not cut back on planting. What he doesn't need, he will sell.

Given the uncertainties of the past nine months, only one thing is clear: Larry and Grayson won't be milking. But many questions remain.

How will Dan, who will be leasing the barn and fields and wants to buy the farm eventually, get from here to there?

At the moment, there is good money in raising heifers. But will it continue?

Forget milking. A biweekly milk check is welcome cash flow, but milking soaks up too much of the day, especially if milk prices return to rock-bottom, below-cost levels.

Not quite the back 40, but with retirement Larry now had the time to expand the back garden, repair the garage, and put in a new wood-burning heating system.

Dan sells all his heifers after being offered a price too good to refuse, with one group headed for Texas. On the 11th, Grayson begins spreading manure on the fields.

Larry has been clearing brush and old fence posts for a new garden behind the house. "It's amazing how much work you can get done when you don't have to steal an hour here and hour there," says Larry of milking-free days.

But the largest unknown remains. Will Jeanne's remission continue? Recent months have been encouraging, but doctors caution that it will require at least another year to determine how well her body has accepted a new immune system.

Help. His brother-in-law, Chris Welch, is an all-around farm handyman. He can milk, fix a tractor, plant a field, and chop the corn. Will he be interested in working full-time?

His son, Jay. At the moment, Dan cannot come close to matching the hourly wage he makes in construction.

Activity around the barn will slow down, but not much. The DeVries' plans to build a barn to house the Wyman herd has fallen through, in part because the builder broke his leg. They are now looking for a barn to rent. Until they find housing, the DeVries will lease the Wyman barn and milk the herd there.

In early April, a Boston checkup indicates that all blood counts look good. Three weeks later the counts look bad. A sinus infection has led to further blood tests, which show a return of her leukemia. Her new immune system has failed. With her body battered by past chemotherapies and extensive full-body radiation, another round of aggressive treatment isn't possible.

Fletcher Allen begins light chemotherapy on the 26th in hopes of slowing the progression of the disease. The prognosis? Two to six months.

Chapter 10

The Family Farm's Future

Farming Has Always Been A Struggle

In the fall of 2006, several members of the Vermont House and Senate agricultural committees held a series of hearings around the state seeking the farming community's ideas on what was and wasn't working in agricultural policy. What could the state, the legislators asked, do both short and long term to provide some price stability for dairy farmers, help stem the loss of family farms, and support all forms of agriculture?

The three hearings followed a particularly difficult year during which recent stronger milk prices had slumped more than 30% to record lows. These low prices coupled with increased energy costs were rippling through nearly all a farm's operating expenses—fertilizers, feed, fuel, transportation, and electricity.

And to create a triple whammy, Vermont's record wet spring had killed or drastically stunted the corn crop of farms around the state. Many farmers were scrambling to find forage for the winter and faced 30% to 50% increases in their feed bills.

Addison County, with its poorly draining clay soils, had been especially hard hit, with many farmers' yields cut in half and more. Not surprisingly, the Addison County hearing was short on optimism for a quick fix and long on the problems the industry faced: the difficulty of finding labor,

aging farm owners, the financial struggles of some vendors that threatened to thin the essential infrastructure in the state's most productive agricultural region, and the high cost of workers' compensation.

The good news was everyone agreed that agriculture was too important to fail. Agriculture generated one out of every six dollars in the state's economy and employed about 15% of the state's workforce in farm and farm-related jobs, about two-thirds in wholesale and retail food businesses.

Each cow could be viewed as a mini-business, generating $14,000 in economic activity annually. Dairying also kept land open, which is critical to the preservation of Vermont's iconic rural image and the health of the tourism industry.

To help farmers ride out the current down period, the state legislature had approved an $8.6 million cash assistance program that would add about $1 per 100 pounds of milk to farmers' milk checks beginning in July. Governor James Douglas, working with the state's Congressional delegation, had also recently asked the U.S. Agriculture Secretary to declare farmers in all the state's counties eligible for federal emergency assistance in the form of low-interest loans. And the Congressional delegation had requested funding in the next Agricultural Appropriations Act for cash grants to help farmers pay for increased feed costs.

Can you start small today? Yes, it's possible but very difficult, says feed dealer Jim Bushey, a member of the 2005 Vermont Dairy Task Force on the future of dairy farming. "It's a major investment, and it's awfully hard to borrow a lot of money for the return you get."

There are hands-on farmers, like the Wymans, who don't want to get bigger than 100 to 150 cows. But once that 100-hour-a-week generation is gone, that farm size is over, say family farm observers. Segregating jobs, specializing, and having time off require the economies of scale of 300 to 400 cow herds.

To underscore that trend, the report charted milk prices from 1995 to 2005. The resulting jagged line resembled the path of a pogo stick, with one year's 10% to 20% increase followed by an even bigger drop the next year. (Cornell researchers, in studying milk price volatility, have charted a 33-month boom-bust cycle. The financial roller coaster would only worsen with 2009's below-cost milk prices, as much as 50% lower than strong 2008 milk prices.)

Over that 10-year period, the number of dairy farms had declined from 2,047 to 1,259, and the number of cows from 157,000 to 143,000. Yet milk production had remained relatively constant at 2.5 to 2.7 billion pounds, reflecting the increased productivity of cows and the absorption of smaller farms by neighbors.

Average herd size had grown from 75 cows to an estimated 114 cows, with more than 12% of Vermont's farms now having over 200 cows. These larger farms were producing over 60% of the state's milk.

In New England, Vermont continued as the region's dairy heavyweight, producing more milk than the other five states combined—with over 80% of the state's production exported as fluid milk or manufactured products, such as cheese, yogurt, and ice cream. In the larger national picture, Vermont remains a middleweight at best, producing less than 1.5% of the nation's milk supply, ranking 15th in milk volume.

Vermont, the task force recommended, should work with its much larger Northeast neighbors, New York and Pennsylvania, then the country's 3rd and 4th largest milk producers, in developing

Those initiatives helped with the short-term crisis. In December of 2005, the Dairy Task Force, a 36-member group appointed by the governor, representing a cross-section of Vermont agricultural interests, had issued its recommendations on longer-term strategies to strengthen the dairy industry. A central finding was no surprise:

> Milk price volatility presents the largest hurdle for all dairy farmers making it difficult to budget and to make financial decisions that affect the farm. Milk price volatility has increased in both frequency and amplitude with little indication of a change in that trend.

regional solutions to the industry's challenges. Closer to home, four task force committees—Business Management; Economic Development; Government, Community Relations, and Information; and Education—were to develop detailed plans to increase farm profitability and the number of dairy cows, to attract new dairy processors, and to educate the public on the importance of agriculture to Vermont.

While the report did not look at national trends, Vermont's changes have roughly paralleled, as noted earlier, those at the national level. Since 1992, the number of commercial dairy farms nationwide has declined 53% from 131,000 in 1992 to 62,000 in 2006. The Northeast lost fewer cows, 17%, during this period than the Midwest, 23%, or the Southeast, 44%. But these regions' losses were offset by the explosion of dairying in the West, where the number of cows increased by 49%, with average herd size increasing from 263 to 706.

Agricultural historians and economists looking at the challenges of the past 10 years would see many parallels in the dairy industry's and family farm's past. Nearly 100 years ago, the Commission on Country Life in a 1909 report to President Roosevelt described the troubled future of agriculture:

> Agriculture is not commercially as profitable as it is entitled to be for the labor and energy that the farmer expends and the risks that he assumes....The farmer is almost necessarily handicapped in the development of his business, because his capital is small…and he usually stands practically alone against organized interests.

Historians would also note that in some eras, such as the Great Depression, which led to the creation of government price support programs, economic threats to the family farm were far greater than they are now. At the low points of the Depression, Vermont dairy farmers were receiving two cents a quart for their milk and the average dairy farm was operating on less than $50 a month.

Library shelves are full of monographs that trace the family farm's evolution decade by decade from labor-intensive, small-plot, diversi-

fied agriculture that fed one's family and a handful of others to today's capital- and technology-intensive agribusiness where a farm's economic survival is determined not just by regional prices but by national and global regulations and market developments. Vermont family farms have not escaped these developments; they are far fewer, as noted, much bigger, and vastly more productive than their predecessors. But Vermont dairy farms, unlike industrialized agriculture—think city-sized beef cattle feedlots in the West—have remained family and extended family operations. This long view, however, is of little solace to today's struggling farmer.

Larry and Grayson Wyman, their milking days over, did not attend the legislators' hearing—few dairy farmers could. As one legislator noted, most dairy farmers were still working when the evening hearing started at 6:30. But they would have been quite at home during the discussion. Long hours and low margins, labor shortages and unpredictable weather, constant technological change and price volatility, Larry and Grayson would have concurred, have been and will continue to be unrelenting challenges to the family farm's survival.

But Larry and Grayson would also argue, as they do in the following narratives, that the family farm, whatever its future, can be a fulfilling way of life. ❧

The trend, larger but fewer dairy farms, is likely to continue, say economists, with very large farms in Addison, Franklin, and Orleans counties and smaller farms elsewhere.

Maybe I Am a Lucky Guy!

LARRY WYMAN: Family farms are a losing battle. Very definitely. Megafarms will produce food for a long time. I'm sure they will. But as far as small family farms, the 100-cow herds, are concerned, I don't see many surviving. The past couple years have been really rough and a lot of farms have disappeared. In the future, I don't think 100 cows will be enough to support a family. That doesn't mean that some won't survive, but it will be hard unless you have a good operation and low debt load.

Even if I were 40, I'd think the same way. In the last five, six years, Grayson and I could see rules and regulations and expenses coming along and were glad that we were getting out. They were going to be the last nail in the casket. Environmental restrictions from the federal Clean Water Act, for one, are getting more stringent all the time. You need a certified planner like an extension agent or a feed company rep now to draw up the plan for your manure management. Regulations haven't changed the way we do things that much, but it's just another expense.

And it seems like every time you turn around there is a new regulation, like the state's proposal that you have to register all your animals. They sound insignificant, but they compound our problems and are expensive for small farms. And oil prices are a bigger issue on the farm than anyone even begins to think about. If you think that we have a problem with oil costs today, you haven't seen anything. Wait until you see your grocery bill.

If the family farm is going to survive, the first requirement is finding people who want to work the hours that it takes. You'll find some. You always do. But it's a real challenge when your kids say, "So and so has just gone to Disneyland, why can't we?" "They're going to the lake swimming, why can't we?" Farmers will say why work 80 hours a week for little or nothing when I can find a 40-hour-a-week job.

Maybe I won't be able to live off that job, but I'll have a few hours to do something else. People don't want to work the hours of a farmer today. If you didn't have Mexicans, where would these big farms be?

Family farms have been the heart of many rural communities, but it is getting to the point where they are part of another phase of Vermont history. Vermont is nowhere near where it was when we came here 50 years ago. It's as different as chalk and cheese. Go to Windsor County. Heavens and earth it's not the same. You notice right off the bat that there are not only many, many more homes in fields but that wide open spaces have grown up.

I can remember driving up Route 7 as a kid and seeing farm after farm after farm. Today, you see remnants of farms and farm buildings here and there. That's what it's going to be. Addison and Franklin and maybe Orleans will be the last of the strongholds. That's where the services are and will be.

No, I don't think I'm dead wrong about the future of family farms. There is no question that we are moving to the megafarm in Addison County. Your megafarms that can spread their costs over a lot more animals will eventually drive the smaller farmer out of business.

Some farms grow because they have to support several families, but why not diversify out of agriculture rather than create more milk and drive the price down. If I were 35 or 40 and had a 100-cow farm that was relatively successful, I wouldn't put money back into more and bigger. I'd take that money and roll it over into another business that could be totally unrelated to farming, even if I had to hire someone to operate it.

Farming for some has become less a "way of life" than a short-term "economic investment." Sustainable farming requires a healthy long-term relationship with the land, one's neighbors, and the larger economic community. The Wymans always managed for this triple bottom line. Larry, above, maintained a wood lot for winter heating.

My feeling is that there's a surplus of milk. Why create more? Allow others to continue to farm just as we did. Very few farmers today think along the lines that we did. If they're not making that transition to bigger and bigger, they think that they won't be able to make the grade when milk prices drop.

That's where we're headed. But the big surpluses aren't in the East, they are in the West and Midwest. Some states are way over what they were a year ago, not 1% or 2% but 10% to 12%. The day will come when more and more farms in the Northeast are gone, then we will see Midwest milk being shipped to Boston.

We're our own worst enemies. We produce more than the market can absorb. Yet we need to make more in order to pay our costs, which we can't control. We buy oil, seed, fertilizers, and services on the open market and pay top dollar for them.

In bad years we had to figure out how to pay our bills, day by day. We had taxes to pay. The vet and the breeding technician and the grain company wanted their money and had a right to it. You paid them and hoped there might be something left for you.

Grayson and I have always been very conservative, but it's rough when milk prices are so ridiculously low. A few years ago the price dropped way down and government under its Milk Income Loss Contract program promised to help. We were promised help in February, but we didn't get a check until the fall. Until you have been there you can't fully appreciate what it's like to work hard, produce a product, and not get the price you were promised.

You only hope you can make enough money when milk prices are good to compensate for bad years. When you can't, you're all done.

I'm not so sure that a lot of people moving into the state aren't just as happy to see farms go by the wayside. There are fewer tractors they have to follow on the way to town. Fewer fields with smelly manure.

I bet many people wouldn't give a rip if there were a farm in the state. I don't think they care.

Why would they? They have what they want. And you have people moving into the state and people who live here with little knowledge of dairying. They won't have the same feeling for family farms that Vermonters once had.

But I have no regrets. I grew up in New Jersey and always wanted to live in Vermont. I never envied people with 9-to-5 jobs. I didn't worry about time off, traveling here and traveling there. I can honestly say those things never played on my mind.

Dan and I and Grayson would shake our heads every so often and ask, "What are we doing this for?" Then we'd laugh and say, "Because we have had some of the best times anyone could ever have had." People just can't understand how farming can be any fun when you face 100 animals every day, have machinery breakdowns and terrible weather. What they don't see is the satisfaction that we see in our crops and breeding and how they all come together in the milk tank.

When Grayson and I got discouraged, we'd look back at the problems we used to have and how far we'd come. When you look at it that way, you figure that you can find a way around anything that gets thrown at you. My feeling is that if you can't make it farming then you should do something else. No one is forcing you to do something that you don't like.

I can remember one time a fellow stopped at the farm, and there were three or four fellows in the truck's cab. As they left, one of them said, "Boy, what I wouldn't give to have what those two fellows have. A barn that's full of cows and the land that goes with it."

I can remember him saying those things just as plain as anything. And I thought, "My God, there is actually someone out there who envies me and what I have! Maybe I am a lucky guy!"

The state's declining milk production, a 4% drop between 2002 and 2006, must be reversed to maintain farming infrastructure and to meet the demand of in-state and out-of-state processing plants, the Vermont Milk Commission reported following a 2007 study. Above, Larry on top of the haylage bunk.

Richmond, Vermont, 1860-1900

And What of Tomorrow?

Does the wealth of the state consist in her commerce? No. Vermont is an inland state and Lake Champlain and its outlets offer but small opportunities for the carrying trade. Are manufactures her chief reliance? There are no beds of coal within her borders for convenient steam power, and the streams are too far away from the maritime ports to base a hope upon them as a source of prosperity.

So then, as neither the winds of heaven will waft our commerce, nor the waters of our streams furnish an industry for our whole people, we must turn to the earth as the source of Vermont's prosperity.

The yesterday of Vermont agriculture is gone. Its dawn witnessed the pioneer farmer cutting his swath of timber with his ax, that his ground might be ready to yield him a crop whose harvest may be gathered by the sickles' gentler strokes. Rude were the implements, rude the agriculture, but abundant were the crops.

Today (1880) we have within the limits of the state near four and a half million acres of land, over three millions of which are improved, making in round numbers, thirty-four thousand farms of one hundred and thirty-four acres each, and valued at one hundred and thirty nine millions of dollars.

Let us ask ourselves whether from this moment we shall advance or recede?

Let us look at our discouragements.

Our acres are depleted. Our native people are replaced by foreigners. Our rural towns are becoming depopulated. Our families are smaller. We are wasteful in our habits, and lack economy on our farms. In spite of all our discouragements the census of the United States shows that Vermont has, decade after decade, been advancing with steady step.

We must make the most of her rugged mountains, and use to the utmost her fertile valleys. This soil has that staying or enduring quality, which renders it next to inexhaustible.

Her hillsides though less productive, still afford the sweetest pasturage for flocks and herds, and the sheep, the horses, and the cows of Vermont have a well-earned and valuable reputation throughout the Union.

And what of tomorrow? As today, but more abundant — yes, as double, and, not in the far future, as treble.

To bring up our agricultural income to the highest point of productiveness there must be a combination of capital, science, skill, industry and economy. While Vermont is fully abreast and even ahead of many of the states, ought we to be satisfied with the present yield of our crops?

It is well known that one large item of income is the hay crop, worth ten millions a year. There is not the slightest room for doubt that the judicious selection and mingling of seed with proper manuring of fields would raise this yield to two tons each acre.

In a herd of native cows only one in three is valuable for the dairy. During this selection and "the survival of the fittest," a race of cows will be raised up whose value will be vastly in advance of those we now have.

The clear-eyed farmer has confidence in Vermont as a farming state. He looks for better results in every respect. He anticipates the time when better pastures, better meadows, better plowed fields will yield better crops of grass, of hay, of grain, of roots, of fruit; that better stock will be better bred, and better cared for.

It is desirable that there be some interchange of population. But the loss of two hundred thousand Vermonters from our state is too great, quite too great to be born without damage.

Those who have gone forth from among us have been mostly those in the prime of youth. Open the eyes of our people to the advantages presented them at home and they will be no longer looking with eager gaze to the mirage that spreads over the breadth of the far away states.

Prof. Henry M. Seely, Secretary,
Vermont Board of Agriculture, 1880

Shelburne Farms, Vermont, 1900

50th Annual Convention:
Vermont Dairymen's Association

In 1869, dairy interests formed the Vermont Dairymen's Association; half of the fifty participants at the organizing meeting were dairy farmers and legislators, signaling the association's intention to seek more support from the state for farmers.

As *Freedom and Unity: A History of Vermont* recounts, state government had provided few services to help the farmer until the 1870s, when the legislature created a state Board of Agriculture. Prior to that informal farmers' groups, agricultural societies, newsletters, and almanacs shared advice on successful farming.

In 1850, farmers held their first state fair, an opportunity to learn about new products and markets and to show off their best crops and livestock. The two-day fair in Middlebury attracted 12,000 visitors and included exhibits of 400 horses, 300 cattle, 1,100 sheep, 50 lots of poultry, and 1,200 "inanimate objects."

In 1920, the association, at its 50th annual convention, met to celebrate the progress and changes in dairying, but also to warn once again that the family farm, as a business and lifestyle, was under siege. The contemporary dairy farmer would be quite at home, with some updating, with the discussions and papers at that three-day convention. Cheaper milk from the Midwest then threatened Vermont's dominance of Eastern markets; youth weren't interested in the long hours of farms and continued to move to higher-paying jobs in the city; and farmers, speaker after speaker warned, needed to become even better businessmen if they were to survive.

Several excerpts from the discussions follow.

Some of Us Are "Striking Twelve"

It is impossible for the farmer, who is obliged to rely on his farm receipts for the maintenance of himself and family, to compete with prices paid at manufacturing centers.

Industries are about operating on an eight-hour day basis, they demand still less hours and more pay, their demands so far nearly all have been granted with this result, higher prices for the necessities of life—every one striking back at the farmer. We hear constantly about the appointment of this or that commission to "investigate" the farmers' price of milk, with the idea in mind that he is profiteering and it is unnecessary to maintain the present price of his products.

Have any one of you known a committee appointed with the idea of reducing those things the farmer is obliged to buy? Every one is striking but the farmer, and I am inclined to think some of us are "striking twelve" to continue in the unappreciated business of farming; nevertheless, I am a firm believer in the ultimate success of the farmer, especially of the Vermont Dairy Farmer.

S.L. Harris, President,
Vermont Dairymen's Association

Let Us Standardize

We farmers have to make up our minds that we are going to give up some of our foolish ideas. I saw in the *Country Gentleman* that there are one hundred and fifty different brands of fertilizer manufactured in this country and it said that twenty-five brands would supply all the needs for all parts of this country.

Let us standardize and have one mowing machine and call it the Farmers' Union. We have standardized on the automobile because we cannot afford to have anything but a Ford.

F.S. Adams, Chief, Division of Markets,
Department of Agriculture, Maine

The West Is Going to Constantly Threaten Your Market

The West with its cheaper feeds is going to constantly threaten your market. The West already dominates your butter and cheese market and you must keep your price to the consumer down or it will dominate your milk market.

What shall be done to meet these issues?

The sires determine the fundamental capacity of your cows to be profitable. There is no factor except the farmer's ability as a manager that has so much effect on profits as the sires used.

Dairymen do not value a tried sire highly enough. We must stop the loss of so many valuable sires. This cannot go on and permit you to meet the competition of the West where they are securing larger production on much cheaper feeds and are making upwards of fifty per cent more profit from their cows than you are realizing. You must have better cows. You must feed your cows wisely. Breeding and feeding cannot be separated.

E.F. Burton, Bureau of Animal Industry,
Washington, D.C.

Each of Us Has a Mission to Fulfill on This Earth

Why is it that so many men—a good many times business men that have been successful—go out and buy farms and spend a large amount of money on them without knowing the first thing about farming? Such people were going to apply business principles to farming. I have never known such a one to make the farm pay for the labor.

There are reasons for that and one is because such a man can't compete with the farmer and his wife, who have been working for nothing in many cases. The war has set the farmers ahead years in their operations; I think they have the largest duty to perform that agriculturists have ever been called upon to perform—to supply the demand and keep the cost down.

The farmer has large responsibilities; greater responsibilities than just to take care of our own. Each of us has a mission to fulfill on this earth; each must help his neighbor.

M.T. Phillips, Member,
State Board of Agriculture, Pennsylvania

"This generation wants to have a life outside of the barn, but this compromise won't allow them to survive at today's milk prices," says vet Walt Goodale of the small dairy farmer's dilemma.

Have We Reached the Limit?

GRAYSON WYMAN: I don't know what will happen in farming in the future. I don't know if we will see the changes in the next 50 years that Larry and I saw. I don't know how much more cows can stand. We have certainly stressed them to a breaking point. When we started in 1959, your average cow produced around 7,000 pounds of milk a year. Today it's over 20,000 pounds in better herds.

The number of cows and farms has been going down but the total production has been increasing. Some farmers are using BST (bovine somatotropin, a growth hormone) to increase production, but we never did. You can argue that you're just injecting them with a protein that they already produce. But what you're doing is kicking up production when nationwide we already have a surplus of milk, mainly because of an increase in size of farms and number of cows in dairy growth states like New Mexico, Texas, Colorado, California, and Idaho. This translates into rock-bottom prices.

If you have a drought in a big-production area like the Midwest and animals aren't producing up to snuff, that affects national prices. Vermont is just a speck in the national scene; New England produces less than 3% of the country's milk so what we do here doesn't have that much of an affect.

You certainly hear more and more about organic farming and how organic milk's higher price can help small farms survive. You do get a higher price, but you sacrifice cow productivity and can't make anywhere near as much milk. You have to buy certified organic cows or feed your cows nearly all organic feed for a year. Organic feed isn't widely available so grain will probably be close to double the cost of regular grain. Plus there's a lot of paperwork to prove that everything is organic.

We never considered going organic. We were totally committed to the way we were. To convert our fields to organic crops would have meant not using commercial fertilizers on them for three years. Our crop yields would have been dropping while we still wouldn't have been eligible for higher milk payments.

Going organic is a 100% commitment. If you use antibiotics on sick cows, they lose their organic status and must be sold or segregated from the herd. Cows aren't under the same production stress, so your chances of health problems are reduced, but they would not be eliminated by a long shot.

Looking back, we have gone through a period when we were lucky to be in the business. There were constant advancements in your seeds, breeding, and machinery. In the last 10 years, we probably made more strides, especially in feeding, than we did in all the other years. We used to have a feed salesman, and you told him what you wanted. Today, we have a team with a Ph.D. nutritionist who tells you what your herd needs.

We're on the edge of knowing so much more about feeding. Experts are telling us now how feeding trace minerals like potassium, zinc, and magnesium can improve herd health and reduce reproductive problems. Even with all these changes, our feeding still hasn't caught up to a cow's genetic potential.

And today, there's a whole new world as far as automation. They're talking about tractors that operate by remote control and robotic milkers. While it sounds very futuristic, what sounds futuristic today can be here tomorrow.

But I think these developments will be too expensive for family farms of our size for a long time. They may work on the megafarms and on the industrial farms of the Midwest, but I don't think we'll see them on the family farm for a while.

There is still a place for the 100-cow milking herd, but whether it can survive economically is the big question. A lot depends on the age of the person. The average age of farmers in Vermont is probably 50 to 55. That doesn't speak well for the future when farms are being run by people not that far from retirement and when you don't see lots of younger guys coming in.

A person who is 55 and is milking 100 cows with part-time help, has managed his debt load well, and isn't making large capital investments can hang on. That was where we were at the end. Over the last 10 to 15 years we had been trying to reduce our debt load so that when we called it quits we wouldn't have a lot of debts to pay off. We knew our tractors were getting pretty tired and some equipment was almost antiquated, but Dan kept it going.

The person who is just starting out with a large debt load and is facing $12 milk will have a hard time of it. Some families will help their children take over the farm. Others are hard-nosed and want to

Cheap food and animal feed have depended on cheap energy. Rising oil costs have offset stronger milk prices and added another economic hurdle in the family farm's survival.

Dairy economists believe that per capita consumption of milk is unlikely to increase in the future—
since 1980 consumption has increased by 1.4% a year while production has increased 2.1%.
"Cheese fatigue," competition from other drinks, and a changing ethnic population are likely to
restrain demand. Increasing population will partially offset these potential losses.

get top dollar when they retire. And a divorce can throw a monkey wrench into any succession when the spouse wants a big settlement that has to come out of the farm.

Your new farmers will need a family committed to farming, be willing to make sacrifices, and accept that they will also be tied down to the farm. Even then surviving tough times is still in question.

Many megafarmers thought that when they built those huge barns and started milking 1,000 cows that they would have more time off, more time for vacations, and more time to spend with their family. But about 99% have found out that they have to be closer to the operation than ever before. They are not only managing animals, they are also managing people. Sometimes managing 30 people is lot more difficult than managing animals.

Whatever your size, managing debt is getting to be more and more of a factor as farms grow in size and the competition for every acre increases. You have to be on top of everything. And I mean right on top. You can't let anything slide.

Larry and I farmed in an era when average herd size went from 30 cows to 100-plus. We were very fortunate when we started; there were still a lot of small farms. We started with a dozen cows and expanded on a pay-as-you-go basis as much as we could. You didn't have to start with a herd of 100 to 150 cows then.

Today, you have to be bigger to cover your start-up expenses because your margins are so much smaller and are getting smaller all the time. Your fuel, fertilizer, and feed costs, which are all tied to the cost of energy, are going up, like it or not. Even if your income is greater, the cost of everything is so much higher. The difference between what we got for cows when we sold out and when we started is staggering. We could buy good-quality cows for $200 to $350 in the late 1950s. When we sold out, good cows ready to freshen brought up to $3,000. That's a lot of money to start a herd.

Go to a bank to borrow money to start a farm with today's costs and they'd probably say, "Here's a good psychiatrist. You must be nuts!" Banks and farm credit will still fund farmers who want to expand, but they want to know your plan to pay it back. Basically, they need to know that you know the road you're going to be traveling.

And a lot of that road depends on milk prices, which are up and down. You have your milk futures that the big investors with lots of money play and economists predicting milk prices. But the farmer still faces big spikes and drops that no one predicts. In the last couple years, we have spiked to nearly $22 and then been in the $13 to $15 range and have been as low as $10 to $12, a price that we were getting 25 years ago.

My concern is that if farmers keep overproducing, there's going to be nothing but more trouble. After World War I, my grandfather had a quota for his milk and got a livable return for it. If he produced above the quota, he was paid next to nothing for it.

I don't know if today's farmer would agree to such a system. But I think the farmers who are left are good enough thinkers to realize that we're going to have to get production under control and live this way. I'd rather be milking in a market that is begging for milk than today's market where you have more milk than buyers can handle.

Before I depart, I'd like to know the answer to another question, How far can we go? Have we reached the limit? Have we have reached a plateau?

My mother used to talk about all the changes that she had seen: the development of the car, airplanes that once carried one person now carried 400. People went to the moon and back in her lifetime (1908-2004). Occasionally when I was plowing I would think about the way my grandfather farmed in Maryland during World War I. He would hitch five or six mules together. I was driving a 200-horse-power tractor.

If I were to make a guess, I'd say you'll never stop "progress." It might slow down, but it will never stop. ◁

May 2005: A List With Lots of Things to Do

"I haven't had my hand in this in years," says Larry, more accustomed to tools bigger than a trowel, of his return to gardening. "He's doing a good job," says Fern, of her new weeding help.

Larry has no regrets in his retirement. "Getting eight hours of sleep makes a difference. When you go to bed at 9 and get up at 5, you feel like a new man. Someone could offer me good cows at $10 a piece, and I wouldn't be interested. It's time for another generation to do the milking," says Larry.

There is now time for attention to a long delayed to-do list, like an extensive spring cleaning and yard sale at the end of May. Among the treasures: an exercise bicycle that Grayson used to rehabilitate his knee; a $10 set of golf clubs, suitable for holding up tomato plants; a 1957 edition of G. W. Stamm's *Veterinary Guide for Farmers* for $5.

The DeVries have found an empty barn to house their herd, but it needs a cleaning and refurbishing before it will pass state inspection. The moving date keeps slipping: mid-April, then the end of April, then early May, mid-May, and finally early June.

Grayson finishes manure spreading on May 5. Corn planting begins May 13 and is completed on the 25th. Larry and Grayson help Dan with the planting.

Lake Champlain is still too cold for fishing.

Jeanne's health is day-to-day and at times, hour-to-hour. Aarin's fall wedding has been moved up to June 10.

"You'd have thought she could have done the milking as if nothing had happened," says Larry following a visit to Fletcher Allen after Jeanne had received an energizing blood infusion. The next visit she is barely lucid.

By the end of the month, her body has lost its ability to fight infection. Jeanne's matter-of-fact approach to her illness doesn't waver; she keeps busy recording stories and sewing clothes for her grandchildren.

"Dan and I have been making a list with lots of things to do," says Larry. "That's what he's going to need. Keep busy. The other night he said planting was awfully long—too much time to think."

June-December, 2005: It Will Be Different

Just past noon on June 2, the Wymans' main barn was still for the first time in 37 years. "I hate to see them go, but the DeVries will take good care of them," Larry reflected, as Sam DeVries headed for Bridport with a final trailer load.

On June 2, after morning milking, Sam DeVries with the help of Dan, Larry, and Paul Barrett moves his 60-odd milkers—six cows at a time—to their new home in Bridport.

Moving 1,500-pound animals that don't want to move can be a rib-breaking business. "I tell you Larry they just don't want to leave," says Sam of the many cows that require urgings much more forceful than "Be a good girl."

Shortly after noon, the DeVries's last four cows are boarded. No one has been injured.

"I wish you all the best," says Larry. "I hope they'll give you some good milk."

"I'm sure they will," Sam replies.

"I hate to see them go, but I'm not going to miss getting up. It'll be nice to sleep in to 5," says Dan who has been helping with the morning feeding.

"You're sleeping in now. The alarm goes off and you turn it off," says Jeanne, who has watched the last of the transfers.

The barn is not totally empty. A Monument Farms Dairy employee is renting space in the heifer barn and is raising eight beef cattle.

Four cows remain in the free stall. "There's the start of our next herd," Dan jokes. "Two has-beens (Bunker and a companion, Beefer) and two bull calves."

Unlike Larry and Grayson, who have made do with sometimes less-than-ideal tractors and equipment in anticipation of retirement, Dan has spent the past year looking for tractors, hay wagons, dump wagons, and trucks, albeit well-used, for expanded field work.

In June, a "new truck," a 1991 delivery truck with 580,000 miles, is converted to haul chop with a 17-foot by 6-foot by 8-foot bin, large enough to hold the silage from a new, bigger 700-cubic-foot dump wagon.

By the end of July, he has leased some barn space and lined up enough heifers, either his own or ones he will board for others, to fill the barn for the winter.

In August, Larry and Grayson clean two no-longer-needed Allis tractors, in anticipation of selling them at a fall auction in northern Vermont, where Allis is a popular brand, especially among Canadian farmers.

Closer to home, Larry installs a new wood furnace and converts the rear section of the house to a garage in late

"When we started we had this bull, Skipper. He weighed 3,200 pounds and when he roared he'd rattle the timbers," says Grayson, recalling one of the farm's legends. "People heard about him and would come out to look. It was like Grand Central Station. When Skipper died, the fellow who came out to pick him up had a new winch with a 3,000-pound capacity. He burned up the winch trying to get Skipper out of the barn. He was that mammoth."

summer. Grayson replaces a shingle roof with a standing seam roof in September. His knees are feeling better, and he will delay a decision on an operation until he sees how they do in colder weather.

In August, Dan stakes a Hay For Sale sign in front of the barn. This has been a good hay year, with the June to August months the hottest in over 50 years. Larry and to a lesser extent Grayson have been helping with the mowing and baling. After September and October's third cutting the hayloft is brimful with over 10,000 bales, a substantial cash crop.

Since the sale of the herd at the end of March, daily feed needs have been cut by more than half. After the bunks off Drake Road and adjacent to the barn have been topped off with corn and grass silage, a new storage pile is needed. A 150-foot-long, 50-foot-wide, 600-ton blimp, causing many double takes from passersby, rises in the corn field south of the Drake Road bunk. The pile will shrink in the coming months with sales to a neighboring dairy farmer and will be gone by spring.

By the end of the year, a new routine has settled in. Dan, free of most barn chores except for once-a-day feeding, can spend much of the day on his repair business. Larry, never idle, mucks out the barn mornings and afternoons just for the exercise.

Missing is Jeanne. April's dire prognosis proved accurate. Jeanne, Larry would reflect later, just kept "going and going." First, Memorial Day. Then her daughter's informal wedding ceremony in June. On August 8, she died, with the end precipitated by a pulmonary embolism.

"In all the time she was sick, and often she was in great pain, I never heard her ask 'Why me?' She never whined. From day one, I never heard her say that she was sorry for herself."

"She had asked her doctor about her disease and he had said there was 'no reason why she was chosen.' It was just 'bad luck.' She accepted that.

"Her church and her faith were very important to her as they have been to Dan.

"Dan has made a supreme effort to stay busy. He hasn't sat around and said woe is me. When Jeanne was dying, she told Dan that he was young (46) and should remarry. She made a list of people that she approved of and a list that she didn't.

"I have told Dan life goes on. But it will be different."

On Labor Day, free of milking, Larry joined Fern, Bev, and Arrin Kehoe for a morning walk. It was his first such walk since coming to Weybridge in 1968 and a prelude, he hoped, to some fall hiking.

Acknowledgments

Assembling a documentary is a little like solving a jigsaw puzzle. There are lots of pieces, and all are essential if the picture is to be complete.

At the heart of this documentary are the Wymans and Kehoes. I cautioned Larry and Grayson Wyman at the outset that their story couldn't be told in a month or several months. Intensive photography went on for a year and a half. Fact gathering and interviewing continued for another year.

They were always patient with my layman's queries during workday note taking and in 25 hours of taped interviews: "Is that orchard grass or brome grass?" "How long do antibiotics stay in a cow's system?" "What's the bunk's internal temperature when the corn is fermenting?" "How much does sexed semen increase the odds of having a heifer? Is it worth the extra cost?"

A photojournalist intent on rendering a faithful account of a life can seem like a pesky mosquito, forever buzzing about. Larry and Grayson and Dan Kehoe never shooed me away in scores of visits or in my weekly phone check-ins: "What's the schedule this week?" "Don't know. All depends on the weather."

Fern and Bev Wyman were similarly forthcoming in providing the perspective of the non-farming members of the family. Dan was reliably good humored and positive during a very testing year when the progression of his wife Jeanne's fatal illness was an omnipresent concern. There was ample cause for long faces, but few were ever seen.

A photojournalist's worst fear is to miss the story and never plumb the complexities of a life's work. Many friends and colleagues were invaluable here. Walt Goodale, their longtime vet, provided a perspective on the challenges facing traditional family farms and endless stories of Larry and Grayson overseeing their cows like mother hens. Harvey Smith, a fellow farmer and former state legislator, provided an historical perspective on the economics and politics of farming. Ken Button, at Yankee Farm Credit, explained the economic choices and constraints in expanding a farm as the Wymans did.

Jim Bushey, their feed dealer and a longtime friend, explained the advances in seed genetics and feeding programs and the constant pressure to do more with less or go out of business. Harold Giard, a state legislator and former farmer, discussed the culture of agriculture and the assumption—faulty he believes—that bigger and bigger is the only path to survival.

Allen Karnatz, a regional director of the Vermont Land Trust, discussed farmers' efforts to preserve their land for future generations in general and the Wymans' effort in particular. Peter James and Millie Rooney of Monument Farms Dairy, next-door neighbors of the Wymans, were helpful throughout the documentation.

Hans Raum, reference librarian at Middlebury College, and the College's Special Collections staff were helpful in my searches for historical accounts of agriculture. Chris Kirby, adult services librarian at the Ilsley Library in Middlebury, and Orson Kingsley, archivist at the Sheldon Museum of Vermont History in Middlebury, were similarly helpful. Larry and Ida Washington shared their knowledge of Weybridge history as did Karen Brisson, Weybridge town clerk.

Many people supplied me with reading material. Kelly Mills, vocational agriculture teacher at the Hannaford Career Center in Middlebury, lent me a copy of *Dairy Cattle Science*, 500 pages on the A to Z of dairying. Jeff Carter, University of Vermont extension agent, lent me historical records and binders covering everything from forage crop management to breeding heifers for profit.

David Girard, from the Farm Service Agency of the U.S. Department of Agriculture, lent me annual reports from the late 1800s and early 1900s. Roger Boise lent me his history of John Deere tractors. Diane Bothfeld at the Vermont Agency of Agriculture and Ellen Ogden and Jane Sakovitz Dale at the Vermont Cheese Council, responded to my requests for dairy data.

Many people read parts of the manuscript and constructively suggested additions and changes. Bob Parsons, agricultural economist at the University of Vermont, responded to my many questions and reviewed all the text covering the economics of dairying. Ken Button also reviewed sections on the economics of dairying. Jan Albers, one of the state's pre-eminent historians of the Vermont landscape, read all my introductory material offering many helpful comments. Peter Ryan, a geologist at Middlebury College, similarly reviewed text on the evolution of the Vermont landscape.

Numerous readers provided a layman's perspective. Bill Orr, as always, was constructively contrary. Don Patterson brought a photo-journalist's eye in assessing the integrity of the photographs and many hours of critical reading of the text. Beth Merritt, who grew up on a dairy farm, and her husband, Edd, responded invaluably to my many questions: "Clear here? Too much? Needs explaining?"

And Larry and Grayson Wyman read the entire manuscript and, with their encyclopedic memories, frequently responded, "That reminds me of the story of...." I hope this documentary is a faithful rendering of their lives.

Steve Jensen brought a professional copy editor's eye to the final book galleys.

In order to share this documentary with as broad an audience as possible, the Vermont Folklife Center has chosen to self publish and to distribute the book at no cost with the help of foundation and community support.

Many people offered fundraising suggestions, among them David Andrews, development director at the Counseling Service of Addison County; John Barstow of the Orton Family Foundation; Elise Annes, Darby Bradley, and Nancy Patch at the Vermont Land Trust; Paul Bruhn, executive director of the Preservation Trust of Vermont: Tim Buskey, director of the Vermont Farm Bureau; Mary Conlon and Scott McArdle of the Vermont Community Foundation.

Jed Davis and Chris Pierson at Cabot Creamery; David Donath of the Billings Farm Museum; Peg Elmer of the Land Use Institute at Vermont Law School; Larry Forcier, then interim director of the School of Natural Resources at the University of Vermont; Gail Freidin, director of the Middlebury Business Association; Chris Graff of National Life of Vermont; Kevin Graffagnino, executive director of the Vermont Historical Society; Gioia Kuss, former director of the Middlebury Area Land Trust; Jolinda LaClair, director of USDA's Rural Development state office.

Also thanks to Steven Larson, managing editor of *Hoard's Dairyman*; Kate McGowan, co-director of United Way of Addison County; Ken Perine, president of National Bank of Middlebury;

Maggie Quinn, development director of Elderly Services, Inc.; Amy Shollenberger, executive director of Rural Vermont; and Enid Wonnacott, executive director of NOFA-VT.

In discussing publishing options, John Barstow, Sally and Upton Brady, John Elder, Paul Erikkson, Bill McKibben, Grant Novak, and Frank Urbanowski provided helpful advice.

Many people provided letters of support in our grant applications, among them Jan Albers; Roger Allbee, secretary of the Vermont Agency of Agriculture; State Representative Chris Bray; Paul Costello, executive director of the Vermont Council on Rural Development; Michael Hendy, co-owner of the local John Deere dealership; Chris Kirby; Douglas Lantagne, Dean of UVM Extension Service; and Nancy Patch.

Support for the book has come from foundations and the community. The New England Dairy and Food Council and the New England Dairy Promotion Board were the principal sponsors, supporting the distribution of the book to every public and school library in Vermont. The Fieldstone Foundation provided a major community challenge grant. The Lintilhac Foundation provided the initial support for the project.

Other support came from Ben & Jerry's Foundation, Brightman Hill Charitable Foundation, Cabot Creamery, Castanea Foundation, Inc., Cerf Community Fund, Co-operative Insurance Companies, Monument Farms Dairy, Merchants Bank, National Bank of Middlebury, Northeast Farm Credit AgEnhancement Program, Preservation Trust of Vermont, Shelburne Farms, University of Vermont Extension Service, Vermont Farm Bureau, and several anonymous donors.

The book would not have been possible without the enthusiasm and support of Brent Björkman, executive director of the Vermont Folklife Center. Center staff, Bob Hooker, Andy Kolovos, Greg Sharrow, and Sarah Stahl, were helpful throughout. The book also would not be possible without the vision of Jane Beck, who founded the Folklife Center 25 years ago.

The Folklife Center is grateful for permission to use photographs from the archives of Shelburne Farms, p. 206; Sheldon Museum of Vermont History, pp. 102 and 120; and the Vermont Historical Society, pp. 69, 144, 181, and 204. The Center would also like to thank the Vermont Historical Society for permission to quote at length from *While the Sun Shines: Making Hay in Vermont 1789-1990* by Allen Yale.

Mason Singer, the book's designer, deserves a very special thanks. I warned him that there was more material than could be stuffed into one book. He met the challenge.

Thanks also to Tom Slayton, who has spent a lifetime thinking about what makes Vermont, Vermont, for his foreword.

David Goodman provided valuable assistence on photographic reproduction. Steve and John Stinehour at Stinehour Wemyss Editions scanned the photographs with care.

Capital Offset Company brought a careful attention to the smallest detail in its printing.

I'm also grateful for my parents' support, direct and indirect, of my documentary life.

Finally, many thanks to my wife Paula, who put up with my barn clothes—they were quickly banished to the garage—and the stacks of *Hoard's Dairyman* throughout the house, and to our daughter Anne, who always wanted to see the latest photographs, read the interview transcripts, and know how the Wymans and the cows were doing.

"Just fine," I'd reply.

Bibliography

Acres U.S.A.—A Voice for Eco-Agriculture, monthly magazine

Albers, Jan, *Hands on the Land: A History of the Vermont Landscape*, Rutland, Vermont, The Orton Family Foundation, Cambridge, MIT Press, 2000

Amber Waves: The Economics of Food, Farming, Natural Resources, and Rural America, newsletter of Economic Research Service, United States Department of Agriculture

Bailey, Kenneth W., *Dairy Outlook*, monthly email newsletter on dairy industry developments, http://dairyoutlook.aers.psu.edu

Bailey, Kenneth W., *Marketing and Pricing of Milk and Dairy Products in the United States*, Ames, Iowa, Iowa State University Press, 1997

Barron, Hal, *Those Who Stayed Behind: Rural Society in Nineteenth-Century New England*, New York, Cambridge University Press, 1984

Becker, Ken; Moser, Mike; Schmidt, Fred; and Sawyer, Will, *Agricultural Handbook for Vermont Counties*, Burlington, Vt., Center for Rural Studies, University of Vermont, 2005

Berry, Wendell, *Home Economics: Fourteen Essays*, San Francisco, North Point Press, 1987

Brady, Alison G., "White Gold in the Green Mountains: The Evolution of Vermont's Dairy Industry," Honors Thesis, Department of History, Middlebury College, 2005

Cuykendall, Charles; Gloy, Brent; and LaDue, Eddy, "Future Structure of the Dairy Industry: Historical Trends, Projections, and Issues," Cornell University, 2003

D'Alusio, Faith and Menzel, Peter, *Hungry Planet: What the World Eats*, Napa, California, Material World Books, 2005

Daniels, Tom and Bowers, Deborah, *Holding Our Ground: Protecting America's Farms and Farmland*, Washington, D.C. and Covelo, California, Island Press, 1997

Ensminger, M.E., *Dairy Cattle Science*, Danville, Illinois, Interstate Publishers, Inc., 1993

Fish, Charles, *In Good Hands: The Keeping of A Family Farm*, New York, Farrar, Straus and Giroux, 1995

Fitzgerald, Deborah, *Every Farm A Factory: The Industrial Ideal in American Agriculture*, New Haven and London, Yale University Press, 2003

Fussell, Betty, *The Story of Corn*, New York, Alfred A. Knopf, 1992

Gardner, Bruce L., *American Agriculture in the Twentieth Century: How It Flourished and What It Cost*, Cambridge and London, Harvard University Press, 2002

Graff, Nancy Price, ed., *Celebrating Vermont Myths and Realities*, Hanover, University Press of New England, 1991

Graff, Nancy Price, *Looking Back at Vermont: Farm Security Administration Photographs, 1936-1942*, Hanover, University Press of New England, 2002

Guither, Harold, D. and Halcrow, Harold, G., *The American Farm Crisis: An Annotated Bibliography with Analytical Introductions, Resources on Contemporary Issues*, Ann Arbor, Michigan, Pieran Press, 1988

Hall, Donald, *String Too Short to Be Saved: Recollections of Summers on a New England Farm*, Boston, Nonpareil Books, 1960

Hanson, Victor Davis, *Fields Without Dreams: Defending the Agrarian Idea*, New York, Free Press, 1996

Hanson, Victor Davis, *The Land Was Everything: Letters from an American Farmer*, New York, Free Press, 2000

Harper, Douglas, *Changing Works: Visions of a Lost Agriculture*, Chicago, University of Chicago Press, 2001

Hastings, Scott E., Jr., *The Last Yankees: Folkways in Eastern Vermont and the Border Country*, Hanover and London, University Press of New England, 1990

Hastings, Scott E., Jr. and Elsie R., *Up in the Morning: Vermont Farm Families in the Thirties*, Hanover and London, University Press of New England, 1992

Hastings, Scott E., Jr. and Ames, Geraldine, S., *The Vermont Farm Year in 1890*, Woodstock, Vermont, Billings Farm & Museum, 1983

Hemenway, Abby, *Abby Hemenway's Vermont: Unique Portrait of a State*, Brattleboro, Vermont, Stephen Greene Press, 1972

Hoard's Dairyman: The National Dairy Farm Magazine, www.hoards.com

Holstein Pulse, quarterly magazine of Holstein Association, www.holsteinusa.com

Ikerd, John, *Small Farms Are Real Farms: Sustaining People Through Agriculture*, Austin, Texas, Acres USA, Inc., 2007,

Jager, Ronald, *The Fate of Family Farming: Variations on an American Idea*, Hanover and London, University Press of New England, 2004

Jenison, Silas H., Address, The Annual Fair of the Addison County Agricultural Society, October 1, 1844, Middlebury, Vermont, J. Cobb Jr. Printer, 1845

John Deere Tractors: 1918-1987, Deere & Company, American Society of Agricultural Engineers, 1987

Johnson, Charles W., *The Nature of Vermont: Introduction and Guide to a New England Environment*, Hanover and London, University Press of New England, 1998

Judd, Richard Munson, *The New Deal in Vermont: Its Impact and Aftermath*, New York and London, Garland Publishing, Inc. 1979

Kessler, Brad, *Goat Song: A Seasonal Life, A Short History of Herding, and the Art of Making Cheese*, New York, Scribner, 2009

Kingsolver, Barbara, *Animal, Vegetable, Miracle: A Year of Food Life*, New York, HarperCollins Publisher, 2007

Klinkenborg, Verlyn, *Making Hay*, New York, Lyons & Burford, Publishers, 1986

Klinkenborg, Verlyn, *The Rural Life*, Boston, New York, and London, Little, Brown and Company, 2003

Klyza, Christopher McGrory and Trombulak, Stephen C., *The Story of Vermont: A Natural and Cultural History*, Hanover and London, Middlebury College Press, University Press of New England, 1999

Kramer, Mark, *Three Farms: Making Milk, Meat and Money from the American Soil*, New York, Bantam Books, 1981

Maroney, James H., Jr., *The Political Economy of Milk: Reinvigorating Vermont's Family Dairy Farms*, Leicester, Vermont, Gala Books, Ltd., 2008

Marsh, George Perkins, *Man and Nature: Or, Physical Geography as Modified by Human Action*, Cambridge, Harvard University Press, 1965

McKibben, Bill, *Deep Economy: The Wealth of Communities and the Durable Future*, New York, Times Books/Henry Holt & Company, 2007

Meeks, Harold A., *Time and Change in Vermont: A Human Geography*, Chester, Connecticut, The Globe Pequot Press, 1986

Meeks, Harold A., *Vermont's Land and Resources*, Shelburne, Vermont, The New England Press, 1986

Miller, Peter, *Vermont Farm Women*, Waterbury, Vermont, Silver Print Press, 2002

Morrissey, Charles, *Vermont: A Bicentennial History*, New York, W. W. Norton & Co., Inc., 1981

"Narratives of the Sufferings of Seth Hubbell & Family," Bennington and Hyde Park, Vermont, Vermont Heritage Press and Vermont Council on the Humanities and Public Issues, 1986

Nestle, Marion, *Food Politics,* Berkeley, University of California Press, 2002

Pistorius, Alan, *Cutting Hill: A Chronicle of a Family Farm,* New York, Alfred A. Knopf, 1990

Pollan, Michael, *In Defense of Food: An Eater's Manifesto,* New York, The Penguin Press, 2008

Pollan, Michael, *The Omnivore's Dilemma: A Natural History of Four Meals,* New York, The Penguin Press, 2006

Roberts, Paul S., *The End of Food,* Boston and New York, Houghton Mifflin Company, 2008

Rozwenc, Edwin, *Agricultural Policies in Vermont 1860-1945,* Montpelier, Vt., Vermont Historical Society, 1981

"Rural Vermont: A Program for the Future by Two Hundred Vermonters," The Vermont Commission on Country Life, Burlington, 1931

Russell, Howard S., *A Long, Deep Furrow: Three Centuries of Farming in New England,* Hanover, University Press of New England, 1976

Schlosser, Eric, *Fast Food Nation: The Dark Side of the All-American Meal,* Boston, Houghton Mifflin, 2001

Sharrow, Gregory, ed., *Families on the Land: Profiles of Vermont Farm Families,* Middlebury, Vt., Vermont Folklife Center, 1995

Sharrow, Gregory, *Measured Furrows: Vermont's Farming History, A Teacher's Guide,* Middlebury, Vt., Vermont Folklife Center, 1996

Sherman, Joe, *Fast Lane on a Dirt Road: Vermont Transformed: 1945-1990,* Woodstock, Vermont, The Countryman Press, Inc., 1991

Sherman, Michael; Sessions, Gene; and Potash, P. Jeffrey, *Freedom and Unity: A History of Vermont,* Barre, Vt., Vermont Historical Society, 2004

Smith, Nicola, *Harvest: A Year in the Life of an Organic Farm,* Guilford, Connecticut, The Lyons Press, 2004

Stilwell, Lewis, *Migration from Vermont,* Montpelier, Vt., Vermont Historical Society, 1948

United States Department of Agriculture, "A Time to Act: A Report of the USDA National Commission on Small Farms," 1998

"Vermont Farms: Some Facts and Figures Concerning the Agricultural Resources and Opportunities of the Green Mountain State," The Vermont Bureau of Publicity, Office of Secretary of State, Essex Junction, Vermont, 1915

Vermont Family Visitor: A Monthly Paper Devoted Exclusively to Agriculture and Miscellaneous Matters, Montpelier, Vermont, E.P. Walton & Sons, 1845

Vermont Milk Commission, reports are available at www.vermontagriculture.com/milkcommission

Visser, Thomas Durant, *Field Guide to New England Barns and Farm Buildings,* Hanover and London, University Press of New England, 1997

Washington, Ida. H., *History of Weybridge, Vermont,* The Weybridge Bicentennial Commission, 1991

Williams, Robert C., *Fordson, Farmall, and Poppin' Johnny: A History of the Farm Tractor and Its Impact on America,* Urbana and Chicago, University of Illinois Press, 1987

Wilson, Harold, *The Hill Country of Northern New England: Its Social and Economic History, 1790-1830,* New York, Columbia University Press, 1936

Wood, Nancy, "Interdependence of Farming and Tourism in Vermont: Quantifying the Value of the Farm Landscape," M.S. thesis, Community Development and Applied Economics, University of Vermont, 2000

Yale, Allen R., Jr., *While the Sun Shines: Making Hay in Vermont 1789-1990,* Montpelier, Vt., Vermont Historical Society, 1991

Yankee Farm Credit, *Annual Northeast Dairy Farm Summary,* www.yankeeaca.com

---

Organizations Involved in Agricultural, Dairy, and Rural Life Issues

Billings Farm & Museum
Route 12 & River Road, P.O. Box 489,
Woodstock, Vt. 05091-0489
www.billingsfarm.org

Center for Whole Communities
Knoll Farm
700 Bragg Hill Road, Fayston, Vt. 05673
www.wholecommunities.org

Cornell University Small Farms Program
www.smallfarms.cornell.edu

Family Farm Defenders
P.O. Box 1772, Madison, Wis. 53701
familyfarmdefenders@yahoo.com

Gund Institute for Ecological Economics
University of Vermont
590 Main Street, Burlington, Vt. 05405

International Dairy Foods Association
1250 H Street, Suite 900
Washington, D.C. 20005
www.idfa.org

Leopold Center for Sustainable Agriculture
Ames, Iowa 50011
www.leopold.iastate.edu

National Family Farm Coalition
110 Maryland Ave. N.E., Suite 307
Washington, D.C. 20002
www.nffc

National Farmers Organization
www.nfo.org

National Milk Producers Federation
www.nmpf.org

New England Dairy Promotion Board
www.newenglanddairy.com

Northeast Organic Farming Association
of Vermont
P.O. Box 697, Richmond, Vt. 05477
www.nofavt.org

Rural Vermont
15 Barre St., Suite 2, Montpelier, Vt. 05602
www.ruralvermont.org

Smart Growth Vermont
110 Main St., Burlington, Vt. 05401
www.smartgrowthvermont.org

United States Department of Agriculture
Economic Research Service
www.ers.usda.gov

University of Vermont Center for Rural Studies
207 Morrill Hall, University of Vermont
Burlington, Vt. 05405
www.crs.uvm.edu

University of Vermont Center for
Sustainable Agriculture
63 Carrigan Drive, Burlington, Vt. 05405
www.uvm.edu/sustainableagriculture

Vermont Agency of Agriculture
Links to state and national organizations
www.vermontagriculture.com

Vermont Cheese Council
16 State Street, Montpelier, Vt. 05620
www.vtcheese.com

Vermont Council on Rural Development
P.O. Box 1384, Montpelier, Vt. 05601
www.vtrural.org

Vermont Farm Bureau
2083 East Main St., Richmond, Vt. 05477
www.vtfb.org

Vermont Land Trust
8 Bailey Ave., Montpelier, Vt. 05602
www.vlt.org

Contributors

GEORGE BELLEROSE, a Weybridge, Vt., freelance photojournalist, has been a reporter at city dailies and rural weeklies and an editor and writer at three colleges. His previous documentaries include *Caring for Our Own: A Portrait of Community Health Care; Facing the Open Sea: The People of Big Tancook Island;* and *Vermont Achievement Center: Forty Years of Service.* He is a neighbor of the Wymans.

BRENT BJÖRKMAN was associate director of the American Folklore Society before becoming executive director of the Vermont Folklife Center in 2007. From 1998 through 2004 Björkman was a folklife specialist with the Kentucky Folklife Program where he oversaw fieldwork, documentation projects, and educational outreach programs for teachers and community scholars. He has advised the National Endowment for the Arts, the National Council for the Traditional Arts, the Southern Arts Federation, and the Maine Arts Commission.

TOM SLAYTON was editor-in-chief of *Vermont Life* for 21 years and is now editor emeritus. He is a regular commentator for Vermont Public Radio. His previous books include *Searching for Thoreau: On the Trails and Shores of Wild New England,* 2007; *A Century in the Mountains: Celebrating Vermont's Long Trail,* which he edited and helped write for the Green Mountain Club, 2009; *Sabra Field: The Art of Place,* 2002; and *The Beauty of Vermont,* 1998. He is a recipient of the Franklin Fairbanks Award, given annually to a Vermonter who contributes significantly to the cultural life of the state.